DEREGULATING

LABOR RELATIONS

Dan C. Heldman
James T. Bennett
Manuel H. Johnson

Foreword by WALTER E. WILLIAMS

Allen County Public Library
Ft. Wayne, Indiana

The Fisher Institute

About the Authors

Dan C. Heldman is Senior Research Fellow in the Graduate School of Management, University of Dallas, and was formerly on the political science faculties at Marshall University (West Virginia) and Texas Christian University. A member of the Editorial Boards of the *Journal of Social and Political Studies* and *Journal of Labor Research,* he has published generally in two fields: labor relations and Soviet politics. Aside from the present volume, Dr. Heldman's most recent book is *The USSR and Africa* (Praeger, 1981).

James T. Bennett is professor of economics at George Mason University in Fairfax, Virginia. He has authored and coauthored many articles dealing with political economy, public choice, labor relations, and public policy. Recent books include *The Political Economy of Federal Government Growth* (Texas A&M University, 1980) and *Better Government at Half the Price* (Caroline House, 1981). He is an Adjunct Scholar of the Heritage Foundation.

Manuel H. Johnson is professor of economics at George Mason University in Fairfax, Virginia, and is an Adjunct Scholar of the Heritage Foundation. He has authored and coauthored numerous articles in various fields of economics including natural resource and environmental economics, public policy, and labor economics. He is Associate Editor of the *Journal of Labor Research*. Recent books include *The Political Economy of Federal Government Growth* (Texas A&M University, 1980) and *Better Government at Half the Price* (Caroline House, 1981).

Preface

There can be little doubt that, today, studies of regulation and deregulation are a growth industry. Why, then, yet another? Indeed, there is a danger that the analysis of government regulations may become so commonplace that the potential reader will become complacent.

We have undertaken this book in part because we believe this may have already occurred. Many Americans now agree that, yes, the regulation of this industry or that industry has turned out badly, been counter-productive, wasteful, inefficient, and so on, but many have not yet grasped the essential reasons for this state of affairs. More likely than not they believe the harm done has been the consequence of laws and rules improperly drawn, of administrators improperly acting, or of conditions unique to that industry. What has not been realized, to the extent necessary for a fundamental re-ordering of national policy, is that the harm done derives from the fact of regulation itself. The industry is irrelevant; the language of the law or rule is irrelevant; the personality or intention of the administrator is irrelevant. These may exacerbate or ease the harm, but the only relevant fact is that government has forcibly intervened in otherwise voluntary market processes to achieve ends which are desirable based on political rather than economic standards.

Though still too small, there is an expanding body of scholars and literature on this point which must somehow be presented unambiguously. With very rare exceptions, no one has studied the regulatory nature of federal labor relations policy: Few, in fact, would even recognize that labor exchanges constitute a vast market which is daily and hourly shaped by almost countless laws, rules, and court or administrative agency decisions. In short, with all the emphasis given to deregulation, no one has yet applied the analysis to the labor market.

If we can make a case for deregulating the labor market, if we can at least start people to thinking about the possibility, then we will have gone a long way toward identifying the essential problem. Portions of the analysis will be more than a little shocking, even heretical, for some readers. If some of the statements seem very unconventional, it is not for effect alone but because these ideas are being implicitly contrasted with decades of conventional wisdom. After all, the emperor may, in fact, have no clothes on.

In all this, we wish to acknowledge our debt to many who have paved the way before us. We trust they will take in good humor the suggestion that no more than the merest mention of labor in their litany of harmfully regulated markets would have helped our task considerably.

We also wish to acknowledge the debt we owe one another. The three authors have known each other over a period of years and have enjoyed an amicable working relationship. It is entirely accurate to say that, while we each brought to the task separate professional experiences and each therefore benefitted from the expertise of the other two, every portion of every draft was read, critiqued, and altered to some extent by each of us. In private, of course, we have the liberty of placing blame for errors of fact or interpretation on an absent co-author but, in truth and for the record, we stand collectively on what follows.

Dan C. Heldman
James T. Bennett
Manuel H. Johnson

Foreword

Deregulating Labor Relations is a powerful, thought-provoking, and convincing book which deals incisively with a critical issue of contemporary public policy: government intervention in the market for labor. For decades the phrase, "labor is not a commodity," has been used to promote practices that would not be tolerated if done by other sellers of services or commodities. By demonstrating that the market for labor is essentially no different from any other market, a major departure from standard teaching in the labor field, the authors are then able to analyze the regulation of the relationships among employers, employees, and unions using the same methods that have been applied to other services.

The theoretical justification for government involvement in markets is carefully explained in order to show that there is little economic basis for government regulation in the labor market. Heldman, Bennett, and Johnson then show that virtually every aspect of the labor market is circumscribed by political interference — labor relations is, it is argued, the most heavily regulated activity in the economy. Not only are the terms of work widely dictated by government actions through such devices as the minimum wage, the Davis-Bacon Act, the hours ceiling imposed by the Fair Labor Standards Act, and the OSHA regulations which specify the work environment, but also the process of negotiating the employment relationship is stringently controlled by government through the National Labor Relations Board and other agencies. As is true for virtually every other instance of government regulation, it is shown that the regulation of labor relations is both costly and ineffective in terms of stated social ideals and effective in unstated objectives, namely, collusion and monopoly for the few at the expense of the many. In fact, as the authors clearly reveal, the regulations actually hurt those workers whom, by conventional wisdom, the regulations are intended to help: youth, minorities, and unskilled laborers. Special interest groups such as the public employees who administer the regulatory programs, union leaders, and union members benefit at the expense of other workers, consumers, and taxpayers.

Deregulation, and its implication, open entry for all, is the appropriate cure for the costly, needless interference of government in the labor market. A number of different deregulation scenarios are proposed by the authors ranging from total decontrol to phased elimination of various parts of the regulatory environment. Though not developed in intensive detail, the implications of deregulation are also considered in order to demonstrate that, although substantial alterations would occur in the way in which labor relations activity is conducted, the changes would produce many positive results and no unmanageable consequences.

It is important to stress that the book is not anti-union or pro-employer, but focuses on the employee — the central participant in the labor relations arena whose interests are all too often submerged in the machinations of large unions, big government, and corporations.

Deregulating Labor Relations should stimulate serious thinking and active debate on a wide range of issues in the field of labor. For the benefit of American workers, a reconsideration and evaluation of public policy with regard to labor relations is urgently needed and long overdue.

Walter E. Williams

Acknowledgements

The authors wish to acknowledge gratefully the financial support provided by the John M. Olin Foundation, Inc., which permitted the research for this book. Outstanding research assistance was provided by Mr. John Dolan, a Scaife Research Fellow at George Mason University. The University of Chicago Press granted permission to reprint the tables in Chapter IV from the *Journal of Law and Economics* and the *Journal of Political Economy*.

Table of Contents

I. **Labor Relations, Regulation, and Public Policy**   **1**
   Labor Relations and Regulations
   Labor as a Commodity
   Overview

II. **The Political Economy of Regulation and Deregulation**   **13**
   The Economic Justification for Government Regulation
   The Extent of Government Regulation
   Is Regulation Effective?
   The Cost of Regulation
   Government Failure as an Explanation of Regulation
   Deregulation: Issues and Evidence

III. **The Regulation of Labor Relations: An Overview**   **41**
   Substantive Regulation of Labor Relations
   Procedural Regulation of Labor Relations

IV. **Economic Costs of Regulating Labor Relations**   **85**
   Minimum Wages and Maximum Hours
   Employer Payroll Taxes
   Federal Manpower Programs
   Occupational Safety and Health
   Employment and Earnings Discrimination
   Collective Bargaining and Union Organizing
   Occupational Licensing
   Summary

V. **Deregulating Labor Relations: Alternative Approaches**   **133**
   Winners and Losers from Deregulation
   Deregulation: The Repeal of NLRA
   Deregulation of Wages and Hours
   Conclusions

VI. **Summary and Conclusions**   **167**

Author Index   **175**

Subject Index   **179**

Chapter I

Labor Relations, Regulation, and Public Policy

A recent commentator, when informed that Americans were not receiving all the government for which we were paying, replied, "Thank God!" It has become a commonplace notion that the United States is not simply a regulated society, but rather an *over*-regulated society. Perhaps, if the observation is reasonably accurate, the situation today is nothing more, nor less, than a natural extension of the notion that we are "a society of laws rather than of men."

This traditional, though cryptic, description of the U.S. political order suggests that society is ruled by positive, written, clear-cut, and recognizable statements about reciprocal rights and responsibilities owned or owed by the two principal components of every society — citizens and government. Moreover, the notion implies further that these statements have wide acceptance because they are produced and modified through procedures in which all persons have an equal right to participate. Actually, the implications of the "laws rather than men" concept are far broader in number and meaning; so broad, in fact, that volumes have been written about each of them. In general, the concept includes such additional ideas as "government is the servant while the people are sovereign," "that government is best which governs least," "absolute power corrupts absolutely," and other similar catchphrases of American politics. Overall, the meaning is simply this: A government of free people should be limited, constrained, checked, unobtrusive, capable of being changed, susceptible to popular influence, with its powers clearly defined in terms understandable to its citizens.

Such a paragon, of course, has never existed in practice. The writers of the Constitution of 1787, for example, were concerned about a government becoming ineffectual if it were *too* constrained, too changeable, or overly sensitive to evanescent public moods: Hence, they instituted such contrary notions as an aristocratic Senate and an almost autocratic judiciary. Nevertheless, it was always perfectly clear what was the ultimate governmental model. Whether the shape of the

American system was determined by economic conditions, revolution-ary fervor, attitudes toward the "Mother country," or by the "great men" of the time, is an issue which could be debated *ad infinitum.* Though such a debate would be intrinsically interesting and perhaps even useful for some purposes, it is beyond the scope of this study.

Rather, it is safe to assert that, whatever the intentions, whatever may have been the "wrong turn" made sometime by some person or party, however natural or understandable the present political econ-omy of the United States, government has grown dramatically in terms of any meaningful measure one may choose to apply. Government at all levels, but particularly at the federal level, is larger, more powerful, more expensive, more intrusive, and more capable of affecting our lives than at any earlier time in our history. And the growth "curve" appears not to be a simple linear function but, rather, an increasingly upward-sloping trajectory that threatens to produce neither the tyr-anny of the monarch (which was so much feared in 1776) nor the chaos of anarchy (Hobbes' "state of nature" where all warred against all). Instead, the expansion of government is producing a myriad of gov-ernment agencies, commissions, boards, councils, task forces, committees, secretaries, undersecretaries, deputy undersecretaries, assistant deputy undersecretaries, and deputy assistants to the assistant deputy undersecretaries — the combination of which is simultaneously tyrannical *and* chaotic.[1]

All government agencies do things that constitute the "output functions" of government. Whereas government has also grown in its "inputs," (i.e., the organizations that collect, analyze, and assimilate the perceived needs of citizens), the greatest growth has occurred in what government does as a result of these and similar activities. In a sense, rampant government is the closest social analogy to a perpetual motion machine. Physicists know that, according to natural laws which appear to be immutable, a perpetual motion machine is impos-sible because, simply put, a device cannot "put out" more than it "takes in"; yet, from one perspective, that is precisely what a burgeoning government does. It translates minor, minority, and special pressures (including those generated internally) into massive, system-wide policies and programs with breadth, impact, detail, com-plications, and even mutual antagonisms so far out of proportion to their source that this behavior constitutes one defining characteristic of government run amok.

In another sense, however, the natural laws which declare physical perpetual motion machines impossible have counterparts in the social realm. While it is always true in any transformation of energy that *some* is irretrievably lost in the process (the principle of entropy), it is equally true that, in obtaining resources and transforming them into programs and services, government always *creates* waste as a byproduct.

The entire body of government output may be viewed as regulation. There is no government act, policy, program, or service that is not regulatory either in terms of the added constraints on those affected or in terms of the constraints on those who must provide the resources for the activity. Such a broad definition of regulation may be thought of as the "purist" position. Not only is the purist definition conceptually valid, but it also is useful in broadening the perspective given to regulatory activity. The common-sense appreciation of regulation encompasses such widely recognized examples as the Food and Drug Administration's rules on the testing and marketing of medical substances, the Federal Communications Commission's licensing of broadcast stations, the Interstate Commerce Commission's requirements on railway rates, and the Department of Agriculture's programs relating to farm production. Under the fundamental definition of regulation as any state activity that constrains market exchanges, other regulatory phenomena, not normally included in contemporary analysis (e.g., the criminal code) can also be investigated, in particular labor relations.

Labor Relations and Regulations

The fundamental definition of regulation strongly points to the field of labor relations as one which has thus far escaped close attention. To our knowledge, there is not one major treatise on government regulation of industrial relations. At most there are only a few passing notes that employment relationships are in fact controlled *at all* beyond certain specific statutes, the impression being that these laws are little more than a general framework within which labor exchanges take place largely in response to traditional market pressures. This impression, as discussed in detail in this study, is utterly false.

The assertion that any particular activity is closely or even *very* closely regulated does not provide sufficient justification for devoting time and resources to an analysis of the consequences and impacts of

3

the regulatory activity. After all, the examples of what is commonly recognized as regulation are so numerous already that the careers of all students of the subject could profitably be devoted to examining just these activities, without adding to the list. If, however, the benefit from analyzing and understanding any particular area of regulation is a function of how extensive the constraints are, how serious are the effects upon the lives of citizens, and how costly they may be for tax-payers and the economy generally, then a strong case can be made that labor relations is a critically important area of investigation that, to date, has not been given the attention it clearly deserves.

The excellent work that has already been done on the regulation-deregulation issue in such industries as airlines, trucking, broadcasting, drug development, railroads, and so forth is important and of great policy significance. The efforts made in these areas provide an excellent basis for advancing what has become a strong public awareness that the growth of government and its interference in economic affairs are potentially far more harmful than beneficial. There is also, particularly in the academic community, a strong and growing attitude that the presence, rather than the absence, of regulation must be justified before being instituted or even retained. Although the regulatory activities that have been investigated are important to the economic system and have significant consequences, the regulation of labor relations is far more pervasive and has much greater impact. Why is it that those who specialize in the regulation-deregulation issue have avoided the labor relations area?

One important reason that the regulatory activities mentioned above have come under scrutiny is that these areas are characterized by well-organized and readily identifiable interest groups representing those in the industry who experience directly the adverse impacts of regulation. This is not the case in labor relations. On the one hand, those parties generally adversely affected by labor exchange regulations either are unorganized with respect to the problem (e.g., employees) or are so diffusely or competitively organized (e.g., employers) as to render ineffectual an aggregating of their deregulation interests. On the other hand, the parties generally affected beneficially by the regulations described later are superbly organized, politically potent, and unabashedly activist: For instance, unions have pushed for the passage of much of the legislation involving labor relations for the past 85 years. Also, unions lobbied for economic and social regulation of industry: The Teamsters and the Steelworkers have joined in common

4

fronts with their respective employer groups, the one to oppose deregulation proposals and the other to lobby for increased regulation as a means of protectionism (by now, of course, the political-economic "deal" between Chrysler and the Auto Workers is also well-known, though under-appreciated).[2] The reasons for these and similar coalitions are not so obvious and probably more varied than might be suspected, but they are beyond the scope of this analysis.

In sum, labor relations is an area of economic activity that has largely been ignored during the contemporary period of increasing interest in the nature and consequences of governmental regulation. Indeed, most analysts have failed even to recognize as regulation those political interventions into the labor market that do exist in vast numbers. It has already been pointed out that labor relations is unique among regulated industries in the pattern in which its participants are organized. Whereas the strength of the competing organized interests in other industries has shifted sufficiently to spur academic, journalistic, and political excitement about regulatory behavior in those industries, the pattern of organized interests in labor relations, unchanged for about 40 years, has stultified research into this subject. In short, those "whose ox is being gored" have yet to find a common ground, they have yet to aggregate sufficient resources (intellectual, financial, political, etc.) to overcome the highly effective power of special interests to maintain the regulatory system from which the latter draw numerous benefits.

Analysts have somehow failed to recognize that government intervention in the labor market is unquestionably regulation of intrinsically and functionally the same sort as found in, say, the airline industry. It should be clear that the Wagner Act (1935) was and is as regulatory in its objectives as the Interstate Commerce Act (1887). Neither the fact that regulation has been viewed in a limited way nor that, in some industries, organized interest groups which benefit from regulation or deregulation can readily be identified provides a satisfying explanation for the lack of professional interest in the regulation-deregulation issue for labor relations. In conjunction with these two explanations is yet another very important factor that has effectively limited the research of competent analysts in labor relations. This factor is the widely-accepted notion, prevalent for more than half a century, that "labor is not a commodity." The importance of this concept as an axiomatic given cannot be overstressed. If "labor is not a commodity," there is no such thing as a labor market and, since there is no labor market, the government can no more regulate labor (in the usual sense of regulation) than it can regulate breathing. Put another way, if there is no commodity, no exchanges can occur and regulation affects only exchanges.

Obviously, labor is a commodity, and government intervention into and political constraints involving labor market exchanges effectively constitute regulation. It is interesting that there are some professionals, particularly economists, who understand the notion that "labor is a commodity" and who therefore analyze labor markets in purely economic terms. However, when the time comes to draw policy implications from their work, they seem to *reject* the idea. This variety of schizophrenia is evidenced in their routine treatment of market influences on labor exchanges (that can be likened to an analysis of the demand curves for automobiles) which are all but meaningless except as intellectual exercises, because the regulatory framework within which those exchanges take place is ignored.

Labor as a Commodity

Since the notion that labor *is* a commodity is so much at variance with the received wisdom of many decades, it is important to explain the concept in detail. The effort to "take wages out of competition" (which is another way of stating the "labor is not a commodity" axiom) has its origins in the 19th century at least, though one can find powerful strains of the movement stretching as far back as the European guild system of the 14th century (or possibly even farther back in Chinese society). It was tied closely to the origins of modern unionism itself and, not surprisingly, those eminent Fabian scholars of the history of British unions, the Webbs, stated that the core function of unions was to strive for "the deliberate regulation of conditions of employment in such a way as to ward off from the manual working producers the evil effects of industrial competition."[3] Traditionally, the arguments advanced for removing wages from a competitive market system have been couched in ethical, humanitarian, ideological, philosophical, and sociological rhetoric, but economic arguments have been conspicuously lacking. Such an objective is nonsensical because it is impossible in economic terms. Labor will always be a commodity, something of value: An employee will always be a seller of labor, an employer will always be a buyer of labor, and wages (or compensation

6

generally) will always be the price of the commodity. This cannot be changed; at most, it might be distorted.

Government intervention into labor markets (just as government intrusions into any industry) can maintain artificially high prices, create artificially low supplies, construct and maintain a seller's monopoly or cartel, and generally inhibit a buyer's search for replacement commodities, but no government act, program, or policy can ever alter the essential characteristics of the exchange of labor itself. No matter how distorted a market, any market, may be as a result of external political forces, it is still a market and it still functions on the basis of demand and supply considerations: Government regulations simply become an additional variable in the equation. They may be more regular than "acts of God" but equally unbalancing in their effects upon the equilibrium toward which markets adjust over time.

The reasons why otherwise perceptive people should fall prey to this blind spot are a mystery. Though one expects to find union publications touting the need to "take wages out of competition" because, for them, it is a matter of self-interest, and though observing the Fabian Webbs arguing likewise should occasion no surprise, why should this notion be found, for example, in the Treaty of Versailles (Section II, General Principles, Article 427, establishing the International Labor Organization)? Why should it be declared, in effect, the public policy of the United States (Section 6, Clayton Act of 1914)?

All the so-called "humanitarian" arguments have been based upon the misconception that treating labor as a commodity somehow implies a pernicious form of slavery. But no economist has ever suggested that buying and selling *labor services* is in any way comparable, conceptually or functionally, to buying and selling people. We totally reject the notion that the laborer is no more than his labor. The fundamental error becomes evident when it is remembered that a large number of American workers routinely engage in offering their labor for sale in an explicit market context. Granted, such people as lawyers, doctors, insurance agents, consultants, dentists, veterinarians, commission sales people, independent plumbers and electricians, writers, and many others are not normally thought of as *employees* but they undoubtedly are *workers* in every sense of the word except that of a Marxian class. For such persons, it is crystal clear that their labor services are bought and sold and that, in the absence of regulations, the exchange value (price) of these services would be determined entirely by market conditions. To say that labor is a commodity is by no means to suggest that human beings are chattel: It is a long-accepted maxim of Western civilization that laborers cannot be sold, but it is just as accepted that every person possesses an inalienable right to offer his or her labor in exchange for whatever remuneration can be obtained.

Nor can it be denied that, conceptually and functionally, such remuneration represents a price of the sort which attaches to every commodity offered for exchange. *A wage is a price.* Rigorous analysis of this whole issue has been impeded from the very beginning by the unfortunate fact that a different word is applied to a particular price. But just as there is no difficulty in perceiving that a *fee* is a price for labor, so there should be no problem in understanding that wages, salaries, fees, and prices are all essentially the same. Of course, a variety of terms can lead the unwary to believe they refer to different phenomena.[4]

Playing hocus pocus with definitions can be an effective propaganda technique. Separating wages from prices and labor from the concept of a commodity no more frees the one from the economic laws that affect the other than distinguishing the human body from a rock somehow frees the body from the law of gravity. "Price," therefore, is the general, inclusive term covering all forms of value that attach to the elements of an exchange by means of which the parties determine how much of one commodity (e.g., wage, salary, or fee in the form of money and nonpecuniary benefits) is equivalent to another commodity (e.g., x hours of personal services in the form of physical, intellectual, creative, or manual labor).

Note further that, all the so-called humanitarian reasons again notwithstanding, it is nowhere argued here that an exchange involving the labor of a person is *exactly* the same as an exchange involving the labor of, say, a horse. People are not horses or machines or rocks, and the assertion that labor is a commodity (or that wages cannot be divorced from competition) is in no way dehumanizing. There is no difficulty in distinguishing the human body from a lump of clay, yet various physical laws apply equally and indiscriminately to both. Apply enough heat and both will be consumed: The difference is that the animated human body can, of its own volition, escape from the heat while a lump of clay cannot. So with labor. What distinguishes labor from other commodities is that, when a potential buyer negotiates a labor exchange, the bargain is struck with the laborer; but when the commodity is a machine, a horse, or stand of trees, the bargain *involves* them, but is not *with* them. Indeed, if there is dehumanization in labor exchanges these days, it may be found primarily in regulations that prevent the laborer from controlling who purchases his services and that prevent him from determining for himself what will be the terms and conditions of the exchange.

Traditional Marxist sociology made much of what was termed "alienation," a condition that arose when those who labored were unable either to benefit from the fruits of their work or to control the nature of their work.[5] As the remaining portions of this analysis argue, however, the impact of government regulations concerning labor relations has been disproportionately felt by those who directly provide the labor; it is *their* choices and options which are most constrained and, to that extent, the regulation of labor relations carries with it an inevitable increase in the alienation of American workers.

This brief detour was occasioned by the observation that, perhaps, one important reason why many students of regulation and students of labor relations have generally failed to connect the two subjects is that both have become imbued with the "labor is not a commodity" notion. The idea that they might be connected is usually dispersed by a Pavlovian reaction induced by "conventional wisdom." The fringes are nibbled but the core is left untouched because to do otherwise would open a host of possibilities until now securely locked in a Pandora's box. The territory, however, is not and has never been totally virgin: A few hardy souls may be found, both in earlier decades and today, but their work has not received the attention it deserves. We acknowledge with appreciation their insights and the paths they sought to explore.[6] Certainly, those earlier investigators worked in an intellectual climate that was both hostile to their objectives and less able to perceive the policy implications of their findings. Today, however, though the climate has become more hospitable and there is greater interest in searching actively for ways in which scholarly analysis can be translated into public policy,[7] it remains true that the interim decades have served only to strengthen further the axiomatic nature of the notions that discouraged explorations into the labor relations field for any who desire to place that area of study in the mainstream of the social sciences. Scholarship on labor relations has largely become dominated by lawyers (partly because labor relations itself has become dominated by statutes and regulations), by unionists, and by others who, for the most part, have all but totally avoided the critical policy issues in the field.

Overview

Though the ultimate purpose of this work is to analyze the possibility of deregulation in labor relations, it will also be necessary to detail the regulatory framework as a proper foundation for any discussion of deregulation. In general, the focus will be on the private sector of labor relations (both as a utilitarian limitation on a broad subject and as a simplifying device). Public sector labor relations could in large measure be included by implication in the discussion, but an explicit coverage of this issue would unduly complicate and overextend the treatment.

Chapter II presents an overview of the regulation versus deregulation phenomenon. Each is a fundamental question in public policy because each represents a different and conflicting view of the proper role of government, the nature of private economic activity, and the consequences of imposing new, extraneous influences upon that activity when the purposes of those intrusions are primarily political rather than economic. Previous studies of regulation in other industries are summarized and assessed, and Chapter II introduces not only the deregulation policies which have been implemented to date but also the dynamics of the deregulation process. Conceptually, regulation and deregulation are not simply opposite facets of the same issue. The former is a condition or state of being related to government-imposed restraints *which are in place*. The latter, if it were nothing more than the other side of the coin, would refer simply to the *absence* of such restraints. While that may be the end result, it is not what deregulation is all about. Deregulation, in fact, refers to the process by which these restraints are withdrawn; it is a winding down, a devolution or dissolution, which may be partial or complete. Viewing deregulation as a *process,* we shall consider the forces promoting or impeding the withdrawal of government from this particular market. The next chapter explores these matters without any explicit connection to labor relations.

Chapter III offers a survey of the myriad ways in which labor relations is regulated, together with the analysis required to identify the economic actors whose market behavior is most affected and the ways in which those consequences are felt. Given the proposition that labor relations is arguably the most heavily regulated activity in the United States and the correlative proposition that this is not generally recognized, Chapter III presents an extensive, though not exhaustive, discussion of the topic. In that chapter, the legal, political, and economic *framework* of modern labor relations regulations is specified. The topic is approached in terms of substantive versus procedural regulations and in terms of which bilateral relationship (between each pair of the three current parties in industrial relations) is principally being affected.

Chapter IV contains an assessment of costs of regulating labor relations. Also, regulatory costs are used to estimate the gains that would result from deregulation of the labor sector. The costs associated with ten different types of labor regulation are evaluated, taking into account such impacts as unemployment, lost income and output, inflation, and resource misallocation.

Chapter V deals with the political economy of the labor sector and considers the process of deregulation in labor relations. In other words, those who stand to win or lose as a result of deregulation are explicitly identified and the repeal of specific regulatory legislation and its effects are addressed.

The final chapter contains a brief summary with particular emphasis on policy implications both for the short and the long term.

One further remark is appropriate. Regulation of industry by government has always been justified on the basis of protecting the interests of the public, particularly those members of the public who deal directly with the industry. The Interstate Commerce Commission Act was specifically designed to protect the interests of shippers from the dominant position held by the nation's railroads in the late 1800s. Similarly, the various pieces of legislation that regulate labor relations were justified on the basis of protecting employees from the then dominant position of employers. It is important to acknowledge that the rationale for *de*regulation is again the public interest. That is to say, there is now a concensus that the public is better served by at least some industries if regulatory constraints are removed than if they are retained. At any rate, airline deregulation has never been viewed as "anti-airline," but rather as "pro-air traveler/shipper;" trucking deregulation is not "anti-trucking." In the same vein, we do not view the deregulation of labor relations as "anti-union" or "anti-employer" but as "pro-employee" and "pro-consumer." If the interests of employees and consumers can be advanced by dismantling or reducing the regulatory environment of labor relations, then our society would be well-served by such a policy because those who work and consume are co-extensive with society itself.

NOTES TO CHAPTER I

[1]See James T. Bennett and Manuel H. Johnson, *The Political Economy of Federal Government Growth: 1959-1978* (College Station, TX: Texas A&M University, 1980).

[2]See Don Erik Farmer, "Enforcing a Cartel: A Study of the ICC and the Motor Carrier Industry," *Southwestern University Law Review.* (1979), pp. 597-639; Thomas G. Moore, "The Beneficiaries of Trucking Regulation," *Hoover Institution Study* No. 76-3, Stanford University; James E. Annable, Jr., "The ICC, the IBT, and the Cartelization of the American Trucking Industry," *Quarterly Review of Economics and Business* (Summer, 1973), pp. 33-47. On the Steelworkers, see *Daily Labor Report,* No. 142 (July 21, 1980), p. A-14, describing the "prompt government action needed to revitalize the industry" as recommended by the "Steel Tripartite Committee."

[3]Sydney and Beatrice Webb, *Industrial Democracy* (New York: Longmans, 1926), p. 807.

[4]The confusion generated by using different terms for prices can also be seen in the case of interest rates. An interest rate is a price, the price charged for the use of one dollar for one year. Many states have "usury" laws which set the maximum rate of interest that may be charged, but other prices are not regulated. Since the price charged for the use of money is given a different name, apparently it is viewed differently by policymakers.

[5]For a contemporary treatment of this notion from a purely Marxist perspective, see Herbert Aptheker, ed., *Marxism and Alienation: A Symposium* (New York: Humanities Press, 1965).

[6]Though the number of persons and works we might cite here is quite small, nevertheless over a period of 40 years it is still too large a number to be treated comprehensively in a footnote. Accordingly, we mention only a sample: Sylvester Petro, *The Labor Policy of a Free Society* (New York: Ronald Press, 1957); Henry C. Simons, *Economic Policy for a Free Society* (Chicago: University of Chicago, 1948); David McCord Wright, ed., *The Impact of the Labor Union* (New York: Harcourt, Brace, 1951); Edward H. Chamberlin, *Labor Unions and Public Policy* (Washington, DC: American Enterprise Association, 1958); F. A. Harper, *Why Wages Rise* (Irvington, NY: Foundation for Economic Education, 1957); Henry Hazlitt, *Economics in One Lesson* (New York: Harper, 1946); W. H. Hutt, *The Theory of Collective Bargaining* (London: King and Son, 1930); Charles E. Lindbloom, *Unions and Capitalism* (London: Yale, 1949); Philip D. Bradley, ed., *The Public Stake in Union Power* (Charlottesville, VA: University of Virginia, 1959).

[7]Witness, for example, the flowering of serious journals having this as their raison d'etre: e.g., *Public Choice, Policy Review, Journal of Labor Research, Public Policy,* and *Journal of Policy Studies.*

Chapter II

The Political Economy of Regulation and Deregulation

Many of the regulations governing employer-employee relationships have been in existence for a number of years. Such government requirements as occupational licensing, unemployment insurance, minimum wages, and collective bargaining date back several decades. In addition, there has been a substantial amount of recent regulation in the labor relations sector. These past and present government regulatory activities seem to indicate that the labor market in the United States is incapable of functioning efficiently, if at all, without large-scale state intervention.

This chapter examines the efficacy of regulation in general, and labor relations regulation in particular, in order to determine whether, in fact, such a public policy is economically and socially desirable. To gain some perspective, it is useful to look at the theory of government regulation and to compare the predicted regulatory outcomes with what actually occurs in practice. Since there is a large and growing number of regulated sectors in the economy, what may be learned from the experiences of various other industries might usefully be applied to the labor relations sector.

The next section deals with the economic theory used to justify government regulation. A survey is then provided of the extent of government regulation in various segments of the economy, including the labor relations sector. Regulation in theory differs widely from that in practice. Research has shown that many regulations are largely ineffective, in spite of the enormous costs imposed on the economy by government constraints. Alternative theories of regulation have been developed to explain why regulation occurs and why regulatory outcomes differ so widely from the original objectives.

The final section of this chapter addresses the deregulation issue and presents the case for removing government controls on the private sector. Case studies of the economic impact of deregulation are presented, and industries and sectors of the economy which would benefit from deregulation are identified. To introduce Chapter III, we specifically evaluate the justification for regulation in the labor relations sector.

The Economic Justification for Government Regulation

The question of whether or not to regulate a particular industry or sector of the economy raises two separate questions: (1) is regulation constitutionally legal, and (2) does regulation make good economic sense?[1] Regarding constitutional legality, the 14th Amendment to the U.S. Constitution prohibits the state from seizing private property without "due process of law." Therefore, because the regulation of a firm or of individual activity reduces prospective income, regulation by the state may deprive persons or organizations of their private property. Such action raises the question of whether regulation is consistent with "due process of law." In the case of *Munn v. Illinois* (1877), the Supreme Court dealt with this issue for the first time. Drawing from precedents within the common law, the Court upheld state regulation of grain storage fees.[2] In so doing, the court contended that industries "affected with a public interest" were subject to regulation. However, the court failed to specify which industries were critical to the public interest so that the courts had to wrestle with this issue time after time. Finally, in the case of *Nebbia v. New York* (1934), the Supreme Court determined that states could, in effect, regulate whatever economic activity they chose (consistent with their own constitutions), provided that state regulations were not preempted by federal authority as, for example, in the case of regulation of currency.[3]

After the *Nebbia* decision, the question of whether or not to regulate an industry or activity shifted from constitutional legality to economic criteria. In effect, the crucial question became: When does regulation make good economic sense? Economists have shown that regulation is justifiable only in the case of "market failure." Market failure, broadly defined, occurs when private markets are unable to transmit accurate information, through prices, about the relative scarcity of goods and services.[4] Two different sets of circumstances may lead to market failure: (1) large-scale operations which have constantly declining unit costs of production and, (2) the existence of "externalities."

Industries in which the technology of production of goods and services requires large, highly specialized plants involving substantial

14

investment and high fixed charges in order to achieve low unit costs may be susceptible to market failure. Plants constructed in such industries must be built in anticipation of demand; however, until demand develops, plant capacity is only partially used. Regardless of initial demand, capacity must be adequate to satisfy demand at its peak level, but during off-peak periods, much capacity is idle. Even when demand is low, fixed costs must be met and, for very large plants, fixed costs are enormous. Obviously, the greater the volume of output the lower will be unit fixed costs (which are the major portion of total unit costs).

Since sales can be increased by reducing prices, there is a strong incentive among large-scale firms to lower prices. Such competition, however, may become destructive, for it will always be to the advantage of a firm to continue cutting prices: It may lose business if it does not. Price warfare, in this case, can drive an industry into bankruptcy. If bankruptcy is not the result, it is likely that combination or collusion will take place among producers — in effect, a monopoly will be formed. Industries with these characteristics are referred to as "natural monopolies" because of the inevitability of monopoly.[5]

Externalities occur when the production or consumption of goods or services affects the interests of other individuals in such a way that no legally recognized rights of compensation or redress exist.[6] Consider the problem of pollution as an example of a production externality. Suppose that firm A dumps waste into a river. By using the river as a sewer, firm A may adversely affect the operations of other firms (B and C) located downstream. B and C may have to incur substantial costs to make the river's polluted water clean enough to use in their production operations. Thus, production costs of firms B and C are higher because of the costs imposed by firm A's pollution. As a result of the higher production costs, B and C produce less output and sell their output at a higher price than would be the case if firm A did not pollute. Similarly, firm A is able to lower its cost of production by dumping into the river so that more is produced and sold at a lower price that would be the case if firm A incurred the cost of pollution control. Output and prices are, therefore, distorted by the presence of externalities.

Externalities that impose costs on third parties are referred to as "negative." Positive externalities occur when benefits are bestowed on others. As an illustration, consider the overseas traveler who obtains innoculations and vaccinations against various diseases. Certainly, the traveler himself benefits because he is protected against ill-

15

ness, but everyone else in society benefits as well because the likelihood of epidemics is reduced when the traveler returns. Society has an important stake in disease prevention and, to encourage innoculation, will often subsidize the provision of such services.

As illustrated above, negative externalities result in a less than optimum determination of prices and outputs, because all the costs of production are not borne by the producer of the negative externality. Profit-maximizing competitive firms produce at a level of output at which price equals the marginal cost of production, i.e., the cost of producing an additional unit of output. This level of output is more desirable from a social welfare perspective: It represents the most efficient level of production of goods and services since unit costs are minimized. In the absence of externalities, the marginal cost schedule of a firm represents *all* the additional costs incurred to produce a given unit of output. If, in fact, all costs of production are private, the profit-maximizing behavior of the firm will yield the socially optimal output.[7] However, it is not always true that the full cost of producing goods and services is internalized by the firm, as shown in the pollution example above. Thus, one can conceive of another marginal cost schedule which includes all the costs of production, both private (internal) and external. This schedule would reflect greater unit costs at all levels of output so that if a firm were compelled to account for all the costs associated with its production, it would equate marginal costs to price at a lower level of output than otherwise.[8]

When individual firms produce negative externalities, supply is increased. If only private costs are considered, a greater quantity of output will be available for sale at each possible price. Since the market demand curve is downward sloping, greater supply will mean lower equilibrium market prices. The end result will be greater production and a lower product price than is socially desirable in the industry not fully internalizing its costs: There will, however, also be reduced production and higher product prices than the socially desirable amounts in those industries that have the external costs shifted to them.

Economically speaking, these two basic forms of market failure, natural monopoly and externalities, may require public sector regulation in order to approximate the competitive market outcome. In the case of natural monopolies, there is room in the market for only one producer. Therefore, the state grants a selected producer the exclusive right to serve a specific market. Regulation takes the form of price controls which are established by regulatory commissions that oversee the operations of the monopolies. Price controls on natural monopolies are usually one of the following two types: (1) average cost pricing or (2) marginal cost pricing by price discrimination.

Average cost pricing allows a firm to cover all its costs since the price is set equal to the average cost per unit of product produced. This price, however, is far from representative of the competitive market outcome. Competition normally leads price-taking firms to expand production to the point where marginal cost equals price. As shown in Figure II-1, the price would be set at p_1 under average cost pricing which would result in output q_1. Clearly, the regulated price, p_1, is greater and the corresponding quantity, q_1, is smaller than the competitive solution, p_2 and q_2. Therefore, marginal cost pricing would allow lower prices and greater output. But, a strategy such as marginal cost pricing presents a problem to the regulators. Because natural monopolies experience continually declining average costs, marginal cost will always be lower, so that setting price equal to marginal cost causes the firm to operate at a loss. If marginal costs are to be used as the benchmark for price setting, regulators must provide a method by which firms can recover their costs plus a fair return. A policy of price dis-

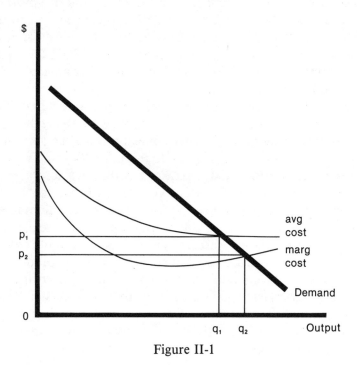

Figure II-1

17

crimination among buyers makes it possible to gain additional revenue from some customers while selling to buyers on the margin at a price approximating marginal costs. Figure II-2 illustrates discriminatory marginal cost pricing with falling long-run costs. A large quantity of output, q_1, is sold to customers who are willing to pay a higher price (p_1) and the remaining quantity, q_1 q_2, is sold at a price, p_2, which is equal to marginal cost. Revenue from the sale of quantity q_1 q_2 is not enough to cover the average cost of its production so losses occur for this block of sales, as shown by the shaded rectangle in Figure II-2. However, these losses are more than offset by the profits received from the sale of quantity q_1 at price p_1 (represented by the lined rectangle in Figure II-2).[9]

The regulation of firms which produce negative externalities requires that government explicitly assume the property rights to all public resources, e.g., air and water, and tax private parties for the use of these resources. Such taxes are essentially rents charged for the lease of rights to dispose of wastes, congest roads, etc., on publicly-owned lands and resources. Economic theory specifies that the correct tax for use would equal the social cost created by the production of an additional good or service. Figure II-3 illustrates the use of government taxation as a remedy for negative externalities created by air or water pollution. Line PBC represents the schedule of marginal social costs from wastes discharged to the environment. Line ABD is the schedule of the marginal costs to the polluting firm of treating discharged waste. In this case, the correct tax to be imposed is the amount P, which is equal to the marginal social costs of waste discharge (PBC). Given the tax, P, a firm will take action to treat internally the first X_1 units of waste discharged to the environment because the tax is greater than the internal cost of treatment up to this point. Beyond X_1 units of waste discharge, a firm would choose to pay the tax since the internal cost of treatment exceeds the social cost imposed due to discharge. Thus, the firm acts along the line ABC, taking internal actions to avoid pollution from A to B and electing to pay a tax on the remainder.[10]

Suppose a firm's total waste load is X_2. The firm would choose to treat X_1 waste units internally so that no externalities are produced and then discharge X_1X_2 units of untreated waste into the environment. Therefore, government would require the firm to pay a tax of P dollars per unit of untreated waste for a total cost of X_1BEX_2 dollars shown by the lined rectangle in Figure III-3. This amount compensates society for the externalities imposed by the X_1X_2 units of untreated waste.[11]

18

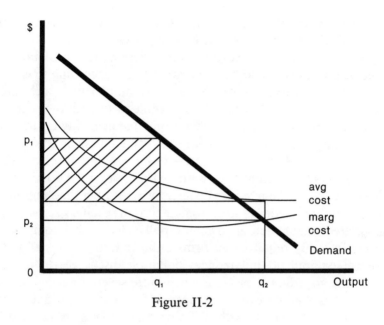

Figure II-2

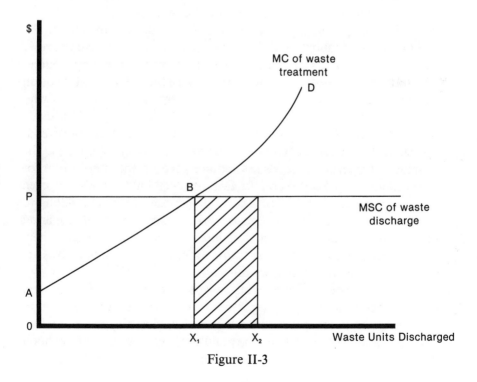

Figure II-3

The government regulation solution to the externality problem, although theoretically correct, is no panacea. The most fundamental problem, as one might suspect, is the determination of the optimal user tax. The tax would have to vary by firm according to each one's contribution to external costs. Due to the complexity of such externalities as pollution, it is practically impossible to sort out the contribution of each individual firm to environmental damage. Any tax imposed by government would likely be arbitrary. Although taxing the production of externalities is the most desirable technique in that social welfare is maximized at minimum cost, we note briefly that the government has dealt with pollution in a very different way. Rather than impose taxes, the government requires firms to take certain specified actions (and the associated costs) such as installing pollution control equipment and technology. By requiring all firms in an industry to install pollution control equipment that reduces pollution discharges to a specified level, the government places a much more severe financial burden on some firms than on others, because different firms produce different amounts of pollutants with differing technologies. A tax that varies with the level of pollution allows the firm the options of installing pollution control equipment or paying the tax.

It is quite possible that externalities can be dealt with through the private market economy if liability rules existed or if private property rights were extended to include all commonly held property (resources that have no defined individual property rights). The legal solution depends on the courts to enforce sanctions on one private party who inflicts external costs on another private party. The law could provide compensation for damages incurred that would internalize for offending parties the external costs of their actions. Coase has shown that the existence of externalities does not require government intervention for a solution to market failure. In fact, market failure does not even occur in most cases of external costs. If private parties are willing to bargain or if liability rules or property rights can be defined, a market solution is obtainable without state intervention. Only in cases where the number of parties is large or transactions and information costs are great will a private solution be difficult to achieve.[12]

When private property rights can be enforced, externalities tend to disappear because profit opportunities for firms encourage them to internalize the externalities. Once a firm recognizes the possibility that damage claims may arise from the pollution it generates, the likelihood of such claims will be taken into account in the firm's profit and loss calculations. The revenue foregone should water be used for waste discharge becomes an internal opportunity cost.

In sum, the traditional economic theory of regulation specifies two narrow situations in which the regulation of business by government may be economically justified: the presence of natural monopolies and externalities. Regulation of externalities must be qualified further to include *only* those cases where liability rules cannot be defined or where private property rights cannot be extended to eliminate external costs.

The industries that might be classified as natural monopolies are: (1) locally-provided services such as electric power, gas, telephone, and transit (all generally regarded as "utilities"), and (2) larger-scale services such as regional electric power generation, pipelines, and long lines telephone service. Industries and activities that produce externalities appear to be more numerous; however, most of the external effects created are small and, in all but a few obvious cases, externalities are internalized through common law sanctions or the establishment of property rights. An obvious area where external effects are large, complex, and difficult to internalize through the private sector is water and air pollution by industrial firms in densely populated regions. Such industries as automobiles, mining, construction, paper, chemicals, stone, clay and glass, primary metals, and electric power generation are the primary sources of air and water pollution. Economic reasoning requires that regulation of the natural monopolies listed above takes the form of average cost pricing or discriminatory marginal cost pricing. Regulation of externalities should take the form of user taxes that vary according to an activity's external costs.

The Extent of Government Regulation

The vast array of regulatory agencies now in existence is surprising in view of the very limited economic justification for regulation: It is difficult to rationalize the degree of government control over the private sector. Until the 1930s, government controls centered on regulating prices and entry in the natural monopolies — interstate transportation, electricity production, and pipelines.[13] The New Deal era, however, saw the introduction not only of further price and entry regulation of natural monopolies, but also regulations designed to pursue social goals as well as to appease special interest groups. Few of the regulatory activities undertaken during the decade of the thirties could claim any real economic merit. Table II-1 lists the major federal regulatory agencies created during the 1930s. Of these seven agencies, only two, the Federal Communications Commission (FCC) and the Food and Drug Administration (FDA), could be considered justifiable based on the economic theory presented above.

The New Deal era was a particularly important time with regard to the regulation of labor relations. In addition to passage of the National Labor Relations Act (1935), which established the National

Table II-1

Federal Regulatory Agencies of the New Deal Era

Organization	Year Established	Activities
Federal Power Commission now part of the Department of Energy	1930	Regulated wellhead gas. Prices and wholesale prices of natural gas and electricity sold for resale in interstate commerce
Food and Drug Administration	1931	Controls the labeling and content of foods and drugs
Federal Communications Commission	1934	Sets prices for telephone and telegraph service. Also controls entry into telecommunications and broadcasting in the U.S.
Securities and Exchange Commission	1934	Regulates investor information and securities exchange transactions
National Labor Relations Board	1935	Regulates all aspects of labor relations-conducts elections, determines fair labor practices, etc.
Federal Maritime Commission	1956	Regulates fares and scheduling of transocean freight shipments
The Agricultural Marketing Service, Dept. of Agriculture	1937	Determines Health Standards for farm products and regulates milk prices in some regions
Civil Aeronautics Board	1938	Regulates airline passenger fares, controls air routes

Source: *The Challenge of Regulatory Reform: A Report to the President from the President from the Domestic Council Review Group on Regulatory Reform* (Washington, DC: U.S. Government Printing Office, 1977).

Labor Relations Board to oversee union elections and to rule on unfair labor practices, many other legislative efforts which, in effect, regulated the conditions of worker employment and wages were instituted. For example, the Davis-Bacon Act (1931) required all private contractors working on federally financed construction projects to pay wages at least equal to the prevailing wages in the region. The Social Security Act (1935) mandated that every state must adopt an unemployment insurance law that would impose compulsory payroll taxes on all employers in order to support workers discharged for reasons other than "cause." Also, in 1938, the Fair Labor Standards Act established the first nationwide minimum wage law.

Between 1940 and 1970, only three new agencies were created with the authority to control private sector activities: the Federal Aviation Administration (1948), the Animal and Plant Health Inspection Service (1953), and the Federal Highway Administration (1966). The 1970s saw a new wave of regulatory activity which affects virtually all private sector firms. Much of this newest regulation was concerned with the environment and workers' health and safety. The principal agencies involved are the Occupational Safety and Health Administration (OSHA) and the Environmental Protection Agency (EPA). The controls of these two regulatory agencies apply to almost all manufacturing firms. Table II-2 lists the major regulatory agencies established during the 1970s and briefly describes their activities.

A better understanding of the extent of government control over the economy can be obtained by accumulating industry shares of national output produced under regulation. On the product side of the market, industries controlled by the price-regulating commissions accounted for 8.8 percent of Gross National Product (GNP) in 1975. The financial sector, which accounts for 3 percent of GNP, typically has had controls on entry, service offerings, and interest rates at either the national or state level. Environmental regulation covers industries that produce about 12 percent of GNP. Mining, construction, and chemical firms were required to divert large parts of their investments to meet mandatory pollution-control equipment requirements. The paper, primary metal, motor vehicle, stone, clay and glass product, and petroleum refining industries were not required to make such investments in plant and equipment, but were regulated because of pollution-emission restrictions on certain production processes and products. Therefore, product market regulations cover firms in the economy which produce approximately 24 percent of GNP.[14]

Table II-2

Federal Regulatory Activity During The Decade of the 1970s

Organization	Year Established	Activities
Federal Railroad Admin., Department of Transportation	1970	Sets safety standards for interstate railroad transport
National Highway Traffic Safety Admin., Department of Transportation	1970	Sets safety standards for automobiles
Environmental Protection Agency	1970	Sets environmental quality standards and approves abatement plans operated by state agencies.
Postal Rate Commission	1970	Establishes classes of mail and rates for those classes; sets fees for other services.
Consumer Product Safety Com.	1972	Sets product safety standards
Mining Enforcement and Safety Admin., Department of Interior	1973	Sets mine safety standards
Drug Enforcement Admin., Department of Justice	1973	Controls trade in narcotics and drugs
Occupational Safety and Health Admin., Department of Labor	1973	Sets and enforces workers safety and health regulations
Energy Regulatory Admin., Department of Energy	1974	Regulates crude-oil prices, sets allocation levels for crude-oil products
Nuclear Regulatory Commission	1975	Controls the construction and operation of civilian nuclear power plants
Commodity Futures Trading Commission	1975	Sets terms and conditions of future contracts and the exchange trading such contracts
Copyright Royalty Tribunal	1976	Sets fees on copyright materials

Source: See Table II-1.

On the factor side of the market, regulations affect virtually 100 percent of the industries in the private sector. Minimum wage and maximum hour regulations currently cover about 65 percent of the non-agricultural work force.[15] Unemployment compensation payments are required from firms that employ roughly 97 percent of all workers.[16] The activities of the National Labor Relations Board (NLRB) can potentially control the employer-employee relations of almost every private firm in the economy. The NLRB is empowered to regulate the actions of virtually any private business that violates a set of guidelines establishing the "proper" relationship between employer and employee. All firms accepting work on federal government projects must agree to pay wages at least equal to the prevailing wage in the region where the work is undertaken. Occupational safety and health regulation applies widely to firms in the mining, manufacturing, and construction industries.[17] Clearly, the coverage of government regulation has become widespread, especially in light of the type of the limited justification for controls based on economic theory. Over the years, the purpose of regulation has shifted more toward social change and away from purely economic objectives. But, regardless of whether society desires regulation to achieve efficiency or other social goals, the critical question remains: Does regulation effectively accomplish the intended objectives?

Is Regulation Effective?

In general, economic and political conditions have been such that the bureaucratic practices used in price, health and safety, environmental, and labor relations regulation have not produced the desired results. Regulation has, in fact, detracted from economic efficiency and growth, not only because many regulations were ill-conceived, but also because the controls have been improperly administered. In health, safety, and environmental regulation the implementation of extremely costly equipment standards has not resulted in the improvement of working and living conditions for which they were designed. Labor relations regulation has had obvious adverse effects on inflation and unemployment.[18]

In terms of natural monopoly regulation, inflationary spirals during the 1960s and 1970s outran agency-allowed annual percentage rate increases so that prices were artificially depressed and demand far greater than in those industries not subject to controls. In other words, average annual rates of price increase in the regulated industries were below those of the nonregulated sector so that the demand for the services of these industries grew more rapidly. Expansions in demand could only be satisfied as long as there was extra capacity to increase production. However, with reduced profitability resulting from price controls during high inflation, there was reduced capacity growth. Therefore, the growth rate of production for the regulated industries declined relative to earlier periods and relative to the nonregulated industries. By the end of the 1970s, the natural monopolies lagged behind the rest of the economy in both investment and production.[19]

Those industries most subject to health, safety, and environmental controls have been characterized by high prices and low output increases indicating that regulation caused production to become more costly: This is the expected outcome when externalities occur. At the same time, however, such regulation should have provided more health and cleaner air and water. But, in fact, the result has been increased costs, increased prices, and reduced production without marked improvements in the quality of working conditions or the environment.

The Environmental Protection Agency and the Council on Environmental Quality have acknowledged that, on a national scale, gains in air and water quality have been quite limited. A recent survey showed that during the 1970s total pollution emissions were reduced for only two of six major air pollutants (particulates and carbon monoxide) while emissions of one major pollutant (nitrogen oxide) actually increased.[20] Even the reductions in two of the pollutants cannot be attributed solely to regulation. Many industry-specific standards were put in place after product and process improvements already undertaken by firms were beginning to reduce pollution. Pollutants were being reduced because it was profitable, given new technology, to conserve products that had been previously discharged as waste. Automobile emissions of major pollutants were being reduced by improvements in fuel burning performance in new car models each year. Regulation of auto emissions may have done little beyond taking credit for the improvements that would have materialized in any event. It is also likely that recent air and water quality changes resulted from cycles in industrial activity rather than regulation. Pollutant emissions are directly related to industrial production and production is determined by economy-wide demand conditions. Therefore, any reductions in pollution that might have occurred during the 1970s were probably due to downturns in economy-wide industrial goods production.[21]

Professor Paul MacAvoy at Yale has shown that environmental regulation has had little effect on the pollutant emissions of industry.

26

Using regression analysis, MacAvoy estimated pollutant emissions per unit of output in six major industries for the period 1968-1976. The general finding was that "new pollution-control regulations did not change the pollution load on the economy."[22] The model he tested hypothesized that industrial pollution per unit of output was a function of technology, the economic business cycle, and regulation.[23] The combined industry equation showed that technology significantly reduced pollution while regulation insignificantly increased the pollution load.

Peltzman has shown that the regulation of automobile manufacturers by the national Highway and Traffic Safety Administration has failed to improve preregulation automobile safety records.[24] To point out government regulatory ineffectiveness, Peltzman projected the automobile death rate, assuming a nonregulatory environment, to 1980 and estimated the rate to be 33 deaths per billion vehicle miles. The federal government, however, has established as its 1980 target a rate of 36 deaths per billion vehicle miles. Peltzman pointed out that

> the implication of all this is that essentially nothing in the post-1965 behavior of the total death rate can corroborate that safety devices provide the kind of lifesaving suggested in safety literature (or, indeed, any lifesaving at all). This behavior can in fact be explained entirely by the forces that explain variation in the death rate before the devices became mandatory.[25]

Grabowski has surveyed the literature examining the effects of government regulation on drug innovation.[26] He asserted that, "a consistent finding is that regulation has had a significant negative effect on the rate of innovation. . . . [T]aken together . . . studies seem to provide considerable support for the hypothesis that regulation has been one of the principal factors responsible for the observed decline in innovation."[27] An influential study also by Peltzman showed that the rate of drug innovation since the 1962 Kefauver-Hariss amendments has been cut in half.[28] Moreover, Peltzman contended that the percentage of ineffective drugs has been constant during both the pre- and post-amendment periods, which implies that a significant decline in the introduction of effective drugs took place. In addition, Wardell has argued that Britain, where the drug regulation environment is less restrictive, has experienced demonstrable benefits from drugs that could not have been introduced in the United States.[29] Viscusi examined the impact of occupational safety and health regulations, using data on industry health and safety investments and injury rates for the period 1972-1975, to determine OSHA's effect on industrial safety. Viscusi concluded:

> what is clear is that the agency's enforcement policies have not had any direct impact on job hazards. Moreover, even if these efforts were effective, their desirability would be doubtful since the preponderance of violations are not for dimly understood health hazards, the type which market forces are well-equipped to handle through compensating wage differentials. In short, policy-makers have paid too little attention both to the potential desirability of the present intervention and to the economic mechanism through which the enforcement activities will exert their influence.[30]

Because the focus of this book is the regulation of labor relations, the following chapter contains a detailed discussion of government controls on employer-employee relationships and the effects of these controls. Therefore, only a brief summary of the extent of regulation on this sector is provided above. As Chapter III points out, labor relations regulation also does not fulfill its objectives.

The Cost of Regulation

In addition to the ineffectiveness of government regulation, government administration of controls has imposed enormous costs on the private sector. According to Scherer, "the regulatory functions at all levels of government have far ranging effects on the operation of the economy, even though these activities require modest amounts of government spending and employment. At the federal level, regulatory activities are broad in size."[31] Because government does not bear all the costs of its regulatory activity, these costs may be regarded as "hidden taxes" that are passed on to the private sector.[32] Some interesting work in the measurement of the costs of federal regulations has been done by Professor Weidenbaum who has stated that,

> when we try to add up the activities of the federal regulatory agencies (comprehensive data on the growing state and local regulation are not available), we find that the operating budgets are on a steep upward trajectory. The budgeted $4.8 billion to run the various federal regulatory bureaus in fiscal year 1979 represents a 115 percent expansion from the $2.2 billion level of fiscal 1974. There are few parts of the private sector that have recorded such

gains in the same five-year period. Government regulation of business literally has become a major growth area of the American economy.[33]

The costs of federal regulation of business are enormous. In 1976, the conservatively-estimated total cost of federal regulation exceeded $66.1 billion, a figure that is about 3.9 percent of total output in that year, or about $307 per capita. Not only are the costs of regulation substantial, but these costs are also growing rapidly. By 1979, according to Weidenbaum's estimates, total costs had exceeded $102 billion — an increase of 55 percent over 1976. About 95 percent of these costs were borne by the private sector so that the administrative costs of the 56 regulatory agencies, which appear in federal expenditures, are only a small fraction of the total.[34] Thus, federal expenditures for regulatory administration severely understate the impact of federal regulatory activity on the economy.

Both the tremendous costs of regulation and its general ineffectiveness cause one to speculate why, if regulation is so bad, government control over the private sector continues to increase in scope and even to flourish. The fundamental issue that must be confronted in considering government regulation is why government, in reality, regulates the private economy. Understanding government regulation requires a recognition that there is a chasm between economic rationalizations for government intervention in the economy and the actual instances of state intervention. While the economic justification of regulation is justified by the market failure rationale, perhaps a more appropriate explanation is the "government failure rationale."[35] The government failure approach is based on the observed imperfections of governmental solutions to private problems and stresses that the market failure argument for regulation (or any other argument) is unrealistic since it fails to consider the political economy of administering controls by the public sector. The market failure model is flawed by the unwarranted assumption that government can correct "imperfect" markets costlessly. As discussed earlier, government is hardly a reliable or cost-effective instrument for carrying out this policy.

Government Failure as an Explanation of Regulation

The government failure thesis of regulation rejects the market failure theory as an explanation of why government regulates the

29

private sector. One would like to think of public sector employees as protectors of the "public interest," but this view is naive and unrealistic. A government employee will no more pursue something called the public interest, as opposed to his own self-interest, than will an employee in the private sector. Therefore, the government failure approach regards regulation as something that occurs through the pursuit of individual self-interest by government bureaucrats, monopolistic labor unions, businesses, and other special interests exercising political power.

In the case of labor unions and a few powerful businesses, regulation comes about as the result of private interest groups lobbying for protection from competition. Powerful labor and producer elements may achieve a cartel through government regulation of entry, wages, and prices in their sector. The cartel operates to the detriment of consumers and society in general.[36] Unions are concentrated enough to make the benefits to the union from lobbying exceed the costs, while consumers, who suffer from protective regulation, succumb to special interests because consumers are many, widely dispersed, and face high costs of organizing to resist regulations in favor of unions or other forms of monopoly.

The public-sector manager who can achieve a rapid expansion in regulatory programs under his supervision can expect to benefit directly in terms of rank, salary, prestige, and perquisites of office. In many agencies the upper ranks of the bureaucracy are accessible only to supervisory personnel. New programs, or old programs with an expanded mission, offer opportunities for additional staff and promotions. The bureaucrat can thus enhance his own interests from the initiation of additional activities by the public sector. Of course, expanded government activity cannot take place without approval, ignorance, or at least apathy on the part of the voting public. Perhaps the most important reason for voters to perceive the expansion of government activity as common to their own interests is that, in creating a new program, the bureaucracy convinces the voter that the benefits far outweigh any reasonable estimate of the costs. This is accomplished by the bureaucracy through the manipulation of crises.

Crises, whether real or imaginary, have become a fact of everyday life in the United States. Examples are commonplace: the energy crisis, the health care crisis, the environmental crisis, the unemployment crisis, and so forth. Crises are generally declared by a government agency (working in tandem with one or more special interest groups) to dramatize some domestic or international condition. These crises are an important component of the search for new government programs: The declaration that an emergency exists implies that, unless the government takes immediate action on a large scale, the consequences for the economic, social, and political system can be catastrophic. Needless to say, when government takes action, it requires enormous infusions of federal (and perhaps state and local) appropriations to hire staff and to implement the courses of action required to deal with the situation. The more "immediate" the action, the greater is the amount of waste likely to ensue from this haste. From the perspective of the bureaucrats who identify the crisis, a warning is given to the public of the existence of a threat to the "public interest" which, given adequate resources and regulatory powers, the bureau can ameliorate or control.

The bureaucrat publicizes the crisis as much as possible to ensure that the public is convinced of its importance and to gain public support for a government program to "do something" right now. Because the bureaucrat, in the view of the public, is working in the public interest, the credibility of government employees far exceeds that of individuals in the private sector whose motivations may be regarded by the public with suspicion because of the profit motive. In emphasizing a crisis, the bureaucrat may well justify a government program to intervene on the basis that the party guilty of creating the crisis is more concerned with greed rather than with the public interest, e.g., private industries that pollute are passing the costs associated with pollution to the general public rather than reducing profits by cleaning up the pollution.

The fact that the public has been willing to accept the notion that civil servants work in the public interest also makes more believable bureaucratic estimates of the costs and benefits associated with whatever government program is being designed to deal with the crisis.

Because bureaucratic self-interest is a major motivating factor in the expansion of regulation, it is axiomatic that crises will hardly ever be solved by regulation; if a crisis disappears, the justification for the agency, its employees, and its appropriations would vanish. Bureaucratic entrepreneurship requires that funding and support must increase over time and, for this to occur, problems must multiply as well. There is no incentive for the careful management of taxpayers' money or the problem (whether real or contrived) at hand, for if an agency does not spend all its money in one budget year, additional appropriations in the following year may be in jeopardy. The pressure is so strong to avoid excess funds at the end of the fiscal year in the federal government that

31

a ". . . spending spree occurs. Billions of dollars are committed in the last days of each fiscal year so that funds are not 'left over.' "[37] Government failure is, from the perspective of the bureaucrat, success. As Professor James Q. Wilson of Harvard has observed, "the regulatory agency will tend to broaden the range and domain of its authority, to lag behind technological and economic change, to resist deregulation, to stimulate corruption, and to contribute to the bureacratization of private institutions."[38]

The crux of the government failure thesis of regulation is that the goal of groups which seek regulation is somehow to transfer wealth to themselves. Such activity is made possible through lobbying by interest groups and through bureaucratic manipulation within an overall context of voter apathy or ignorance. Monitoring government actions is costly, and individuals will let their wealth be taken away from them as long as the costs of overcoming political decisions are greater than the amount of wealth taken away or they *perceive* as taken away. As the cost of monitoring political decisions increases, a larger quantity of wealth will be transfered through regulation from the general public to special interest groups and government bureaucrats.

Deregulation: Issues and Evidence

In light of the evidence presented above, the performance of regulation over the years can hardly be described as impressive. Regulation's dismal record practically precludes its recognition as a "necessary evil." The record strongly supports the government failure thesis of regulation over the market failure theory. Therefore, it is not clear that government should even attempt to regulate those activities which obviously inflict social costs, for it may be that the cure is much worse than the disease.

While the private sector may not resolve every problem perfectly, market forces are vastly superior to bureaucratic planners for the purpose of allocating resources in an efficient manner. Probably the best examples are cases where government controls have been lifted from private sector functions. A comparison of the performance of an industry under regulation with its performance after deregulation provides evidence of the relative effectiveness of government and the market. As one might suspect, there are not many instances of deregulation simply because bureaucrats and special interest groups have fought "tooth and nail" to resist the dismantling of government controls.[39] However, there are two recent cases, commercial airlines and natural gas production, which were made possible by voter-consumer pressures and the persistence of a few political appointees.[40] In both situations, deregulation has not been complete (e.g., state regulations on natural gas production remain in place), price controls are being phased out over a period of time, and entry to these industries is still somewhat restricted. Thus, benefits from partial deregulation, more than likely, indicate further economic gains from total decontrol.

Deregulation of the airlines by the Civil Aeronautics Board (CAB) in 1978 offers strong evidence of the superiority of market competition over government control. As a result of deregulation, normally scheduled airlines have instituted new flights in over 100 cities, and 231 completely new routes have been added by as many as 35 commercial carriers.[41] The increased competition due to deregulation has led to a tremendous number of discount fares. About 50 percent of all commercial airline customers receive price discounts on air travel. Discount fares and increased service to Florida have resulted in an increase in passenger demand at Miami Airport by 21 percent. Air traffic nationally was up by 13.5 percent for the first nine months of 1979 and an increase of 17 percent was reported during 1978.[42] Basic fares have increased due to escalating fuel costs. When adjusted for inflation, however, the real price of air travel has become relatively cheaper. According to Rakowski and Johnson, "the empirical evidence is overwhelming that the price of air transportation can be significantly reduced and that passenger traffic is quite sensitive to changes in fares."[43] Loss of service by communities was a major argument against deregulation, but many studies have shown that this has not materialized and that new firms and commuter carriers have picked up any slack in service that may have resulted.[44]

Throughout most of the 1960s and well into the 1970s, the Federal Power Commission (FPC) fixed the price of natural gas at approximately one-third the price of its energy equivalent in crude oil. This below-equilibrium price encouraged consumers to use more natural gas while greatly reducing the incentives of producers to discover additional supplies. Needless to say, a policy of stimulating consumption and discouraging production is an ideal strategy for the creation of shortages. Due to regulation, proved reserves of natural gas declined to a 10 year supply (given annual consumption rates) by 1974 compared to a 20 year supply before major regulatory initiatives. Natural gas shortages in the early 1970s were as great as 20 percent of the total demand.

In 1976 the first major step toward reducing shortages was undertaken by the Federal Power Commission. FPC rate proceedings allowed increases in new contract prices of about one dollar per million cubic feet, almost double the previous level. Following this decision, there was a dramatic increase in new exploration and development activity and a reduced growth in consumption. Demand-driven price increases provided new investment incentives, thus increasing production and causing consumers to practice conservation. Practically overnight the political and economic disruptions brought about by regulation-induced shortages were eliminated. Presently, there are plentiful supplies of natural gas and the price, in real terms, has become relatively stable.

It would be hasty to argue on the basis of two case studies of deregulation that all government-regulated activities in our economy should be decontrolled. However, there is a significant body of evidence to show that the costs associated with the regulatory process are extremely high. Several studies mentioned earlier found not only that the costs of regulation were high, but also that the benefits from regulation were negligible. In cases where the net benefits from regulation are obviously negative, decontrol should be a completely noncontroversial policy. Even in situations where the benefits are not known, the burden of proof that regulation is useful should fall on the regulators, and voters should carefully monitor such activities for evidence of bureaucratic self-interest.

Without doubt, our economy has become over-regulated and would vastly improve as a result of deregulation. The most obvious areas for deregulation are those activities that are currently controlled but do not possess the characteristics of market failure. No rational economic argument can be made to preserve regulation in these areas and its existence can be attributed only to the influence of special interests.

Currently, railroads, airlines, trucking, and oil and gas producing firms are operating under phased or total deregulation. Our analysis has suggested that further efforts along these lines should be undertaken by legislation which abolishes the activities of the Interstate Commerce Commission at the present stages of decontrol. It is also necessary to eliminate corresponding state regulatory agency controls.

Additional government regulatory functions that could be unambiguously phased out or eliminated are automobile safety requirements, control of drug innovation, industrial health and safety requirements, and many industry environmental standards. Other activities where control or decontrol is more ambiguous are electric utilities, gas pipelines, telecommunications and broadcasting, and some areas of environmental pollution. Again, it must be stressed that the burden of proof that regulation is desirable should be on government regulators, for the additional costs of their activities are well documented and have been shown to be excessive, while the additional benefits from their actions are dubious, at best. Unless the benefits from a specific regulatory activity can be shown to exceed the associated costs, there is no justification for its existence. Therefore, although the regulation of natural monopolies and externalities can be justified based on the pure economic theory of market failure, its efficacy is questionable when the more comprehensive theory of government failure is applied.

The preceding review of regulation produces useful policy implications for the labor relations sector. Hardly any labor relations regulation can be justified based on the market failure theory. Certainly, no labor sector activity can be classified as a natural monopoly. Thus, price and entry regulation is not a legitimate function for government agencies that oversee employer-employee relations; yet, minimum wage-maximum hour policies and government-sanctioned collective bargaining effectively control the wages paid by employers.

NOTES TO CHAPTER II

[1]Most studies that trace the evolution of regulation in the U.S. tend to focus on these two major issues. See, for example, Leonard W. Weiss and Allyn D. Strickland, *Regulation: A Case Approach* (New York: McGraw-Hill Book Co., 1976); and, Frank M. Scherer, *Industrial Market Structure and Economic Performance* (Chicago: Rand McNally & Co., 1970).

[2]*Munn v. Illinois,* 94 U.S. 113 (1877).

[3]*Nebbia v. New York,* 291 U.S. 502 (1934).

[4]The economics literature is replete with discussions of market failure. For a complete treatment of this topic, see Francis Bator, "The Anatomy of Market Failure," *Quarterly Journal of Economics* (August, 1958), pp. 351-379.

[5]A more thorough discussion of this argument can be found in Jack Hirschleifer, *Price Theory and Applications,* 2nd ed., (Englewood Cliffs, NJ: Prentice-Hall Inc., 1980), pp. 349-350; and, Clair Wilcox, *Public Policies Toward Business* (Homewood, IL: Richard D. Irwin, Inc., 1971), pp. 276-277.

[6]A comprehensive treatment of externalities is available in James M. Buchanan and W.C. Stubblebine, "Externality," *Economica* (November, 1962), pp. 371-384; and, E.J. Mishan, "Reflections on Recent Developments in the Concept of External Effects," *Canadian Journal of Economics and Political Science* (February, 1965), pp. 1-34.

[7]See Joseph J. Seneca and Michael K. Taussig, *Environmental Economics* (Englewood Cliffs, NJ: Prentice-Hall, Inc., 1974), pp. 32-35.

[8]Ibid., p. 35.

[9]The above argument is taken from Hirschleifer, *Price Theory and Applications,* p. 349; and, Scherer, *Industrial Market Structure and Economic Performance,* p. 552.

[10]See Seneca and Taussig, *Environmental Economics,* pp. 236-237.

[11]Ibid., p. 237.

[12]Ronald Coase, "The Problem of Social Cost," *Journal of Law and Economics* (October, 1960), pp. 1-44.

[13]Passage of the Act to Regulate Commerce (1887), which established the Interstate Commerce Commission (ICC), gave the federal government jurisdiction over railroad rates and service. Later, the ICC gained jurisdiction over all interstate surface transportation (trucks, bus lines, oil and gas pipelines, and domestic water carriers).

[14]For documentation of the percent of GNP produced by regulated industries see Paul W. MacAvoy, *The Regulated Industries and the Economy* (New York: W.W. Norton & Co., 1979), pp. 21-25.

[15]See Neil W. Chamberlain, Donald E. Cullen, and David Lewin, *The Labor Sector,* 3rd ed. (New York: McGraw-Hill Book Co., 1977), p. 507

[16]Ibid., p. 496.

[17]See MacAvoy, *The Regulated Industries,* p. 22.

[18]Dwight R. Lee, *The Inflationary Impact of Labor Unions* (College Station, TX: Texas A & M University, 1980).

[19]MacAvoy, *The Regulated Industries,* p. 22.

[20]U.S. Environmental Protection Agency, "National Air Quality and Emissions Trend Report, 1976" (Research Triangle Park, NC, 1976).

[21]The above discussion draws heavily from MacAvoy, *The Regulated Industries,* pp. 101-104.

[22]Ibid. p. 102.

[23]The variable for technology was accounted for by using a time trend over the years 1968-1976. The business cycle variable was constructed from an index of capacity utilization for industry taken from Federal Reserve Board data. The regulation variable was represented by a dummy variable which equalled one for the presence of regulation of pollutant i, and zero otherwise.

[24]Sam Peltzman, "The Effects of Automobile Safety Regulations," *Journal of Political Economy* (August, 1975), pp. 677-725; also, Sam Peltzman, *Regulation of Automobile Safety* (Washington, DC: American Enterprise Institute for Public Policy Research, 1975).

[25]Peltzman, *Regulation of Automobile Safety,* p. 45.

[26]Henry Grabowski, *Drug Regulation and Innovation* (Washington, DC: American Enterprise Institute for Public Policy Research, 1976).

[27]Ibid., p. 37.

[28]Sam Peltzman, "The Benefits and Costs of New Drug Development," *Regulating New Drugs,* ed. Richard Landau (Chicago: University of Chicago Center for Policy Study, 1973), pp. 9-20; also, see Sam Peltzman, *Regulation of Pharmaceutical Innovation: The 1962 Amendments* (Washington, DC: American Enterprise Institute for Public Policy Research, 1974).

[29]William Wardell, "Therapeutic-Implications of Drug Lag," *Clinical Pharmacology and Therapeutics* (January, 1974), pp. 73-96.

[30]W. Kip Viscusi, "The Impact of Occupational Safety and Health Regulation," *Bell Journal of Economics* (Spring, 1979), p. 136.

[31]Joseph Scherer, "How Big is Government?" *Challenge* (September/October, 1975), p. 61.

[32]For a thorough treatment of the costs of hidden taxes see James T. Bennett and Manuel H. Johnson, *The Political Economy of Federal Government Growth* (College Station, TX: Texas A & M University, 1980); also see James T. Bennett and Manuel H. Johnson, "Paperwork and Bureaucracy," *Economic Inquiry* (July, 1979), pp. 443-444.

[33]Murray L. Wiedenbaum, *The Future of Business Regulation* (New York: Amacom Books, Inc., 1979), p. 15.

[34]Ibid., pp. 22-23.

[35]The government failure hypothesis of regulation has been advanced by a number of scholars. Generally, two approaches to this theory are found in the literature. One approach focuses on the self-interest of those who are regulated and stems from the work of George Stigler, "The Theory of Economic Regulation," *Bell Journal of Economics and Management Science* (Spring, 1971), pp. 3-21; and, Sam Peltzman, "Toward a More General Theory of Regulation" *Journal of Law and Economics* (August, 1976), pp. 221-240. A second approach concentrates more on the self-interest of the regulators and, to some extent, takes account of both parties to the regulatory process. This vein of the theory can be found in the work of Gordon Tullock, *The Politics of Bureaucracy* (Washington, DC: Public Affairs Press, 1965); James M. Buchanan and Gordon Tullock, *The Calculus of Consent* (Ann Arbor, MI: University of Michigan Press, 1962); Paul Craig Roberts, "The Political Economy of Bureaucratic Imperialism," *Intercollegiate Review* (Fall, 1976), pp. 3-11; Paul Craig Roberts, "Idealism in

Public Choice Theory," *Journal of Monetary Economics,* (August, 1978), pp. 605-610; James M. Buchanan and Richard E. Wagner, *Democracy in Deficit* (New York: Academic Press, 1977); Morris P. Fiorina and Roger Noll, "Voters, Bureaucrats, and Legislators: A Rational Choice Perspective on the Growth of Bureaucracy," *Journal of Public Economics* (April, 1978), pp. 239-254; William A. Niskanen, *Bureaucracy and Representative Government* (Chicago: Aldine-Atherton, Inc., 1971); Susan Rose-Ackerman, *Corruption: A Study in Political Economy* (New York: Academic Press, 1978); and, Bennett and Johnson, *The Political Economy of Federal Government Growth.*

[36]A previously overlooked, but highly significant, cost associated with the cartel behavior of regulated groups is the waste of resources employed to effect a pure transfer of wealth from consumer and other groups to the cartel. Such a phenomenon is referred to as "rent-seeking" and occurs when interest groups expend resources to influence regulators in order to gain a monopoly position and obtain additional rents. These expenditures do not contribute to the real productive activity of the economy. They are merely expenditures to bring about a transfer of income. The cost to the economy of such rent-seeking expenditures is the value of the output that they could have produced had they been productively employed elsewhere. Research on rent-seeking can be found in Gordon Tullock, "The Welfare Costs of Tariffs, Monopolies, and Theft," *Western Economic Journal* (June, 1967), pp. 224-232; Anne O. Krueger, "Political Economy of the Rent-Seeking Society," *American Economic Review* (June, 1974), pp. 291-303; and, Richard A. Posner, "The Social Cost of Monopoly and Regulation," *Jouranl of Political Economy,* (August, 1975), pp. 807-827.

[37]For documentation and a discussion of the effects of this spending spree, see James T. Bennett and Manuel H. Johnson, *Better Government at Half The Price* (Ottawa, IL: Caroline House, Inc., 1981), esp. Chapter III.

[38]James Q. Wilson, "The Rise of the Bureaucratic State," *The Public Interest* (Fall, 1975), p. 97.

[39]Although much attention is drawn to the private lobbying groups on Capitol Hill, much less is known about the efforts of government agency lobbyists. Peter Woll, *American Bureaucracy,* 2nd ed. (New York: W.W. Norton & Co., 1977), p. 194, has summarized these activities as follows:

> The ability of administrative agencies to marshall support in favor of particular programs is often severely tested, and as a result the agencies have frequently created public relations departments on a permanent basis to engineer consent for their legislative proposals. It has been estimated that the executive branch spends close to half a billion dollars a year on public relations and public information programs. Not all of this expenditure is for political purposes, for there are a number of legitimate public information programs that administrative agencies must undertake. But whatever the percentage may be for non-political purposes, it is obvious that agencies are expending huge amounts of funds, time, and effort on indirect and direct lobbying activities. Administrative personnel engaged in public relations are not so open about their activities as their counterparts in private advertising and public relations firms, for the myth that the bureaucracy is "neutral" must be maintained, if possible. However, through what might be called undercover devices, the bureaucracy engages in extensive lobbying and propaganda activities.

[40]Although the President has recently signed a bill to deregulate the trucking industry, time has been much too short to determine the effects of this deregulation effort.

[41]"Dividends From Regulation," *Time* (November 12, 1979), p. 113.

[42]Ibid.

[43]James P. Rakowski and James C. Johnson, "Airline Deregulation: Problems and Prospects," *Quarterly Review of Economics and Business* (Winter, 1979), pp. 65-78.

⁴⁴"For example see Rakowski and Johnson, "Airline Regulation"; John C. Panzar, "Regulation, Deregulation, and Economic Efficiency: The Case of the CAB," *American Economic Review* (May 1980), pp. 311-315; and, Paul MacAvoy and John Snow, eds., *Regulation of Passenger Fares and Competition Among the Airlines* (Washington, DC: American Enterprise Institute for Public Policy Research, 1977).

Chapter III

The Regulation of Labor Relations: An Overview

As noted in Chapter I, labor relations is perhaps the most heavily regulated economic activity in the United States. Based on the most fundamental definition of regulation, i.e., constraints upon decision-making imposed by "the machinery and power of the state,"[1] regulatory constraints can be easily identified in all facets of the employment relationship. To facilitate the analysis, however, the regulation of labor relations is divided into two categories. The first is termed "substantive" regulation and identifies state-imposed constraints upon the final product or the outcome of the employment relationship. These restrictions involve such matters as wages, hours, working conditions, and contractual obligations. The second category is termed "procedural" regulation and consists of restraints on how the employment relationship is conducted, i.e., the procedures and mechanisms by which two or more parties attain the status of employer and employee: in this category are such matters as unionization, bargaining, grievances, and strikes.

From the outset it is important to emphasize that the discussion of regulation is limited solely to the context of government action: All decision constraints imposed by the parties themselves or which emanate from the market, for example, are excluded. The market is the ultimate regulator of all economic activity in the sense that it gives each decision maker a set of choices and concomitant set of consequences from which a person can elect a course of action based upon personal goals. Since market transactions are, by definition, interchanges, it follows that there must exist at least one other party who has certain goals.

Moreover, each party to any particular transaction is enmeshed in a seamless web of additional relationships with others — all of whom are pursuing maximizing strategies. Accordingly, employment relationships are constrained by the same types of market factors that affect any sort of transaction. These are excluded from the analysis precisely because regulation, being a government interference with

41

market constraints, involves choice restrictions which are by definition external to the market and which are therefore antithetical to individual maximizing strategies. The regulation problem does, however, have a market approach because regulation also involves transactions in political power. This "political market" overlays the labor market, and references to it are inescapable from time to time.

It should also be noted that all forms of particular government action will be considered together. Regulatory behavior can, of course, have its locus at the state or national level; it can stem from judicial, legislative, or executive action; and it can emanate from various private agencies operating under government authority. Labor relations in the private sector are regulated principally at the federal level by virtue of a generally broad latitude given to the interstate commerce rationale of the Wagner Act and its later amendments. By now, there are very few private employment situations that are so small or limited in scope as to fall below the test for coverage by the federal National Labor Relations Board. The Board itself creates regulations directly affecting labor relations, putatively under authority of congressional legislation, though the frequency with which it has been overruled by the courts suggests that Board members may occasionally be substituting their personal versions of how labor relations should be conducted.

Furthermore, such purely private agencies as labor unions regulate a variety of procedural aspects of employment relations and they do so under the authority of federal law. All these specific sources of regulatory action are, naturally, part of the state (directly or, as in the case of unions, indirectly) and all are discussed together. Insofar as employers and employees are concerned, there is seldom any important difference in constraints upon their choices whether the state regulations affecting them derive from the NLRB, the AFL-CIO, the Eighth Appeals Circuit, the Congress, or the Department of Labor: The result is almost always the same.

In a society ruled by law, statutes (together with their judicial interpretations) constitute the first line of state action and the discussion therefore begins with that subject in this survey of the ways in which labor relations are regulated. Following this, attention is given to such secondary sources of regulatory behavior as executive agencies and private groups. Throughout, the discussion continues the categorization described at the beginning of this chapter; namely, substantive and procedural regulation.

Substantive Regulation of Labor Relations

Perhaps the most obvious form of substantive limitation upon transactions in the employment relationship can be seen in the requirement that labor services must not be compensated below a certain level (minimum wage) nor provided beyond a certain time amount (maximum hours) unless, in the latter case, an overtime differential is charged. This is, of course, a governmentally-set floor price for a product and a ceiling upon the quantity that can be purchased. Since the federal government's basic legislation on this subject in 1938 (Fair Labor Standards Act), episodic amendments have produced higher minimum wage levels, lower maximum hours permitted, and a wider coverage through the addition of employee groups formerly exempted.[2] The FLSA itself specified certain sub-minimum rates for a few special classes of employees, and legislation other than FLSA sets considerably higher minimum rates for other employee groups.[3] Over 50 million employees are presently governed by federal wage and hour standards, with some 5.5 million more covered by comparable state legislation: This total represented over 70 percent of the nonagricultural civilian workforce employed in 1975 and is likely a low estimate at that since employees not otherwise under FLSA (or parallel state legislation), but covered instead by the Davis-Bacon, Walsh-Healey, or O'Hara-McNamara Acts, have been excluded from this calculation. Congress attempted to bring state and municipal employees under FLSA-type coverage in 1974, but this was found to be unconstitutional by the U.S. Supreme Court in 1976 as a violation of the federal principle.[4] Thus, a large majority of the labor market is regulated and economic exchanges between employer and employee must conform to a minimum price and a maximum amount of sale. Moreover, the political trend is toward increasing the first, decreasing the second, and increasing the number of those who are limited by these constraints.

The available evidence and research are persuasive that the chief effect of this particular variety of regulation is to limit the employment opportunities of youth, women, racial minorities, and the not yet skilled; to reduce the viability of smaller firms; to add an upward pressure on all wages; and to increase marginally the general price level. The effect on youth, women, racial minorities, and the not yet skilled is fairly straightforward: It can be detected for example, in the unemployment rates of these groups[5] and signifies an apparent belief that it is better to be unemployed at the minimum rate than to be employed at some lesser wage more consistent with their lower productivity due to lower skill and experience levels. Yet the connection between their inability to find work and the legislation that produces this difficulty has historically been obscured by social welfare payments. There is also a strong indication that the disemployment effect of the minimum wage shows up not only in higher unemployment levels for certain groups but also in their increased vulnerability to unemployment cycles.[6] The viability of smaller (and/or newer) firms is reduced because their vitality is more a function of a lower price (where the larger and/or longer established companies can more easily rely upon consumer perceptions of "quality" or brand name identification): Since labor costs for such companies are usually the major factor in prices, ever higher minimum wage floors can be more readily absorbed by larger or older firms. Facing rising labor costs, a firm may turn to mechanization, which has the long-term effect of permanently displacing or obviating the need for certain labor skills altogether — an alternative that is also less available to the smaller or newer company.

Against these consequences, all of which are generally negative in an efficient labor market (because imposed politically from without), is the by now discredited argument that minimum wages serve as a cure for "poverty." There may be some beneficial effects upon employee efficiency in the sense that a wage that produces family income above the subsistence level is likely as well to reduce the employee's fundamental concern for the necessities of life — thus permitting greater concentration upon the requirements of the job. And it may also be true that, as labor costs rise in partial response to rising minimum wage levels, employers become more conscious of the overall importance of employees — thus possibly creating a pressure for a more solicitous employment relations policy. Both propositions, however, have never been directly tested and, at this point, are still highly speculative.

Organized labor has traditionally lobbied strongly for minimum wage legislation (in all its forms, not just in regard to FLSA): Its public position has always been couched in the most humanitarian language involving principles of social and economic justice. Indeed, to cite only one instance, recognition of the youth employment displacement had grown sufficiently strong by 1974 that a potentially successful effort to amend the FLSA to permit a "youth differential" (subminimum) was initiated that year, but the effort failed due largely to the influence of the AFL-CIO. It is safe to suggest that the federation opposed not so much the concept *per se* of a lower minimum wage for unskilled, inexperienced young people as it opposed the argument underlying that proposal — namely, that the minimum wage *in fact* has a disemployment effect.[7]

As for the ceiling on hours worked (at "straight-time"), this too is a regulation of economic activity which remains surrounded by considerable mythology and contending claims. Traditionally, the limitation was grounded on arguments that recalled the "sweatshops" of the late 19th and early 20th centuries. While recognizing that, when Americans were pioneers, they labored far longer hours than prevailed in any factory, proponents of this form of regulation asserted that the factory was nonetheless an unnatural setting, unhealthy over long periods of work time, and disruptive of family relationships. Moreover, safety considerations were mentioned in connection with trades which were thought dangerous or which were conducted by women or children. Whatever the merits of such health and welfare arguments then, one major rationale advanced in modern times for limitations on hours and/or days worked is that shorter standard work periods leave more time for employees to function as consumers (thus to aid the economy) and that less work time is conducive to greater efficiency.

With respect to the first of these, it is said that more leisure time (holding income constant) leads to greater consumer spending in that employees have more time to be customers. The proposition is open to considerable challenge, however, for there is little evidence that the volume of family spending on goods other than necessities is a function of leisure time: The question particularly arises when, in the case of a family unit, one member of the family may be the main source of income while other family members engage in consumer activities (a situation somewhat reduced as more American families consist of two or more employed persons). Further, a loosening in the hours worked ceiling does not translate directly, if at all, into a reduction in hours worked. There is, for example, the possibility of the employee limited in this fashion who works additional hours at the mandated *premium* rate (i.e., "time and a half" or "double time") or who may even acquire additional employment by "moonlighting." There is evidence that limits on hours worked is simply an extension of wage bargaining.[8]

At the same time, information on the efficiency argument is either lacking or dated. As Bloom and Northrup have noted, while the "reduction in hours of work has been accompanied by increases in productivity," it is important to remember that "productivity and worker efficiency are not necessarily synonymous terms." The former is a measure of what comes out of the worker-equipment interaction, but "efficiency" is solely a measure of what the worker alone does. "Hence an increase in labor efficiency will result in an increase in productivity, but an increase in productivity does not necessarily mean that labor efficiency has increased." The relationship between lower hours worked and worker productivity is a statistical correlation only — with capital replacement, management effectiveness, technological innovation, *plus* (possibly) worker efficiency accounting for improved productivity. The studies that *have* been done on the effect of hours worked on labor efficiency have suffered the shortcomings of having looked particularly at an increase in hours worked over 40 (rather than at reductions below 40), of having based the findings on data related to the rather abnormal conditions of World War II, and of having found a distinct difference in the effects of the number of hours worked per day versus the number of days worked per week.[9]

Needless to say in the face of these arguments regarding regulations on the maximum amount of labor an employee may "sell" at the standard rate, it is obvious that such a limit accomplishes also the important task of making room for others in the labor market. If it is assumed for the moment that the total amount of labor a society can employ at any one time is both finite and fixed, it follows that the number of people who can be employed in the absence of a limit is smaller than when each prospective employee is prevented from working at his optimum level. Suppose a task requires no more than 120 man-hours of work per day and suppose people generally are willing and able to devote 12 hours per day to gainful employment.[10] With these parameters, the task would employ ten persons. Then assume that a regulation is imposed limiting the hours worked per day to ten: The consequence is that the same task now *must* employ two additional persons and, as a political matter, these two people would have a powerful incentive to see that such a regulation were imposed (so far, the cost to the employer is assumed to be constant so he has no reason to oppose this change). The lower the maximum hours ceiling, the larger is the number of additional people employed at the task and the larger is the number of people who have an incentive to advocate the reduction.

Now, suppose that people can work over the ceiling only if they are paid a premium wage. First of all, a reason has just been created for an employer to resist the imposition of the ceiling (labor costs could rise). On the one hand, the employer could control the situation by requiring that no one work overtime at the premium rate. On the other hand, the cost of permitting current employees to work overtime might well be less than the cost of finding and training additional personnel. Second, the number of people with a beneficial interest in the regulation has been vastly increased. Before, only those additional people who would be employed under a reduced hours ceiling had an incentive to support the change; now, all presently employed people have an incentive as well since, before the fact, they might anticipate extra income from working more hours at a premium rate.

It is not difficult, therefore, to understand why the number of hours worked (both per day and per week) is regulated and why that sort of regulation is strongly supported by labor unions. Unions in particular create their own, more restrictive ceilings which are embedded in a plethora of work rules promulgated by the union itself, made judicially enforceable in union-negotiated contracts, or achieved through political pressure in the form of local codes governing work, e.g., construction specifications. Any limitations on the *amount* of work a person may do is equivalent to an hours ceiling. Thus, work rules that specify the maximum width of a paint brush, the maximum number of brick to be laid per hour, the size of a cargo sling net, the weight of a hammer, or who may perform which particular tasks with how many helpers are all devices that, whatever may be their formal rationale, serve to spread work around and to increase the number of people who must be employed to achieve a given work result.

Note that an extreme form of this sort of regulation is the licensing law — which, by the way, unions have also supported vigorously.[11] Licensing laws go beyond maximum hour limits, "make work" rules, and construction codes in that they totally constrain entrance to a profession or a craft. With entry thus limited (by registration fees, experience requirements, apprenticeships, examinations, recommendations from established practitioners, so on and so forth), those already "in" are more certainly guaranteed a larger and more stable amount of the available work. It also follows, under these circumstances, that prices will be higher and that any strike will likely be more successful, because there are fewer alternative employees to work in place of strikers.[12]

While one may regard as desirable the collective goal of providing some amount of gainful employment to the maximum number of those willing to take it, it is not at all clear either that the damage done to individual preferences is worth it or that the collective goal is attainable in light of the system inefficiencies produced by such regulations. The first problem is easily recognized but difficult to analyze since the answer depends ultimately upon one's values. The second problem is more amenable to empirical study and is dealt with in later chapters. Note, however, the possibility that people who are not working at all due to minimum wages, who are employed below their capabilities due to an hours ceiling, or who are restricted in the scope of their employment due to work rules, are ready sources of inefficiency, bitterness, and alienation. It is further possible that eliminating these difficulties by removing the regulated limits on individual work preferences might well introduce such vitality to the economic system that additional capital and jobs would be generated to compensate for the absence of mandated employment. There may, indeed, be immediate net savings resulting from reductions in a multitude of government welfare and support programs which today undergird system inefficiencies. And there is an increasing number of respected economists who suggest that a revitalized national economy could generate sufficiently greater revenues even at lower tax rates to fund necessary government programs.

The discussion above deals with "substantive" regulations regarding labor relations — government-imposed restrictions upon the particular terms or conditions of employment — in contrast to the "procedural" regulations considered below. This treatment given to substantive regulations should not be taken as an implication that the topic has been exhausted. Far from it. Much more, for example, could be said about the substantive regulatory impact of such measures as Davis-Bacon or Walsh-Healey, of paperwork requirements imposed by equal employment requirements,[13] or of numerous licensing restrictions which prevent or hinder entry into a variety of professions and trades. Nor can space be devoted to such relatively minor regulations as the setting of mandatory nationwide holidays or regulations which, as of this writing, are merely prospective in nature (as, for example, proposed limitations on the geographic flow of capital and jobs through restrictions on business relocations).[14] Each and every one of these constitutes an impairment of the individual's right to engage in economic activity through the sale of his labor on terms and conditions determined solely by the mutual preferences of seller and buyer.

Procedural Regulation of Labor Relations

Some regulations are called "procedural" in view of their application to the *process* by which employers and employees come together and reach agreement as to terms and conditions of employment. For organizational purposes, procedural regulation is viewed here primarily as restraints created through the institution of unionization: Aside from the substantive restraints deriving from governmental legislation and rules on wages, hours, conditions of employment (e.g., workplace health and safety), equal opportunity, and the like, the process by which employees come together with employers to agree on a mutual exchange of economic goods of value to each is a process that remains largely unregulated in the absence of a union. The employment contract may be formal or informal in the nonunion relationship but, in either case, there is an established body of law available to hold either party to the terms of the agreement. In the presence of a union, however, the state enters the calculations in myriad ways — directly through its express regulatory agencies (e.g., the National Labor Relations Board), or indirectly through its regulations applied to the unions themselves. In fact, this direct-indirect distinction is sufficiently useful to serve as a categorization for the discussion that follows.

Direct regulations on the procedures involved in the employment relationship cover virtually all aspects; only the most important can be highlighted for review. First and foremost, while similar legislation often exists at the state level, the main statute affecting unionization for the private sector is the National Labor Relations Act.[15] Applying to all industries except railroads and air transport (which are governed, insofar as labor relations are concerned, by the Railway Labor Act of 1926), the NLRA sets the basic ground rules for union involvement in how employees and employers within its purview come together and reach agreements about their economic relationships.[17] What the NLRA does is expressly and purposely to encourage unionized collective bargaining on the assumption that employees desire to be unionized and are perpetually frustrated in this goal by obstinant employers. Moreover, the Act assumes that collective bargaining itself is impossible, infeasible, or impractical without a unionized context, i.e., that only a union is able to engage in collective bargaining. Accordingly, the NLRA makes unionization the "natural" state of affairs, with all procedures designed to facilitate or to promote its achievement and to frustrate those who would oppose it. This carries a host of conse-

49

quences as regards the subject of regulating labor relations for it inter-jects between employer and employee a third entity, the union, with governmentally-protected powers to affect that relationship.

The public policy of the United States is declared to be the protec-tion of employee rights (freedom of association, self-organization, and designation of representatives of their own choosing) when these rights are exercised with respect to "negotiating the terms and conditions of their employment or other mutual aid or protection." In the body of the Act itself, however, this policy became somewhat more limited in nature: Notably, for example, these rights were implicitly defined by a series of examples (Section 7) which gave them an organizational and union context ("to form, join, or assist labor organizations"), and a further limit was placed on the activities protected by requiring that they be "for the purpose of collective bargaining and other mutual aid or protection." As a consequence, and in spite of later Taft-Hartley language purportedly emphasizing individual employee rights, it would appear that the main employee "rights" being protected and encouraged are those that can be exercised only collectively and only through a union.

An employer engages in an unfair labor practice if he restrains or coerces employees in their Section 7 rights — rights that have been very broadly defined operationally. Moreover, the NLRB has declared that violations of this sort depend neither upon motive (i.e., whether an action had the *intent* of restraining or coercing) nor upon whether an action in fact *did* restrain or coerce (i.e., its success or failure). "The test is whether the employer engaged in conduct which, *it may reason-ably be said* [by the NLRB?], *tends* to interfere with . . . employee rights under the Act."[18]

The Taft-Hartley Act sought to protect the employee rights listed in Section 7 of the Wagner Act against encroachments by unions but, while this added language seemed to parallel the prohibition against *employer* encroachments, the NLRB has made it clear that, in the Board's opinion, the limits on union restraint of employees are consid-erably more narrow. In other words, though the provisions are com-parable in language, unions are permitted more leeway to encroach upon employee rights than are similarly regulated employers. Thus, to take one example, if an employer refuses to bargain with a certified union, this is a *"per se"* restraint or coercion of Section 7 employee rights: not so if a union refuses to bargain.[19]

The Act also permitted unions to be exempt from these provisions to the extent that a union may freely prescribe its own rules regarding membership. This has been taken to mean that unions are declared not to be restraining or coercing employees if the action or threat involves internal union rules (e.g., fines, suspension, or expulsion). Such fines may be enforced by the courts, and the threat to apply these penalties may even be for the purpose of punishing a union member for failing to do something that would be unlawful under the Act.[20]

The NLRB had originally (and as late as 1946) required that employers maintain a strict neutrality as regards unionism. An employer could not, for example, argue about, exhort, or persuade employees to reject a union's bid to become a certified agent. This seemed particularly galling in view of the assumption rampant in federal labor policy that unions and employers were natural antagonists with conflicting interests: Such a restriction, in effect, gagged the employer. The Supreme Court had recognized (partially) the absurdity of the imbalance by pointing out that employers had a constitutionally protected right to free speech, provided the speech was not coercive.[21] The Board developed, backed by Section 8(c) of Taft-Hartley, a policy of permitting employers to voice objections and opposition to unionization so long as the employer's speech contained "no threat of force or reprisal or promise of benefit." Since then, the Board has tended to interpret broadly what might come within the meaning of those terms: It has condemned, under this language, "threatened loss of employment, . . . closing of plant or going out of business, . . . moving of plant to new location, . . . loss or reduction in pay or overtime, . . . loss of promotion . . ."[22] Yet the result turns upon an impossible distinction imposed by such findings between a threat and a prediction. While the line of demarcation is difficult to draw in practice, the Board and the Courts have tried to distinguish among statements according to whether or not the employer would have discretion regarding the consequences: If the employer himself could bring about the future situation, it was a proscribed threat. Nevertheless, this merely begs the question because such a scheme necessitates some definition of "control" or "discretion." It would be extremely difficult, for example, using this distinction, to evaluate an employer's statement that, were his work force to be unionized, the company would go out of business and the jobs would disappear. In the extreme case, a showing that company profits were so large that even a doubling of the wage bill would not lead to bankruptcy (assuming no increase in productivity and no product price increases) might well indicate that the statement was a threat. But what is the time span? Perhaps the employer was thinking not of one or two years in the future but of ten years. And except for involuntary bankruptcy proceedings forced by creditors, couldn't it be said that the closing of a business is *always* at the owner's discretion? After all, the owner could operate at a loss so long as the company's or his own personal assets were sufficient to cover the deficit.

Clearly, both employers and employees — the former generally much more so — are closely regulated as they engage in the ritual that precedes formal unionization. The NLRB, backed by a court system which more often than not prefers to grant deference to the Board's presumed industrial relations expertise and knowledge, appears to believe that employees are incapable of assessing for themselves what are their best interests, what are the costs and benefits of unionization, and who can be believed when faced with conflicting assertions from employers, unions, and other employees. One recent study of Board regulations concerning the electioneering activities of employers and unions prior to a Board-administered union agent election disclosed that these pervasive restrictions have little basis in reality; indeed, virtually every assumption underlying NLRB regulation in this area was disproved by direct measurements of employee opinions, beliefs, and decisions.[23] Quite apart from these empirical findings, however, which the Board briefly considered and then rejected as irrelevant to its superior experience and knowledge,[24] one might well ask why it is that employees must be so assiduously "protected" from the welter of conflicting claims about unionization when almost the entire constitutional structure is designed to *prevent* such protections when it comes to the realm of politics.

Put another way, the freedom to speak and hear a broad range of political statements is considered a sacred principle of a free, democratic system: Those statements may be sublime or ridiculous, true or false; they may even be rash, contentious, irrelevant, vague, threatening, and vulgar. The values of our political system, and the legal principles in which they are embedded, assume that citizens are (or must of necessity be considered) fully qualified to judge the content of political speech. Yet such an assumption is lacking in the case of "labor relations speech." One could fairly suggest that employees are so uniquely subjected to external limits on what they may hear during a union agent election campaign because, being putatively incompetent to judge such speech, they might make the wrong decision.

Every restriction on what employees may *hear* demands equivalent restrictions on what other people *say*. Nor must very much research be conducted to discover that the courts have permitted these uncharacteristic intrusions upon the increasingly protected constitutional guarantee of free speech, even though these same courts have developed various complex formulae which permit forms of speech (e.g., defamation and pornography) most Americans would find difficult to judge worthy of protection. Apparently, people can elsewhere say just about anything; only the ears of employees must be kept from hearing what the NLRB believes is evil. One may truly wonder how it is that a voter's decision on who should be President of the United States is less crucial or less in need of government's solicitous regulation than an employee's decision about who (if anyone) is to represent him in his employment relationships.

This assumes, of course, that employees are even given a decision. Federal labor law permits employers to grant a union "exclusive agent" status with no action needed beyond that union merely requesting or demanding this privilege. An *election* is required (with attendant NLRB administration of the procedure) only if an employer challenges or rejects a union's claim that it has the support of employees. Traditionally, a union gathers "signature cards" from employees and presents these to an employer; if the employer disagrees with this evidence and if it is verified by the Board that the union has such cards from at least 30 percent of the employees,[25] a formal election will normally be held to decide the issue. However, none of this is really necessary under the law. An employer can grant recognition to a union without an election, without a showing of signature cards, or without, as a matter of fact, a union request for this privileged status.[26] Nor is it impossible for an employer to grant recognition without the employees knowing this has actually occurred until after the fact.[27] There are, in short, many reasons why an employer might totally bypass the input of employee opinion as to unionization — and almost as many ways in which an employer might choose to do so.[28] Unfortunately, despite an intrinsic interest in analyzing the circumstances and frequency of this phenomenon, the basic data are unavailable: Being outside the direct auspices of the Board and being on occasion for reasons, moreover, which the parties would prefer to keep hidden, it is simply impossible to say just how often this occurs and precisely why an employer may choose to avoid his employees from deciding for themselves whether to unionize. All that *can* be said at this point, in the absence of considerably more pertinent research, is that federal labor law (as well as parallel state laws for the public sector) permits it and that the practice appears to be on the upswing.[29]

It is also true that an employer can be *ordered* to grant recognition if the Board feels the employer has committed some "unfair labor practice" which, in the Board's opinion, would "interfere with the election process and tend to preclude the holding of a fair election."[30] Such an order can be issued even when an election has been held and the union has clearly lost. The conclusive presumption is that, but for the employer's "unfair" behavior, the union would have won. The Board may look to the signature cards as an indication of employee desires, though there is a disconcertingly obvious difference between a manifested affirmative employee desire to be represented by a particular union and the practical context surrounding a union agent thrusting a card upon an employee with an explanation ranging from "sign this, everyone else has" to "this is just a request for an election" to "sign this and, if we win, you won't have to pay any initiation fees."[31] There is here an asymmetry: If the Board finds the existence of certain employer unfair labor practices, it can lead to an order against the employer requiring that a union loss be reversed and that the union be recognized, but union unfair labor practices will seldom result in the Board reversing an election win by the union.

If an employee vote occurs, however, Section 9 of the NLRA states that a union, to succeed, need receive no more than a majority of the employees in the unit — a requirement which, on its face, would seem to call plainly for a majority of all employees, i.e., both those voting and those not. Years ago, though, the Board analogized from the political system and asserted that the Congress really didn't mean what it had plainly said. Since legislators are routinely elected only by those voting, irrespective of those failing to vote, a parallel rule should control the selection of unions as employee agents (yet the majority requirement was retained, rather than replaced with the sort of plurality arrangement that is also found in the American political arena). Thus, no matter how few employees may have participated in an election relative to the total number who could vote, a majority would determine the matter for the whole body. Even a cursory review of NLRB-administered elections would reveal many in which substantially less than a majority of the whole had made the decision binding on all. According to recent records, an affirmative vote of as few as 20 percent of all employees has constituted the "majority" as defined by the NLRB.[32]

Having achieved this majority, what has a union won? Briefly put, the result is "exclusive representation." By law and subsequent interpretation, this status carries with it a series of special privileges which, in many respects, are similar in effect to the inherent advantages of legislative incumbency. In summary form, it may be said that the "exclusive representative" or "exclusive agent" has acquired the protected privilege of serving as the sole channel of communication between the employer and all affected employees. No other person or agency is permitted to discuss the terms and conditions of employment: Only the union can bargain or negotiate on these questions and it would be an unfair labor practice for the employer to bypass the union channel. If an employee and an employer meet to resolve any matter involving employment, the union's presence must be invited and any resolution must be within the existing union contract terms.

Because the analogy to government is considered a telling argument for the voting rule and for exclusivity, several points should be briefly noted. First and foremost, government is a bad analogy because government is unique: Alone among all institutions of society, government is set apart as the single agency possessing a lawful monopoly on the ultimate use of coercive force. This is the defining characteristic of government. As a consequence of this single fact, all activities of government are hedged about with a multitude of limitations. When government coerces through its policies of conscription, taxation, spending, and regulation, it is exercising sovereign powers it cannot share. Assuming various procedural requirements are met, government policies apply to all even if made or influenced by some. The fact that all citizens must accept and be bound by those policies (while retaining the democratic right to work for changes) is the essence of sovereign government. Nowhere else is this true. All other organizations, groups, collectives, and structures may operate in any manner they choose, adopt any policies, prescribe any voting procedures (or none at all), and construct any system of representation! Groups in a democratic society can exist in this freewheeling fashion because any participant can exit from any organization that has ceased to further his interests. The only exceptions to this are government and labor unions: The first exists by definition and is the result of more than two thousand years of political philosophy; the second exception exists by law and is the result of less than 50 years of growing political influence. Who can doubt, under the circumstances, that exclusivity is an organizational privilege jealously guarded by every established union?[33] A final point is in order: Despite all the rhetoric about a union being "like a Congressman" in that each "represents" an entire constituency even though some members of that constituency may have not voted or may have voted for someone else, the facts of life are quite different. In no way can it be said that any legislator represents (in the sense contemplated by "exclusivity") all of his constituents. Every citizen is guaranteed in law and practice a variety of ways to approach agencies of government (including the legislature). He may, of course, go through his legislator, but he may alternately employ an attorney, represent himself, or join any number of groups which have among their functions activities designed to influence the governmental process. The analogy to government or to the position of Congressmen is simply untenable and it would be well to relegate this particular argument to the trash-can of fatally extended analogies.

The benefits to be derived from this status are manifold. The relationship between the two *real* partners in the enterprise (employers representing capital and entrepreneurship, employees representing labor) is sundered — quite possibly irreversibly. From this point forward, the opportunities for any substantive dialogue are sharply reduced, and the habit of communication becomes increasingly rusty. Moreover, the employer is likely to lose whatever perspective he may have had on employees as individuals: In other words, the work force becomes an undifferentiated mass, a collective, treated in terms of its average member at best or, at worst, its lowest common denominator. With most union contracts geared to a "standard wage," there is little advantage (at times, a positive danger) for any employee to stand out from the crowd. Nor is it an accident that unions, through their multitudinous work rules, seek to prevent individual employees from rising above this crowd.[34] Thus, one consequence of exclusivity is the estrangement of employers and employees, a separation that could well become permanent, thus tending to perpetuate unionization. While it is often true that unions are more likely to be successful against a backdrop of poor employer-employee communications, it is *more* often true that the advent of unionization not only freezes that condition but also acts to prevent any significant improvements. Another consequence of exclusivity is a leveling of the work force, a result partly of collectivization and partly of union rules which hold superior abilities to a lower denominator. As can be seen, the insertion of a union, with governmentally-protected powers, between employers and employees has an impact upon both parties which could best be described as serving principally the organizational interests of the union.

Given, however, the conclusion of this whole process by which a union obtains "exclusive agent" status and given the consequent creation of a three-party relationship where there had been only two before, what in fact is the next step? The answer points to one of the most overworked, least understood, and most troublesome catch-phrases in American labor relations — "the duty to bargain in good faith."[35] This phrase has three critical parts: "duty," "bargain," and "good faith." As befits a significant component of state regulation of labor relations, the duty (as administered) imposes numerous constraints upon the choices available to the parties in an economic transaction.

It is worth reiteration, though, that as a consequence of government action, the parties to the economic transaction have forcibly changed. Whereas before the parties were employers and employees, unions have supplanted employees as the party, indeed the *only* party, with which an employer can transact a labor exchange. Where does this leave employees? Simply to suggest that this is a "good question" might be considered overly flippant; it is nonetheless accurate to say that employees are (since the Wagner Act, at least) a forgotten element in labor relations. In this sense, the regulation of employees has become virtually total because their choices have become almost totally constrained.

Nevertheless, the duty to bargain in good faith is specifically a constraint upon employers. Though Section 8(d) of NRLA affirmatively applies the duty against both the employer and the union ("representative of the employees") and Sections 8(a) (5) and 8(b) (3) make it an unfair labor practice for either party to refuse to bargain collectively, it remains an irrefutable fact that charges under 8(a) (5) or 8(b) (3) are weighted disproportionately in favor of union claims against employers. In other words, the NLRB routinely is, and throughout most of its history has been, faced with far many more union charges that employers were failing to bargain in good faith than with comparable employer charges against unions allegedly failing to engage in good faith bargaining. While some might say that this massive imbalance is due to an employer perception of NLRB bias and a consequent unwillingness to bring otherwise worthy 8(b) (3) charges, an alternative interpretation is that the good faith bargaining duty is, in fact, a duty applied in practice far more often against employers than against unions. Further, this asymmetry was built into the duty from the beginning: Interpretations thereafter only served to strengthen or extend the accuracy of this observation.

Yet, in a sense, this ought not to be overly surprising since it is equally clear collective bargaining was sought by unions and imposed upon employers. The original Wagner Act, Section 8(5), plainly stated that it was the employer who was required to "bargain collectively with representatives of his employees," not the other way around.[36] It was not until the Taft-Hartley amendments of 1947 that Wagner's employer duty was, on paper at least, made mutual in what is now NRLA's Section 8(d) and 8(b) (3). Since the labor laws *define* collective bargaining in union terms (i.e., as an activity or relationship involving employers and employee *representatives*), it is not unreasonable to conclude that the duty to engage in bargaining is more onerous for the employer. After all, the employer has various options in regard to employment relationships, of which unionized collective bargaining is only one, whereas unions have no option except collective bargaining. The essence of regulation being the subtraction of options, it is thus virtually inescapable that imposing a duty of good faith bargaining is principally a regulation of employers.

Consider now the second element of this phrase, "bargaining," and an analysis of its meaning in a regulatory context. One of the earliest formal expressions of what constitutes collective bargaining may be found in a decision of the War Labor Board where the parties were told they must meet to "take up the differences that still exist in an earnest endeavor to reach an agreement on all points at issue."[37] Merely coming together (meeting and/or conferring) was insufficient; the parties had to identify their areas of disagreement and to seek actively some aggregate compromise. While most Congressmen (during the legislative debates) disavowed any suggestion that the language of what would become the Wagner Act necessitated the signing of a formal compact or contract as the end product of bargaining, the Supreme Court took only three years after the Act passed to declare in fact that the whole purpose of collective bargaining as contemplated by the Wagner Act was the making of contracts with unions.[38]

The conclusion seems to be that "bargaining," while it is a process involving interdependent activities engaged in by employers and unions, is nevertheless regulated in large part with regard to what that process produces, i.e., what happens as a result. If it were otherwise, agencies of labor regulation would measure the collective bargaining requirement solely in terms of whether the parties communicated with each other (through meetings, correspondence, etc.) and whether or not the subject of that communication was terms and conditions of employment. This is manifestly *not*, however, how the state regulates the bargaining requirement in labor relations. Instead, the state has imposed various requirements upon collective bargaining which can only be operationalized by an inspection of the *ends* rather than the *means* of bargaining. Thus, such phrases as "good faith," "earnest endeavor," "reasonable effort," and the like acquire particular importance.[39]

To say that the parties who are bargaining must do so in "good faith" generally meant that they had to negotiate with the aim of reaching an agreement; yet the Taft-Hartley amendments specifically removed from the Board any authority to use the making of concessions an indication that good faith bargaining was occurring. How, then, is "good faith" to be measured? One clue was made available when the NLRB itself admitted that the particular conduct of the employer (the "position taken . . . on substantive contract terms") might well have failed to provide sufficient basis for finding that the employer had violated the good faith bargaining rule: The Board decided it would look at the "totality of circumstances reflecting Respondent's [the employer's] bargaining frame of mind."[40] In other words, an employer can have a correct or acceptable stance on the issues being bargained but can still be found guilty of "bad faith" bargaining because he doesn't have the right "frame of mind." One is entitled to wonder if, despite the Taft-Hartley protestations to the contrary, what is legally impermissible has been outflanked through an implicit definition of a "bargaining frame of mind" as one in which the willingness to make concessions is a major component.

As administered, the duty to bargain in good faith can be abrogated in two general ways — by refusing altogether to engage in bargaining (also known as a *per se* violation) or by substituting sham for substance (i.e., going through the *forms* but lacking the intent to try to reach agreement). Needless to say, these abrogations are as defined by the NLRB and the courts; the terms are susceptible to varying interpretations. One company, for example, was found to have committed an unfair labor practice when, having failed to find common ground with the union's international negotiators, it proposed a settlement directly to the union locals.[41] Another company was determined to have avoided demonstrating "bad faith" in bargaining because there was a record of extensive negotiations, proposals, counter-proposals, and concessions;[42] but, if an employer presents at the beginning of negotiations the very same contract terms which would result from "proposals, counterproposals, and concessions" (perhaps because the employer has successfully anticipated and taken into account the probable course of negotiations), then it is likely he has committed an unfair labor practice.[43] In other words, an employer may find that the only way to avoid a *per se* violation of the good faith bargaining duty is to engage in sham bargaining. Thus, a company that has carefully estimated its market future, the availability of labor, and numerous other factors determining the upper limits of what it could pay in a total compensation package would be skating on thin regulatory ice if it simply laid its best proposal on the table at the outset and said, in effect, "we have taken into account all the factors and arguments you are likely to raise and, short of presenting facts of which we are unaware, this is the best we are prepared to do." Indeed, the emphasis of the NLRB and the courts on seeing a record of *negotiations* as an indication of good faith bargaining encourages each party to start the proceedings by laying on the table proposals considered unacceptable — even outrageous — by the other party so that there would then follow the creation of the desired record of "proposals, counter-proposals, and concessions."

As a matter of dynamics, however, this situation tends strongly to favor the union over the employer because, as already noted, the *duty* to bargain (as legislated, but notably as administered) falls more heavily on the latter. The degree to which this is so has been supported in previous references to Board or court language which more commonly related the onus of bargaining in employer terms.[44] The classic *Reed & Prince* decision provides yet another example in the area of concessions: ". . . the Board cannot force an employer to make a 'concession' on any specific issue or to adopt any particular position" but "the employer is obligated to make some reasonable effort in *some* direction to compromise his differences with the union. . . ."[45] The cases are very few and far between regarding a union making concessions, so the message to employers comes through fairly clearly — union proposals must be accommodated to some nontrivial degree. *Some* compromise must be made by the employer because compromising is a prime indicator of good faith. Thus, again, one is led to the inescapable conclusion that the regulation of bargaining works in such a way as virtually to require that employers start with the least expensive compensation proposal which it can reasonably justify (to the examiners, hearing officers, and members of the NLRB or to the courts), while the union forsakes important dynamic advantages if it fails to launch the bargaining process with a set of demands which, in the aggregate, would be considered objectively as predictably unacceptable.

Consider what further is being implied here regarding concessions. It is worthwhile to point out the obvious fact that a concession (or, for that matter, a counterproposal) is possible if and only if there is disagreement. The existence of disagreement depends entirely upon the stance of *both* parties: In no way can only one party be designated as responsible for the gulf separating it from another party without a concomitant evaluation of the respective stances and a determination that one of them is somehow unreasonable, untenable, or otherwise intended solely to frustrate the bargaining process. To declare that no *particular* concession is required in order to show good faith, only *some* concession, is no solution. That immediately suggests several questions. Must both parties make some concessions? What if one party makes fewer (substantially fewer?) concessions than the other? Suppose the number of concessions is approximately equal on each side but there is a difference (substantial difference?) in their subject matter or importance — for example, the employer offers to repaint the lunchroom if the union will agree to eliminate its demand for a wage increase. Suppose the importance of a concession is measured relative to the original proposals — for example, the union offers to reduce its demand that employer contributions to the pension fund be tripled in size if the company will agree to an additional day of paid vacation time.

The above examples were deliberately constructed to lead most readers to agree that the imbalance described is obviously unreasonable, untenable, and probably designed to frustrate any rational process of reaching an agreement. But real world situations are far more complex because the meaning, implications, consequences, and impact of a counterproposal are determined through highly subjective processes. In any bargaining process, there are such matters as inertia, psychological mind-set, the symbolic importance of what are perceived to be defeats or victories, and so forth. Thus, in sum, there is no effective way objectively and even-handedly to regulate the bargaining process without simultaneously intruding on someone's estimation of what results from the process, i.e., how someone else feels about the outcome, the substance of the proposals, or both. In other words, no one can administer a requirement that bargaining be undertaken in "good faith" without going far, far beyond the original characterization of this term by Sen. Walsh as involving nothing more than a means to "escort representatives to the bargaining door, not control what goes on behind the door."[46] The record of the NLRB and the courts is replete with indications that "what goes on behind the door" has increasingly become the crux of how these agencies regulate collective bargaining: The record indicates, moreover, that the options available to employers in this regard have been more consistently constrained than have union options.

Thus far, attention has been given to government regulation of the relationship between employers and employees (e.g., wages, hours, unionization, etc.) and the relationship between employers and unions (e.g., exclusivity, elections, and negotiations). Consider now the relationship between employees and unions. Not surprisingly, this area is subject to various regulatory restraints, but there is also a similar imbalance in the degree to which the options of each party have been constrained in practice.

Though discussed in the context of employers and unions, that aspect of labor relations regulation known as "exclusivity" has a fundamental impact upon employees. Being in effect a privilege or right enjoyed only by unions, exclusivity redirects and reduces the number of channels of communication and makes the union the sole permissible nexus for employers and collectivized employees. Inevitably, placing unions in this position involves a reduction or elimination of choices for the employee. No longer can the employee negotiate terms and conditions of employment based more precisely upon individual tastes, preferences, and abilities. Such an option is totally foreclosed, as the *J.I. Case* decision made abundantly clear.[47] As a result, for a certain proportion of employees, employment terms are lower than they might otherwise be — with a potentially concomitant reduction in overall productivity. While this in turn may have serious consequences for the nation's economy, our concern is for the individual employee now submerged in a collectivity which, in the context of exclusivity plus a standard contract compensation schedule, engages in massive redistributions of income perhaps in excess of all governmental transfer payments programs combined. Its magnitude really is beyond measurement. Assuming a roughly standard distribution curve for ability within an employment contract category, it follows that a standard wage overpays one half at the expense of the other half. Moreover, there is little incentive for any particular employee to increase his productivity (even were he able to do this in light of various union-imposed work rules) because rarely would such an effort lead to any increase in benefit. As the *J.I. Case* decision put it,

> the practice and philosophy of collective bargaining looks with suspicion on . . . individual advantages. The workman is free, if he values his own bargaining position more than that of the group, to vote against representation; but the majority rules, and if it collectivizes the employment bargain, individual advantages or favors [e.g., superior ability, experience, training, knowledge, etc.] will generally in practice go in as a contribution to the collective result.[48]

The essence of regulation, of course, is that one could not by any stretch of definition call what happens to "individual advantages" a "contribution"; it is, simply and forthrightly, a coerced redistribution of employee benefits under union auspices within a framework of governmentally-imposed regulations.

In consequence, the very initiation of the relationship between employees and unions is bounded by various constraints stemming from the principle of exclusivity. As a matter of fact, such constraints appear even *before* an election triggers the institutionalization of exclusivity. Note in this regard the NLRB's ability under Section 9 of the NLRA to determine the "appropriate unit" in which an election may be had and over which a union can exercise exclusivity if it wins the election. In carrying out its right to shape the election/bargaining unit, the Board need not (and rarely, if ever, does) consult with employees on the matter: its only input comes from unions and employers. If these two parties agree that employee group x, y, or z is to be in the unit, the Board usually complies; if a union and an employer disagree, the Board will base the decision on its own self-proclaimed experience and expertise without any particular regard to possible evidence from employees. Normally, however, when faced with competing requests for unit determinations, the Board is heavily influenced by the desires of the union since the NLRA defines "appropriate unit" in terms of a so-called "community of employee interests" and the Board presumes the union knows or reflects better employee interests.[49] Thus, the creation of an election/bargaining unit, which may significantly affect at the outset the aggregate employee vote on unionization or decertification (much as the gerrymandering of a legislative district can influence who gets elected), is left almost entirely to the "good offices" of the NLRB which, in turn, bases its perceptions about the mutuality of employee interests upon how the employer happens to have structured his business, or upon what the union wants (an objective not difficult to specify), or upon what the Board's own view happens to be.

Assuming a union becomes a certified bargaining agent, the following discussion may be divided into three parts as regards the application of regulations to the relationship between the two parties which are the present focus. The first area to be discussed is the union's duty of fair representation, which applies generally to all employees in the bargaining unit whether or not they are formal members of the union. The second consists of those regulations relevant to the relationship between a union agent and employees who are *not* members of the union. The third area of discussion is aimed at regulations affecting unions and their members: By and large, this last subject need not presuppose that the union is a certified bargaining agent, i.e., this third area of regulation applies to union members generally whether or not the union is bargaining or administering a contract on their behalf.

The duty of fair representation is a doctrine totally constructed by the judiciary (later adopted by the NLRB) because exclusivity would have been unconstitutional without it. Nowhere can the phrase or any equivalent language be found in the statutes governing labor relations; yet the "duty of fair representation" has become as ridden with controversy and as riddled with ambiguity as the concept of the "duty to bargain in good faith" discussed earlier.

The origin of this duty, so the Supreme Court said, was the statutorily-mandated principle of exclusivity.[50] Because unions "control" all communications with and access to a unit of employees and because it is their sole permissible spokesman, grave constitutional dangers are created *unless* (though Congress nowhere said this) the union were required to represent fairly all employees in the unit. What does this mean? Following the *Steele* language, it was said that the union could not discriminate among employees in a manner that was "irrelevant and invidious."[51] Nearly a quarter century later, the Supreme Court enunciated a different test; namely, refraining from actions that were "arbitrary, discriminatory, or in bad faith."[52] Notice that both definitions are stated in the negative; even the Supreme Court has apparently not been willing to venture beyond describing what unions must *avoid* doing. Perhaps the reason why fair represen-

64

tation cannot be defined affirmatively is because its connection with reality is tenuous at best.

Unless a group of people is completely homogeneous, it must be true that the group will contain interests that conflict or at least diverge. What does it mean to say that a union "represents" these interests, much less represents them fairly? Given the conceptually necessary proposition that a union cannot simultaneously advance two or more employee interests which are divergent or mutually inhospitable, one must conclude that a union must somehow either choose among them or aggregate them into one bargaining position. Both alternatives, however, involve some degree of foreclosure regarding employees. In other words, with an even slightly heterogeneous employee unit, the interests of *some* employees will *not* be represented, while others will be represented adversely. No other conclusion is possible: "the complete satisfaction of all who are represented is hardly to be expected."[53] The question of representation, therefore, inevitably resolves itself into issues that are pre-eminently political in nature. *Which* interests are asserted? *Whose* interests prevail? By what formula are competing interests to be amalgamated? This is the essence of politics, of claims, groups, and pressures, of choices by decision-makers, of ruling and being ruled. It is no wonder that neither Congress nor the courts have said what affirmatively constitutes fair representation. It is completely inconceivable, for example, how a duty of fair representation could be applied to Congress: The totality of our political and philosophical traditions declares that it is the voter who decides how and when the political representation of his interests has been "fair," and what he should do if it has not been. The usual argument in this regard is that, like the political voter, the employee can express his dissatisfaction in a comparable manner, i.e., by voting a union out through what is known as a decertification petition. Yet this analogy is fundamentally faulty. The union-as-government analogy has been shown false earlier in this chapter, but this particular use of the analogy calls for an additional point. While decertification movements have been increasing in number (and have been increasingly successful), it remains true that such petitions touch only an extremely small proportion of all bargaining units. Whereas some would say that this is the case because most employees are satisfied with their union representation,[54] it is also possible that this situation occurs because certification, once obtained, is difficult to reverse for a variety of structural and procedural reasons, regardless of employee opinions on the matter. A certain degree of support for this latter possibility is deducible from the very rationale for the fair representation duty; namely, that the duty is a necessary prescription for the constitutional infirmities of exclusivity. Yet, since the *political process* is taken automatically to be a sufficient solution to "unfair" political representation, it requires no great leap in logic to suggest that the courts have imposed a duty of fair representation upon unions based on an unspoken but possibly widespread concern that, in fact, with a certified union agent, there is no viable counterpart to the political process for divesting oneself of an undesired representative. In other words, there would be little need to graft the fair representation duty upon the exclusivity privilege if there were no roadblocks to changing or removing a union agent which did not represent the aggregate interests of an employee unit. Despite the acknowledged difficulty of unseating an incumbent legislator, unseating an incumbent union must be far more difficult. If nothing else, the union-as-government analogy does alert us to the apparent fact that crucial elements of government responsiveness (and the factors impelling that responsiveness) are considerably weakened or altogether missing when it comes to the relationship between a union and the employees it purports to represent.

Nevertheless, decertification is reserved for the most egregious situations because it is successful only when backed by an absolute majority of employees in the bargaining unit. Suppose, however, that the majority consists of both those who accept the union's representation and those who are indifferent at the margin. What of the others? What of various shifting minorities who, on one issue or another, are not being represented in any usual sense by their union agent? Again consider the implication of the heterogeneous employee unit.

The duty of fair representation is either impossible to apply on its face[55] or limited in some fashion by a shifting distinction between which sorts of discrimination are permissible and which are impermissible. While we are inclined to the former view, for more reasons than can be discussed here, the courts have tended to the latter view because only the existence of such a duty (no matter how strained its specification and application) saves the exclusivity principle from the graveyard of constitutionally defective doctrines, and exclusivity is, as already noted, the cornerstone of the U.S. system of unionized industrial relations. Consequently, the NLRB and the courts have labored mightily to produce some sort of viable distinction between fair and unfair discrimination — given the premise that discrimination is inevitable.[56]

The result was the further specification that, where union actions (e.g., the making of a contract) involved terms which were unfavorable to some employees being represented by virtue of statutory exclusivity, the *J. I. Case* principle[57] validates such individual harm as simply a necessary "contribution" to the common good when employment relations have been collectivized; *provided,* however, that the harm delivered by the union was not the result of invidious discrimination, bad faith, irrelevance, or personal animus. The problem with proceeding beyond this point is that the effort to distinguish between reasonable and unreasonable discrimination is grounded on specific cases with precise factual situations which, taken together, provide few, if any, guidelines for generalization.

Racial discrimination has generally been taken as almost *prima facie* evidence that fair representation has not occurred,[58] though in recent years historical patterns of such discrimination have run afoul of union-negotiated seniority provisions which are so steeped in tradition that the concrete in which they are embedded may be sufficient to defeat a duty of fair representation claim.[59] And there seems little doubt that discrimination based on religion would be equally irrelevant; though, again, there are some shifting legal winds. It would also appear that, whereas the practice is probably more widespread than the case records would indicate, union discrimination based on an employee's difficulties *within* the union (i.e., internal union politics) contravenes the duty.[60] Other bases are far less clearcut.

In general, both the Board and the courts have granted to unions a fairly wide discretion in deciding for themselves when to institute discriminatory representation: In somewhat different terms, not only is the category of reasonable discrimination relatively wide but also the agencies of regulation have normally deferred to the presumed expertise and unselfish interests of union organizations in accepting that some particular form of discrimination promotes the common good or is necessary to the process of collective bargaining.[61] It should further be understood that, since so frequently does a charge of unfair representation depend upon an inquiry into personal motivations, questions of evidence and proof become exceedingly complex: Employees contemplating such actions must surely be discouraged by the difficulty, time, and expense involved — not to mention the potential repercussions from a failure to sustain the charge and to obtain a realistic remedy.[62]

Curiously, though it is the employee bringing suit and it is the union that allegedly has failed to represent fairly, an *employer* may be found liable for the employee's damage and may, in fact, be required to provide compensation. Despite union demands (embodied in the statutes) that an employer must not interfere in a union's internal affairs, the courts have held that an employer may nevertheless be the party that provides a "make whole" remedy to an employee wronged by a union that has failed properly to represent his interests. While it cannot be said that the explanation for this anomalous situation is very sensible (the employer is supposedly in a better financial position than the union), it does suggest that employers are caught between the "must not interfere" provisions of the NLRA and the need to protect their own liability by somehow ensuring that unions process grievances competently.[63]

This duty of fair representation, then, emerges as a fundamentally far-reaching incursion into the employee-union relationship, an incursion moreover that constricts the options of employees as a result of its inherent ambiguities and the clear intent of regulatory agencies to resolve those ambiguities in favor of union institutional needs to the detriment of individual interests. Combined (as it necessarily is) with exclusivity, the duty further places employees at a decided disadvantage with regard to the procedures and requirements for seeking its enforcement. Calling this doctrine a "duty" of a union is therefore an excellent example of misleading semantics: To the extent it is judicially recognized and applied, it works to expand a union's latitude of action; to the extent it might impose a realistic or important restriction upon union behavior, it cannot be enforced (or, alternately, an enforcement effort is very difficult for an employee either to undertake or to conclude successfully).[64]

The relationship between a union and its membership has received less attention because for many years it was assumed that the interaction between the two did not affect industrial relations to a significant degree. Put another way, the regulatory framework had as its locus the work place and the issues that revolved about *employment,* whereas the organizational connection between two of the parties (employees and unions) was considered a purely private arrangement extraneous to that situation. Except for compulsory unionism (to be discussed briefly later), the regulation of labor relations ignored the question of union membership as being irrelevant to the scheme of government intervention. Any aspect of the employer-union-employee relationship could be treated with no special regard taken for whether particular employees were members of the union: Conceivably, a union could receive 100 percent employee support as the certified bargaining agent and not have a single member in the unit. And exclusivity had the effect of making an employee's membership in any other organization (including any other union) an even less important piece of information.

Historically, as with any other private group, a union could prescribe such rules and regulations for membership as it wished (subject ultimately only to the requirement that its rules could not contemplate certain kinds of illegal acts). A person joined a union by fulfilling the prescribed conditions, and the courts generally said that such a membership thereafter became a contractual matter based upon the reciprocal obligations spelled out at the time of the joining or as modified later in accordance with established procedures. None of this excited much extended analysis or close inspection since, by and large, the law governing individuals and purely private groups was well-settled and based upon such commonly accepted principles as voluntary action, free exit, and the absence of overriding state interests.

As unions became increasingly critical actors in the realm of national economic life, as the government became more actively participatory in the labor market (through regulations of the sort described earlier), and as unions claimed a special status for themselves above or beyond other private groups, however, the regulatory impetus began to touch upon the issue of union membership. One of the first questions to be raised in this regard was, what constitutes membership?

Following a series of court decisions, it is now well-established (though little known, less publicized, and even obscured among employees, the personnel offices of employers, local agents of unions, and, curiously, lawyers specializing in labor law) that no "union security" arrangement, no matter how stringent on its face, can compel formal membership. This is true without regard to the existence of a right-to-work law. To accomplish this result, given the apparent working of the NLRA (which uses the term "membership" in several places with respect to permissible forms of "union security" in the absence of a right-to-work law), the courts (with the NLRB following) have distinguished between full or formal membership and "financial core" membership.[65] Full or formal membership involves the filing and acceptance of an application which, in turn, normally calls for the completion of some assertion of allegiance or obedience to the union and its rules; whereas "financial core" membership (a misnomer under the circumstances) involves only the payment to a union of some amount of money (e.g., initiation fees and dues). Clearly, the former includes the latter. The former grants such access to internal decision-making as the union rules permit (e.g., depending on the *specific* union, voting for union candidates, voting on contract proposals, access to union facilities, etc.) but carries with it various reciprocal responsibilities (e.g., principally, the obligation to pay fines and assessments, to submit to the union's disciplinary action, and to abide by its constitution or by-laws). "Financial core membership," since it entails only the payment of money (even if the sum required is exactly equivalent to and is measured by union dues), relieves employees of both the rights of access and the obligations of discipline. Though it would seem from the foregoing that the employee is being permitted a choice based upon his balancing of perceived costs and benefits associated with access and discipline, the employee seldom has this choice as a matter of practice. Thus, whereas the choice is a matter of settled law, employees generally know only what they are told, and those who do the telling in this regard usually fail to describe what the law actually permits either through ignorance or intent.

An employee's sources of information respecting his contractual rights and obligations are mainly three: the employer, the union, and the contract itself (if one exists and is available to him). Despite the distinction, built over nearly two decades, between these two types of membership, it remains true that most contracts containing a "union security" provision utilize only the term "member" or "membership" and no one could fault the average employee who, upon reading such a provision, gives these terms their normal meaning. Furthermore, for reasons explained earlier in this chapter, it is in the interests of unions to avoid where possible giving these terms any more exact or accurate definition since union organizational purposes are more effectively served by formal membership (which includes dues) than by "financial core" membership (which provides only dues, and possibly even less than this). The employer, finally, has no particularly compelling interest in providing employees with information which conflicts either with their normal reading of the contract (or the statutes, for that matter) or with what they might be told (or implied to them) by the union's business agent.[66] Indeed, having presumably already agreed to a "union security" contract provision, it is a matter of economic indifference to an employer (except, perhaps to those few who are sufficiently astute to appreciate the union's organizational interests in full membership and the effect of those interests upon future strike capabilities) whether an employee is a full member or a "financial core" member of the union. In any event, just to avoid "unrest," the employer may simply accede to whatever meaning the union wishes.

As a consequence of this situation, it can be concluded that many of the traditional assertions about union members based solely upon the fact of membership are likely inaccurate because some unknown proportion of union members are not associated with the union and its policies by voluntary choice. This, alone, introduces a major disturbance in any calculation which utilizes "level of union membership" (or changes in that level over time or across industries) as an indicator of anything at all. Unlike other aspects of labor regulations discussed so far, this matter of what constitutes membership is one of the few important areas where the options have actually been *increased* (though they are still less than optimal because the need to distinguish varieties of membership arises only from the imposition of the more broadly limiting condition of "union security"), but few affected employees can take advantage of this wider latitude because few are aware of the possibility. Moreover, there are virtually no parties to the employment relationship who would find it strongly in their interest to supply the information.[67]

Suppose an employee, given the option, decides that formally joining a union is on balance the preferred course of action. The courts have generally assumed that this relationship has been entered upon voluntarily and thus the member has activated a set of mutual obligations which is controlled mostly by the union itself, i.e., through its constitution and by-laws.[68] The extent of direct government regulation in this situation is minimal and limited to certain requirements imposed by what is known as the "union members' Bill of Rights."[69] Nevertheless, due to the presumption of voluntariness of entry and exit unmitigated by the practical considerations described above, the very fact that government by and large will use its coercive machinery (e.g., the courts) to enforce the regulations imposed by union rules becomes significant when the overall framework is considered. Thus, for example, a full member is assumed to have given implicit consent to each and every expenditure of money by a union's leadership, so long as the leadership followed its own prescribed procedures in making and disbursing the appropriation: A (full) member generally has no recourse to any court or administrative agency if he believes his union is doing improper things or doing things improperly, provided the leadership can point to a constitutional or by-law provision which authorizes the action.[70] His only options are either to work within the union's structure for change or to resign.[71] Within certain limits, which remain the subject of conflict in court interpretations, the member may also be required, even in the case of an alleged violation of the union's own established procedures, to exhaust avenues of challenge and appeal *within* the union before even being permitted to launch any external legal attack upon the claimed impropriety.[72] Yet it is clear that these internal challenges and appeals, in addition to constituting a lengthy process when the final "verdict" is rendered only by a union convention which meets just once every two, three, or four years, are automatically suspect as models of fairness precisely because they are internal and may be controlled by the very people with whom the member has his dispute.[73] For this reason, a few unions (notably the Auto Workers) have instituted "public" review boards which, being staffed by supposedly neutral (but union-paid) public figures, are intended to answer the issue of inherent bias.

As a further indication of the degree to which government regulates the member's relationship with his union by enforcing the union's own rules, note that a union's disciplinary actions can be backed by the courts. For example, courts can be called upon to collect a union-imposed fine if the fine were imposed through the procedures established properly by the union.[74] While the offenses giving rise to such a penalty are uncountable, fines are normally imposed for refusing to go out on strike, returning to work before a strike has ended, crossing another union's picket lines if that strike has been sanctioned, exceeding limits on work or productivity,[75] and so forth. The only way a member can remove himself from any danger of these penalties being imposed by the union and/or enforced by the courts is to resign *before* taking the action that might lead to the penalty (resigning after the action but before the penalty is imposed is usually insufficient protection, though it does prevent the penalty from accumulating further).[76] But, as already stated, many employees would fear to take this step on the belief that their full, formal membership was a condition of employment. There is the additional question, so far unresolved, whether a union can properly prevent member resignations, e.g., by a constitutional provision which grants a right to withdraw only during a certain period of the year (say, the last two weeks) or denies withdrawal during or in anticipation of a strike.[77]

The issue of "union security" (or compulsory unionism) has already been mentioned and, while numerous questions still need to be addressed, they are beyond the scope of this work.[78] In any event, exclusivity is logically a more fundamental concern. Yet one aspect deserves at least a brief mention; namely, the extent of the obligation owed by the nonmember to a union agent that enjoys a "union security" clause. Given that formal membership cannot be required, the practical consequence is that (where it is enforceable at all) the only form of union security permissible in the United States is functionally equivalent to what is known as the "agency shop." The "agency shop" obligation is normally met by an affected nonmember paying to the union a sum of money equal to the dues and fees (but not fines or assessments) that members pay. The theory is that, because the union must expend its resources to represent fairly the nonmember under exclusivity, it is only "just" (and supportive of the union's general ability to engage effectively in bargaining) that the union be repaid for producing the benefits enjoyed by these "free riding" nonmembers. The notions of universal benefits, of "free-riders," and of the union's costs in providing services have been analyzed (though still insufficiently) elsewhere, but it appears that, where a dues equivalency obligation has been imposed, such charges are at a level that is much greater than the existing law permits.

The ambiguity arises from the possibility that the putative solution to "free riding" (paying an amount equal to dues) is not justified by the theory. In other words, if the justification lies in compensating a union for the *additional* costs it incurs in providing services to a group that is larger than its membership in the bargaining unit, it follows that those additional costs are the measure of what nonmembers might be required to pay. When members of the union pay their dues, however, they are providing funds that the union uses for many activities, of which only some may reasonably be termed "collective bargaining, contract administration, and grievance adjustment." Moreover, even analysts who generally approve of "union security" have conceded that, as a matter of fact, a union incurs virtually *no additional costs* in bargaining and administering the contract when the employee unit includes nonmembers.[79] It would appear, therefore, that the existence of nonmembers in a bargaining unit theoretically constitutes a financial burden (in the sense of having to provide certain services without compensation) only with respect to the adjustment of grievances for nonmembers. But, the "agency shop" form of union security is normally applied in such a way as to require the payment of what amounts to full dues and fees. This issue is still in the early stages of litigation but at this point it is possible to say, first, that the *principle* of requiring nonmember compensation only for the union's legally essential services has been established in the public[80] and private [81] sectors of employment and, second, that the question of precisely how much should be paid (i.e., the portion of a union's total program of activities and interests which is properly subsumable under the rubric of collective bargaining) remains the subject of major controversy.[82] It would appear overall that unions spend relatively small sums in connection with representing employee interests through collective bargaining: A court-appointed Special Master (a sort of "fact finder") in one major case recently determined that only 19 percent of the budget of the Communications Workers of America was devoted to this purpose.[83] The prospect is thus raised, once a definitive and final judicial solution is reached, of the nonmember eventually having to compensate a certified union agent only so much proportionally as the union in turn devotes to his interests.

Because "labor relations regulation" is so broad a topic, only a few of the more significant areas of employee-employer-union relationships affected by government regulation can be discussed in any detail. It should again be emphasized that a major premise of this entire work is the surprising degree to which such regulation exists and the concomitant degree to which little note has been taken of it among those involved in contemporary analyses of "regulation" or "deregulation." Among the standard, heavily used tools of the labor specialists' trade are (as of 1980) 250 volumes of NLRB decisions, 87 volumes of *Labor Cases*, 103 volumes of *LRRM (Labor Relations Reference Manual),* 11 volumes of *Federal Regulation of Employment Service,* 26 volumes of various publications of the Bureau of National Affairs dealing with labor relations, 22 volumes of *Fair Employment Practice Cases,* literally untold volumes of cases and decisions emanating from state-level employment relations boards and commissions, and a virtual avalanche of materials on private and public sector arbitration decisions. It is possible that no other topic enjoys (if that is the right word for it) the massive amount of legal reference materials as that which must be mastered if any particular party in an employment relationship is to act in accordance with the standards of behavior laid down by agencies of government.[84] This short chapter can, therefore, hardly do justice to the variety and complexity of its subject.

The body of labor relations regulations has been approached in two parallel ways. Some regulations are mainly substantive in their effect upon the very nature of the relationship between the parties involved in the commercial exchange of the labor commodity while others are procedural in that their effect is upon an ongoing process. An example of the former is the protected intrusion of a union into what, at one time, had been a relationship solely between sellers and purchasers of labor; other examples are wage and hour limitations and exclusivity. Procedural regulations are exemplified by the duty to bargain in good faith, the duty of fair representation, and government enforcement of union discipline. Another conceptualization of this large body of government rules which has been used is the particular bilateral relationship being primarily affected — e.g., employee-employer, employer-union, and union-employee (with the latter divided by employee members and nonmembers). These two perspectives overlap in that both substantive and procedural regulations may be found in each one of these bilateral relationships.

Since the regulatory process, by definition, consists of government-imposed constraints upon the market options available to participants in economic exchanges, this chapter has also identified how, where, and to what degree market decisions are restrained. It seems self-evident that any specific regulation has an asymmetrical impact upon the parties to an economic exchange; furthermore, specific regulations are expressly and intentionally drawn so as to be asymmetrical in effect. Two observations are in order in this regard. First, a regulation's *actual* impact may be quite different, in fact diametrically different, than what was intended. Second, a *body* of regulation (as opposed to any particular element) may on balance be symmetrical in effect: It may, overall, constrain all parties to roughly the same degree, though each party is affected in quite different ways. It is important, as a consequence, to assess regulatory impact not only in terms of which parties are being affected and how, but also in terms of whose choices are *most* restricted in the general regulatory framework. A second continuing theme of this analysis is that labor relations regulation falls most heavily upon the employee. Either by the express terms of most regulations involving market exchanges of labor or by the manner in which they are applied, it is the individual employee — not the employer and not the union — whose options are most constrained. We cannot claim credit for this conclusion: It may be found stated as long ago as in the language of *J.I. Case* and as recently as 1979 when the Associate General Counsel of the United Steel Workers said, "If you believe in the principle of collective bargaining you must believe in the collective interest and not the individual interest."[85]

NOTES TO CHAPTER III

[1]George J. Stigler, "The Theory of Economic Regulation," *Bell Journal of Economics and Management Science* (Spring, 1971), p. 3.

[2]The minimum wage, as of January 1, 1980, was set at $3.15 per hour and increased to $3.35 on January 1, 1981.

[3]Thus, separate legislation defines a complex wage formula for airline pilots and sets their hours of work at no more than 85 per month: Workers on federally-supported construction projects are paid in accordance with "prevailing wages" as determined by the Department of Labor.

[4]*National League of Cities v. Usery,* 97 S.Ct. 2465 (1976).

[5]See the work of Walter Williams; e.g., "Government Sanctioned Restraints that Reduce Economic Opportunities for Minorities," *Policy Review* (Fall, 1977), pp. 7-30; also John T. Addison and W. Stanley Siebert, *The Market for Labor* (Santa Monica, CA: Goodyear, 1979), esp. pp. 212-220.

[6]Marvin Kosters and Finis Welch, "The Effects of Minimum Wages on the Distribution of Changes in Aggregate Unemployment," *American Economic Review* (June, 1972), pp. 323-332; Robert M. Bednarzik, "Involuntary Part-time Work," *Monthly Labor Review* (September, 1975).

[7]For the AFL-CIO's position on a youth subminimum, see U.S. Senate, Subcommittee on Labor, *Fair Labor Standards Amendments of 1971, Hearings* (1971), pp. 75-116.

[8]As one union official noted, more grievances arise from disputes over who gets the premium overtime work than over being forced to work overtime: See George Brooks, "The History of Organized Labor's Drive for Shorter Hours of Work," *Daily Labor Reports,* No. 177 (September 11, 1956). For the possibility of moonlighting as evidenced in the rubber industry's Akron experiment, see *Business Week* (March 18, 1972), p. 67.

[9]Gordon F. Bloom and Herbert R. Northrup, *Economics of Labor Relations,* Eighth Edition (Homewood, IL: Richard D. Irwin, Inc., 1977), pp. 512-513.

[10]Remember, we are not saying that people ought, should, or can be required to work that much or that little: In the absence of regulation, such decisions become individual matters of choice.

[11]We should note that the licensing supported by unions is the sort of licensing over which they exercise control: They normally oppose licensing (medical, dental, legal professions) when that control has traditionally been lacking. Nevertheless, licensing is licensing, whether practiced by plumbers or doctors, and with few exceptions the same arguments apply to either sort.

[12]Only a brief sample of some recent references on this interesting topic is possible. See, for example, Benjamin Shimberg, *et al., Occupational Licensing: Practices and Policies* (Washington, DC: Public Affairs Press, 1973); Addison and Siebert, op. cit., pp. 299-300.

[13]It is not unlikely that these paperwork costs could, if mitigated, result in lower prices, higher wages, or both. We accordingly classify these paperwork-promoting regulations as potential *substantive* restrictions on the terms and conditions of employment. It will be noted that we also ignore the regulatory impact of equal employment requirements themselves. For a detailed treatment of paperwork and its costs, see James T. Bennett and Manuel H. Johnson, "Paperwork and Bureaucracy," *Economic Inquiry* (July, 1979), pp. 435-451. A discussion of the cost of all types of regulation can be found in Murray L. Weidenbaum, *The Future of Business Regulation* (New York: Amacom Press, 1979).

[14]See Richard B. McKenzie, *Restrictions on Business Mobility* (Washington, DC: American Enterprise Institute, 1979).

[15]The NLRA embodies the original Wagner Act of 1935 (which replaced the National Industrial Recovery Act of 1933, declared unconstitutional in 1935), the Taft-Hartley Amendments of 1947, the Landrum-Griffin Amendments of 1959, and several other less significant amendments, at other times.

[16]Landrum-Griffin (1959) was, however, a series of amendments to *both* the NLRA and RLA.

[17]In the description which follows, only the *current* language of the NLRA will be discussed: We shall not be concerned with changes that have occurred over the years, even when those changes produced important alterations in the regulatory framework. This will also be the case as we come to other examples of procedural regulation.

[18]*Cooper Thermometer Co.,* 154 NLRB at 503 (1966) (emphasis added).

[19]*National Maritime Union,* 78 NLRB at 985 (1948).

[20]*NLRB v. Allis-Chalmers,* 388 U.S. 175; *American Newspaper Publishers' Association v. NLRB,* 193 F 2d 782 (1951).

[21]*NLRB v. Virginia Electric and Power,* 314 U.S. 469 (1941).

[22]NLRB, *Annual Report,* Vol. 27 (1963), p. 89.

[23]Julius Getman, *et al., Union Representation Elections: Law and Reality* (New York: Russell Sage, 1976).

[24]See *Shopping Kart,* 228 NLRB 190 (1977), followed by *General Knit of California,* 239 NLRB 101 (1978).

[25]This, by the way, is not a statutory requirement: The 30 percent was chosen and instituted by the NLRB, with the particular percentage chosen possibly because 30 percent *is* a statutory requirement for de-authorization petitions.

[26]Though relatively rare, employers have been known to seek out a union because of outside pressures (e.g., organized crime) or because they are faced with the prospect of being organized by a union that they consider less desirable than the one they are approaching. In either case, the result is usually a "sweetheart" contract, i.e., an agreement advantageous to the employer and/or union, but not to employees.

[27]Again, this is relatively rare, particularly in these more sophisticated times, but neither can it be denied that various decisions of the NLRB permit a union to acquire recognition rights solely because an employer has unwittingly acted in certain ways that the Board has determined effectively constitute the granting of recognition.

[28]For a discussion of this, see James T. Bennett and Manuel H. Johnson, *Pushbutton Unionism* (Fairfax, VA: Contemporary Economics and Business Association, 1980).

[29]Ibid., p. 25.

[30]*NLRB v. Gissel Packing,* 395 U.S. at 594 (1969).

[31]This "card," it may be noted, can actually be any number of things: a regular membership application, a membership card, an authorization for dues check-off, a card designating a union as the signer's bargaining agent, or some combination of these. A union may collect such cards over a period as long as a year and does not have to identify itself (either a local or international union name) on the card except in the most general terms (merely "AFL-CIO" can be sufficient). See Charles A. Morris (Editor-in-Chief), *The Developing Labor Law* (Washington, DC: Bureau of National Affairs, 1971), pp. 254 ff., for additional details.

[32]E.g., Case #07-RC-15536 (20 percent of eligible voters approved union representation), *NLRB Election Report,* ER-217 (June 6, 1980). Overall, for example, out of 106 single union elections in which the union was successful (as listed in the report cited above), fully 20 per cent were won by a vote of less than a majority of eligible employees in the unit.

[33]An indication of the degree to which exclusivity is in fact a cornerstone for a union's ability to become and *remain* "established" may be seen in those few instances where a union has not supported this concept. An excellent contemporary example of this is the case of a small, primarily black union of postal workers which vigorously opposed legislation intended to replace Executive Order 11491 (see Statement of the National Alliance of Postal and Federal Employees, reported in 707 *GERR* 9, May 9, 1971). See generally Herbert Hill, *Black Labor and the American Legal System: Race, Work, and the Law* (Washington, DC: Bureau of National Affairs, 1977).

[34]The examples are legion of unions rigorously enforcing their work limitation rules for fear of revealing the extent to which productivity could be much greater than it is. Even more devastating would be an increased pressure for wage differentials based on ability, a concept that has historically been anathema to the union movement. See, for example, "Low Productivity: The Real Sin of High Wages," *Engineering News-Record* (February 24, 1972), pp. 20-23; Sumner H. Slichter, *et al., The Impact of Collective Bargaining on Management* (Washington, DC: Brookings, 1960), pp. 317-335; Robert D. Leiter, *Featherbedding and Job Security* (New York: Twayne, 1964); William Gomberg, "The Work Rules and Work Practices," *Labor Law Journal* (July, 1961), pp. 643-653; Addison and Siebert, op.cit., pp. 300-304.

[35]NLRA, Section 8(d): ". . . to bargain collectively is the performance of the mutual obligation of the employer and the representative of the employees to meet . . . and confer in good faith and with respect to . . . terms and conditions of employment. . . ."

[36]As further indication of this asymmetry, note the language used by the National Labor Board (created under the later superseded NIRA): "The employer is obligated by the statute [the NIRA which, in this respect at least, did not differ much from its successor, the Wagner Act of NLRA] to negotiate in good faith with his employees' representative; to match their proposals, if unacceptable, with counter-proposals; and to make every reasonable effort to reach an agreement" [*Houde Engineering Corp.,* 1 NLB 15 (1934)]. Thus, it was the *employer's* obligation: Clearly, the union was seen as the initiator and employers had a duty to respond *constructively* (a point taken up in more detail below).

[37]*Western Cold Storage,* NLB, Docket No. 80 (1919).

[38]*Consolidated Edison Co. v. NLRB,* 305 U.S. 197, 3 LRRM 645 (1938).

[39]Whereas the concept of "good faith" was lacking in the NLRA from its inception as the Wagner Act, until it was added through the Taft-Hartley amendments, the NLRB almost immediately began on its own to attach this requirement: see Morris, op. cit., pp. 273-276.

[40]*Rhodes-Holland Chevrolet Co.,* 146 NLRB 1304, at 1304-1305, 56 LRRM 1058 (1964).

[41]*General Electric Co.,* 150 NLRB 192, 57 LRRM 1491 (1964); enforced in *NLRB v. General Electric Co.,* 418 F 2d 736, 72 LRRM 2530 (1969).

[42]*Proctor and Gamble Mfg. Co.,* 160 NLRB 334, 62 LRRM 1617 (1966).

[43]*NLRB v. General Electric Co.,* op. cit., at 759 and elsewhere.

[44]See note 36, *infra.*

[45]*NLRB v. Reed & Prince Mfg. Co.,* 205 F 2d 131, at 134-135. Emphasis in the original.

[46]*Congressional Record,* Vol. 79 (1935), p. 7660.

[47]321 U.S. 332 (1944).

[48]Ibid., at 338 and 339.

[49]See *NLRB v. Metropolitan Life Insurance Co.*, 380 U.S. 438 (1965).

[50]*Steele v. Louisville Railroad*, 323 U.S. 192 (1944). It should be noted that *Steele* was decided with reference to the Railway Labor Act, but the essence of the holding was thereafter applied also to the NLRA in *Ford Motor v. Huffman*, 345 U.S. 330 (1953) and *Syres v. Oil Workers International*, 350 U.S. 892 (1955).

[51]*Steele*, op. cit. at 203.

[52]*Vaca v. Sipes*, 383 U.S. 171, at 190 (1967).

[53]*Huffman*, 345 U.S. at 338 (1953).

[54]But see Dan C. Heldman and Deborah L. Knight, *Unions and Lobbying: The Representation Function* (Washington, DC: Foundation for the Advancement of the Public Trust, 1980), esp. Ch. 3.

[55]We observe in passing that, despite *Steele* in 1944, *Huffman* in 1953, *Syres* in 1955, and numerous other judicial actions regarding "fair representation," it was not until 1962 (*Miranda Fuel*, 140 NLRB 181) that the NLRB acknowledged any ability to remedy a violation of this duty as an unfair labor practice.

[56]Note that we are using "discrimination" in its traditional definition, i.e., making choices. The word, though perfectly meaningful and useful, acquired a pejorative connotation in the context of racism and this connotation continues to infect an otherwise valuable idea. When we say that a union discriminates, we mean nothing more than that a union represents some employee interests but not others or that, in aggregating interests, a union produces a representation position which is at variance with that of at least one individual employee. Of course, a union may also discriminate in the contemporary pejorative sense, but that is another matter.

[57]See notes 47 and 48, *infra*.

[58]*Steele*, op. cit.

[59]See, for example, *Teamsters v. U.S.*, 431 U.S. 324 (1977); M.J. Levine, "The Conflict Between Negotiated Seniority Provisions and Title VII of the Civil Rights Act of 1964: Recent Developments," 29 *Labor Law Journal* 352 (1978).

[60]*IUEW (Automotive Plating Corp.)*, 170 NLRB no. 121 (1968).

[61]For example, negotiating a seniority preference for union officials in the case of layoffs is permissible (*Aeronautical Lodge 727 v. Campbell*, 337 U.S. 521 [1949]); a union's insistence upon basing compensation upon distance from work is permissible (*Millwright's Local 1102*, 144 NLRB 798 [1963]); pressing for the allocation of work to persons "not at trade" as opposed to those already employed full-time elsewhere is permissible (*N.Y. Typographical Union Local 6* [*N.Y. Times Co.*], 144 NLRB 1558 [1963]); seeking to fine and suspend members for being more productive than the union's work rules would permit is permissible (*Scofield v. NLRB*, 394 U.S. 423 [1969]).

[62]For a good discussion of this particular problem, see Paul H. Tobias, "The Plaintiff's View of '301-DFR' Litigation," *Employee Relations Law Journal* (Spring, 1980), pp. 510-532. Tobias develops the thesis (p. 510) that "the labor-management establishment [employers, unions, and attorneys representing them] has influenced the courts to be hostile toward rank-and-file claims. . . . the record of plaintiffs [employees] in court is abysmal. Most . . . cases are dismissed."

[63]*Hines v. Anchor Freight,* 424 U.S. 554 (1976); see also C.P. Barker, "The Employer's Stake in the Union's Duty of Fair Representation: A Form of Liability Without Fault," *Labor Law Developments,* ed. M.L. Langwehr (NY: Bender, 1978), pp. 61-87. The idea that the union's financial strength should not be undermined by employees charging unfair representation can be found not only in *Hines* but also in *IBEW v. Foust,* 99 S.Ct. 2121 (1979).

[64]Among many other reasons employees find it difficult to sustain an unfair representation charge is the fact that the employee bears the burden of proof: *Motor Coach Employees v. Lockridge,* 403 U.S. 294 (1977). As Tobias has noted (op. cit., p. 513), "individual rights remain illusory and virtually nonenforceable as a practical matter." That this is by no means a recent problem is attested to by the remark, in 1960, by Archibald Cox that "individual workers who sue union officials run enormous risks, for there are many ways, legal as well as illegal, by which entrenched officials can 'take care of' recalcitrant members." See Cox, "Labor Reform Act," 58 *Michigan Law Review* at 853 (1960).

[65]The two leading cases here are *NLRB v. General Motors,* 373 U.S. 734, 53 LRRM 2313 (1963); and *Retail Clerks v. Schermerhorn,* 373 U.S. 746, 53 LRRM 2318 (1963); the latter on reargument, 375 U.S. 96, 54 LRRM 2612 (1963).

[66]We add to this litany the observation that few attorneys are sufficiently informed about labor law, much less about labor law from the perspective of *employee rights,* to provide accurate advice on this matter — assuming they were approached to do so in the first place. Most lawyers in this field of specialization developed their expertise in connection with and/or are otherwise obligated to represent the interests of employers or unions, not the interests of employees. An unnamed Justice Department attorney, specializing in union problems, was quoted by *Washington Post* reporters as observing "the individual union member doesn't have the money to get a lawyer." Anyway, most labor law specialists work either for the unions or for management." Haynes Johnson and Nick Kotz, *The Unions (Washington Post* National Report) (New York: Pocketbook, 1972), p. 164.

[67]The case of *Buckley/Evans* is instructive in this respect. The union involved (AFTRA) has long required a "membership as a condition of continued employment" clause in its broadcast industry contracts. Plaintiffs sued, based upon the established precedents, and only after numerous hearings did the union admit that, of course, formal membership could not be required. The court, as part of the settlement, required AFTRA to issue a letter stating this fact to each and every broadcaster with which it had a contract: see *Buckley v. NLRB,* 76 Civ. (S.D. of N.Y.) 2212 (1978). Subsequent to all this, AFTRA contracts still used the term "membership" with no qualifications, and certain employers were still declaring (in conjunction with AFTRA) that a new, covered employee had to join the union within 30 days. The situation is unique neither to broadcasting nor to AFTRA.

[68]See Clyde Summers, "Legal Limitations on Union Discipline," 64 *Harvard Law Review* at 1055-1056 (1951), for a critique of this situation.

[69]This is to be found in Title I of the Landrum-Griffin (Labor-Management Reporting and Disclosure) Act of 1959: Included here are provisions relating to the right of members to equal participation in union affairs, free speech and assembly, reasonable dues, fair treatment in disciplinary hearings, etc. Title II involves the financial obligations and arrangements of unions, Title III deals with trusteeships over union locals, Title IV regulates internal elections, and Title V seeks to remedy the problem of infiltration by Communist and/or organized crime groups. See, for a generally approving commentary, Benjamin Aaron, "The Labor-Management Reporting and Disclosure Act of 1959," 73 *Harvard Law Review* 851 (1960).

[70]See *McNamara v. Johnston,* 522 F 2d 1157 (1975); *Gabauer v. Woodcock,* 594 F 2d 666 (1979). The courts have, however, occasionally refused to enforce a union constitutional provision which, no matter how "democratic" the procedure by which it was instituted, violates in

application common-sense notions of democracy as well as particular portions of the Landrum-Griffin Act. The IUE, for example, has a requirement in its constitution that "laid off" members *cannot* pay dues; but the payment of dues happens also to be a requisite for being in "good standing" which is, in turn, a requisite for participating in union affairs. This situation was tested in *Alvey v. GE and IUE* (CA 7, Case No. 79-1636 [June 11, 1980]); decision and analysis in *DLR* (No. 136 [July 14, 1980], at F-1 and A-8) where the union prevented from participating (through this rule) the very people whose interests were most affected (the union was deciding on a plan for recalling laid-off employees based on seniority): The application of the rule was found wanting.

[71]We have already indicated why a member might believe (however wrong the belief is from a purely *legal* point of view) that the option of resignation is not available in the face of a putative "union shop" requirement.

[72]Indeed, some union constitutions provide that a member may not sue the union on pain of expulsion, suspension, or some other severe penalty: It was such a requirement, for example, which produced *NLRB v. Industrial Union of Marine Workers*, 391 U.S. 418 (1970).

[73]One study, for example, discovered that, out of nearly 2000 internal union appeals carried to the final level, less than 2 per cent were resolved in favor of the employee/member. When the member's complaint involved penalties against him for "political dissent or other acts 'disloyal' to the union and its leadership," the study found that appeals were "uniformly denied." Charles Craypo, "The National Union Convention as an Internal Appeal Tribunal," *Industrial and Labor Relations Review* (July, 1969), p. 498.

[74]*Local 756, UAW v. Woychick*, 5 Wis. 2d 528, 43 LRRM 2941 (1958).

[75]A leading case which permits a union to levy fines for exceeding union-imposed productivity limits is *Scofield v. NLRB*, 394 U.S. 423 (1969): The Supreme Court explicitly declared that union rules limiting productivity and individual ability were entirely legitimate (Ibid. at 425, 431).

[76]*NLRB v. Granite State (Textile Workers)*, 409 U.S. 213 (1972); *Booster Lodge (IAM v. NLRB*, 412 U.S. 84 (1973); but see, on the untimely resignation issue, *United Construction Workers (Erhardt Construction)*, 187 NLRB No. 99 (1971).

[77]*UAW (General Electric)*, 197 NLRB No. 93 (1972); see also cases cited in note 76, above.

[78]Some of the questions have been outlined by Dan C. Heldman, "Making Policy in a Vacuum: The Case of Labor Relations," *Policy Review* (Fall, 1979), pp. 75-88. See also James T. Bennett and Manuel H. Johnson, "Free Riders in U.S. Labour Unions: Artifice or Affliction?," *British Journal of Industrial Relations* (July, 1979), pp. 158-172.

[79]Curtis Mack and Ezra Singer, "Florida Public Employees: Is the Solution to the Free Rider Problem Worse than the Problem Itself?" *Florida State University Law Review* 1347 (1978), note 34 at 1353.

[80]*Abood v. Detroit Bd. of Educ.*, 431 U.S. 209 (1977).

[81]Under the RLA, see *Ellis v. Railway Clerks*, 91 LRRM 2339 (1976); under NLRA, see *Beck v. CWA*, 468 F. Supp. 93 (1979).

[82]The controversy stems in no small part from the unwillingness of most unions involved in a case of this sort to reveal, through its books and records, just how much it spends for what. The *Beck* case, op. cit., is notable in this regard. The *Ellis* case has actually produced a calculation of impermissible costs (*Ellis*, op. cit., 88 L.C., paragraph 11,986 (1980)).

[83]Report of the Special Master, *Beck v. CWA* (Civil No. M-76-839) (August 18, 1980); full text reprinted in *Daily Labor Report*, No. 166 (August 25, 1980), pp. D1-D17.

[84]"This observation must certainly be true if the amount of material were somehow correlated with the time over which it had been produced: Labor relations regulation is, after all, a comparative newcomer to the list of legal topics.

[85]Carl Frankel, quoted in *Business Week* (August 13, 1979), p. 76.

Chapter IV

Economic Costs of Regulating Labor Relations

Chapters II and III contain discussions of the disadvantages of regulation in general and the regulation of labor relations in particular. A common feature of all types of government regulation is that the costs are enormous and are shared by everyone while the benefits are few and are misdirected to a small number of special interest groups. Therefore, regardless of the good intentions of regulation, the resulting benefits are often not realized by those persons who should be protected. Instead, economic gains perversely accrue to the regulators and, in some cases, to those regulated.

Regulation in the labor sector provides no exception. Those who bear the costs of government control over labor relations are the consuming public, employees, businesses, and job seekers. The beneficiaries are the employees of government agencies that administer the regulatory programs (NLRB, OSHA, Department of Labor, EEOC, similar state agencies, etc.) and the labor unions (more the union officials than the members) that obtain special privileges.

The deregulation of labor relations would not only eliminate the costs to taxpayers of supporting a huge regulatory bureaucracy, but also would reestablish the market as the allocator of labor resources. Therefore, the economic benefits associated with deregulation of the labor sector are both savings of taxpayer/consumer dollars and additional employment/income that would be generated in the absence of labor regulation.

This chapter assesses the economic gains to society that would result from the deregulation of labor relations. Estimation of these gains involves compiling empirical evidence regarding the social costs associated with the myriad constraints on employer-employee relations. The social costs of regulation in the labor sector represent the benefits that would result from deregulation in the sense that these costs include the employment and income that would occur in the absence of regulation. The remainder of this chapter, therefore, deals with an assessment of the costs of various labor regulatory programs.

A thorough analysis of the impact of minimum wage-maximum hour regulations is provided in the second section. Studies that determine the employment and income effects of wage and hour laws are surveyed and an attempt is made to assess the magnitude of the benefits that would result from their repeal. The effects of repeal of the Davis-Bacon and Walsh-Healy Acts are also discussed.

The third section deals with the impact of payroll taxes on employers, employees, and consumers. Economic gains from the elimination of mandatory unemployment insurance payments and social security contributions are discussed. Costs and benefits of government manpower programs are addressed in the fourth section. The proliferation of federal programs is documented so that a price tag can be placed on these activities. Occupational safety and health regulation is evaluated in the fifth section. Both direct budgetary costs and the indirect private sector burden of OSHA are reviewed. The sixth section contains an analysis of the costs of affirmative action programs. Benefits due to the elimination of hiring quotas are estimated in terms of gains in worker productivity and wage differences.

An assessment of the gains from removing the special union protection clauses of labor legislation is undertaken in the seventh section. The economic effects of exclusive union representation, granted by the National Labor Relations Act, are estimated in order to determine the social costs created by this protective measure. An accounting of tax dollars budgeted for NLRB regulatory purposes is also provided.

Minimum Wages and Maximum Hours

The first minimum wage law in the United States went into effect with the adoption of the Fair Labor Standards Act by Congress in 1938 which initially set the legal minimum at 25 cents per hour for a limited segment of the work force.[1] Since 1938, a series of amendments has raised the minimum to $3.35, effective January 1, 1981. Coverage of the minimum wage law has also expanded over time. Today, approximately 52 million workers, or 65 percent of the labor force, come under coverage of the FLSA. The law was purportedly established to reduce poverty by raising wages to a level above that for mere subsistence.[2] A typical appraisal of the positive aspects of raising minimum wages and expanding coverage is contained in the following statement, in 1968, by then Secretary of Labor Willard Wirtz:

Minimum Wage Legislation went a long way toward the development of a philosophy . . . consistent with . . . the attack on poverty. Increases in the minimum wage level . . . brought it roughly in line for the first time with at least the low side of what is considered a minimal decent subsistence income. . . . The extension of coverage . . . reflected the Congress' recognition that the human needs of the principal contributors to the economy were entitled to at least as much consideration as the enterprises involved. There was clear indication that the self-interest pressure groups which have been responsible for the large scale exemptions and exclusions from the coverage of the Act will have an increasingly difficult time in the future in pressing their claims against the broader national interest in seeing to it that a day's work gives whoever does it a day's decent living.[3]

While such pronouncements by government officials and politicians sound encouraging, conclusions drawn from economic theory suggest a much less promising result from minimum wages. According to economists, a legislated minimum wage, if it is to have any effect at all, raises the price employers must pay for low-skilled labor above the level that would have occurred in the market.

In a free market for labor, firms will hire workers at a wage equal to the value of the additional output they produce.[4] Therefore, employees will be paid an amount equal to their individual contribution to the firm's profit. Competition among firms for workers will ensure that labor receives its fair share of the economic pie; no more and no less. If, on the one hand, a firm attempted to pay individuals a wage lower than their productivity, it would lose them to other firms that were willing to pay the appropriate wage. On the other hand, if a worker attempted to command a wage above the value of his or her productivity, other job seekers willing to work at the going wage would be hired instead.

Congress may possess the power to legislate a wage increase for low-income workers above that which could be obtained in the market, however, they have not discovered a way to legislate an increase in productivity. If, therefore, the established minimum wage exceeds the value of the productivity of some workers, a firm will adjust to this rise in labor cost by eliminating from its work force those persons whose productivity is below the minimum.[5] Unlike public officials and politicians, the majority of economists believe that the minimum wage adversely affects those workers who are most disadvantaged in terms

87

of income and marketable skills.[6] Walter Williams, a well-known labor economist, has pointed out that

> in the U.S. labor force, there are at least two segments of the labor force who share the marginal worker characteristics to a greater extent than do other segments of the labor force. The first group consists of youths in general. They are low skilled or marginal because of their age, immaturity and lack of work experience. The second group, which contains members of the first group, are some racial minorities such as Negroes who, as a result of racial discrimination and a number of other socioeconomic factors, are disproportionately represented among low-skill workers. These workers are not only made unemployable by the minimum wage, but their opportunities to upgrade their skills through on-the-job training are also severely limited.[7]

Williams has also indicated that, as one might expect, young people in general and black youth in particular are disproportionately represented in unemployment figures. Even in relatively prosperous periods, the youth unemployment rate has been as much as three times that of the total labor force. The black youth unemployment rate has been about five times that of the general labor force. Tables 1 and 2 provide interesting statistics showing that increases in the minimum wage are consistent with greater youth unemployment. In Table 1, column 3, the unemployment rate for teenagers (ages 16-19) relative to the overall unemployment rate is shown to rise steadily over time with increases in the minimum wage. Table 2 contains figures showing that nonwhite youth unemployment has increased over time relative to white youth unemployment, thus suggesting that Williams was correct in asserting that nonwhite teenagers are hardest hit by escalating minimum wages.

Fortunately, there have been numerous empirical studies investigating the impacts of the imposition of minimum wage laws, beginning with the establishment of the first minimum of 25 cents per hour in 1938.

A short time after the FLSA became law, it was reported by the Department of Labor that 30 to 50 thousand persons became unemployed as result of the Act.[8] About 90 percent of the laid off workers were concentrated in low-wage, labor-intensive industries in the South, e.g., pecan shelling, tobacco, and lumber. Research findings showed that in such industries, the substitution of capital for labor created substantial technological unemployment; an average of three to ten workers were displaced by a single machine.[9] Studies of the hosiery industry by Hinrichs and Douty showed that between 1938 and 1939

Table IV-1

Comparison of Teenage and General Unemployment Rates
(Averages of Monthly Seasonally Adjusted Data)

	Unemployment rates (percent)		Ratio teenage/ general	Minimum wage
	Ages 16-19	General		
February 1949-January 1950	13.9	6.2	2.2	$0.40
February 1950-January 1951	11.6	5.0	2.3	.75
March 1955-February 1956	11.0	4.2	2.6	.75
March 1956-February 1957	11.0	4.1	2.7	1.00
September 1960-August 1961	16.4	6.6	2.5	1.00
September 1961-August 1962	15.4	5.8	2.7	[1]1.15 (1.00)
September 1962-August 1963	16.4	5.6	2.9	1.15 (1.00)
September 1963-August 1964	16.6	5.4	3.1	1.25 (1.00)
September 1964-August 1965	15.6	4.8	3.3	(1.15)
September 1965-August 1966	13.2	3.8	3.5	(1.25)
February 1966-January 1967	12.6	3.8	3.3	1.25
February 1967-January 1968[2]	12.9	3.8	3.4	1.40 (1.00)
February 1968-December 1968	12.7	3.6	3.6	1.60 (1.15)

[1]Minimum wage figures in parentheses are for jobs not currently covered prior to September 1961 and February 1967.

[2]Not comparable with earlier data because of the exclusion from the unemployment count on those seeking future jobs and not currently available for work.

Source: Yale Brozen, "The Effect of Statutory Minimum Wage Increases on Teenage Unemployment," *Journal of Law and Economics* (April 1969), p. 116.

low-wage firms were forced to raise wages by 35 percent. This increase in labor prices led to increased spending on capital equipment and a decline in employment of 12.8 percent by 1940.[10] The imposition of a $1.00 minimum wage in 1956 was found to have had a severe impact on employment. At that time, a large number of industries maintained substantial employment at wage rates under $1.00. Douty showed 16 industries experienced a decline in employment of from 10 to 25 percent.[11] In 1961, the minimum wage was raised to $1.15 and by September 1, 1963, it had increased to $1.25. In addition, the FLSA was extended to cover an additional 3.6 million workers. Those industries hardest hit by these increases were labor-intensive southern firms which had absorbed every escalation in the minimum wage since its

Table IV-2

*Comparison of Teenage Unemployment Rates, Nonwhite and White
(Both Sexes, 16-19)*

	Teenage Unemployment rates (percent)		Ratio nonwhite/ white
	Nonwhite	White	
February 1949-January 1950	17.4	13.4	1.3
February 1950-January 1951	14.8	11.2	1.3
March 1955-February 1956	15.8	10.2	1.5
March 1956-February 1957	18.1	10.0	1.8
September 1960-August 1961	27.4	15.0	1.8
September 1961-August 1962	25.3	13.9	1.8
September 1962-August 1963	29.2	14.9	2.0
September 1963-August 1964	23.4	15.0	1.9
September 1964-August 1965	26.1	14.2	1.8
September 1965-August 1966	26.5	11.9	2.3
February 1966-January 1967	25.1	11.1	2.3
February 1967-January 1968[1]	26.3	11.0	2.4
February 1968-December 1968	25.4	11.0	2.3

[1]Not comparable with earlier data because of the exclusion from the unemployment count on those seeking future jobs and not currently available for work.

Source: Yale Brozen, "The Effect of Statutory Minimum Wage Increases on Teenage Unemployment," *Journal of Law and Economics* (April 1969), p. 116.

beginning in 1938. Prior to 1961, average hourly earnings in the southern lumber industry were $1.18 per hour; however, after the 1961 increase in the minimum, wages averaged $1.25 and employment had declined from 173,000 to 141,000.[12]

The expansion in coverage of the minimum wage law in 1961 and 1963 included for the first time many employees in retail trade. As a result of increased coverage, affected retail employment in nonmetropolitan areas of the South declined from 160,000 in June, 1961 to 143,000 in June, 1962. Interestingly, retail trade employment in southern establishments *not* covered under the FLSA increased from 549,000 to 574,000 over the same time interval.[13]

A 1960 study by Macesich and Stewart examined 11 industries in which data were classified by region and wage level. Their findings showed that the 1956 increase in the minimum wage produced effects on employment precisely the same as those predicted by the economic theory of competition in the labor market. Worker layoffs were greatest among firms that employed large numbers of low-skilled persons — exactly where theory predicts minimum wages would have the largest impact.[14] In a later study, Peterson and Stewart found that, following the establishment of a new minimum wage, firms using low-skilled labor substantially increased their capital investments and correspondingly reduced the size of their labor forces.[15] The authors also discovered that a significant number of firms were violating minimum wage laws by maintaining some low-skilled workers at wages below the legal minimum. This result reconfirmed a similar conclusion drawn by Peterson in analyzing three low-wage industries covered by the FLSA and three occupations subject to state minimum wage laws.[16]

Two studies by Brozen have documented the employment and income effects of minimum wages on unskilled workers. In his earliest research, Brozen found that persons in occupations adversely affected by the FLSA tend to crowd into uncovered areas, such as domestic service work, thereby increasing employment and competing down equilibrium wages. The displacement of workers from covered occupations was shown to have an especially severe impact on low-skilled women.[17] A later article by Brozen indicated that successive increases in the legal minimum wage were reflected by rises in the teenage unemployment rate and that nonwhites were disproportionately represented among this group, a phenomenon illustrated in Tables 1 and 2.[18]

Moore conducted a statistical analysis of the effects of minimum wages over time for the period 1954-1968.[19] In this study he allowed for the measurement of impacts by both changes in the level of the minimum wage and its coverage of the labor force. A summary of Moore's findings is reported in Table 3 below. Inspection of the table clearly shows that the youth population is severely affected by increasing the minimum wage and the coverage of the law. In addition, nonwhite youths were shown to be most adversely affected. The unemployment rate of nonwhite teenagers age 16-19 was found to increase 1.76 percent for each 1.0 percent increase in the ratio of the minimum wage to average hourly earnings of production workers in the nonagricultural work force. Also, the unemployment rate for this group increased .25 percent for each 1.0 percent increase in the coverage of the minimum wage law. As shown below, increases in the level and coverage of the minimum wage have led to increased unemployment among all other

Table IV-3

The Impact of Minimum Wages on Teenage Unemployment, 1954-1968

Worker Group	%Increase in Unemployment for Every 1% Change in:	
	Minimum Wage as Proportion of Hourly Earnings	Workers Covered by Minimum Wage
Nonwhites, 16-19	1.7593%	.225%
Whites, 16-19	.5846	.077
Males, 16-19	.6165	.080
Females, 16-19	.7399	.171
Males, 20-24	.0535	− .063

Source: Extracted from regression results in T. G. Moore, "The Effect of Minimum Wages on Teenage Unemployment Rates," *Journal of Political Economy* 79 (July/August 1971), p. 901.

teenage subgroups as well as nonwhites; only males ages 20-24 enjoyed higher employment as a result of increased coverage of the FLSA.

Examining the same time period as Moore, Kosters and Welch discovered that the minimum wage caused a decline in job opportunities for teenagers during periods of normal employment growth and caused their jobs to be of a more temporary nature during short-run changes in the business cycle. In the words of Kosters and Welch,

> our evidence indicates that increases in the effective minimum wage over the period 1954-68 have had a significant impact on employment patterns. Minimum wage legislation has had the effect of decreasing the share of normal employment and increasing vulnerability to cyclical changes in employment for the group most "marginal" to the work force — teenagers.[20]

In a study of the effects of minimum wage legislation for the period 1954 to 1968, Welch concluded that, before the FLSA amendment in 1956, minimum wages had only a minor impact on youth unemployment but increases since that time have produced severe effects.[21] According to Welch, the teenage/adult employment ratio was only about 1.5 percent below what it would have been in the absence of minimum wages just prior to the 1956 amendment. However estimates showed that in 1968 minimum wages had reduced teenage employment relative to adult employment by 15 percent of what it otherwise would have been. Welch also asserted that minimum wages increased the vulnerability of youth employment to changes in the business cycle. On average, teenagers represented about 6 percent of total employment over the 1954-1968 period. But, among employment variations produced by the business cycle, teenagers accounted for 22 percent. Welch stated that "the evidence is that a substantial part of the discrepancy between 22 and 6 percent is attributable to minimum wages."[22]

A 1974 survey article by Goldfarb revealed a growing consensus on the adverse effects of minimum wages.[23] Goldfarb examined four studies completed between 1971 and 1974. All of the research showed that wage increases decrease teenage unemployment. In particular, a 25 percent rise in minimum wage rates was shown to lower teenage employment by approximately 3.5 to 5.5 percent.

In a more recent study, Gramlich evaluated additional empirical research estimating the impacts of minimum wages.[24] These studies, in general, suggested that a 25 percent increase in the minimum wage would reduce youth employment by, at most, 6 percent. Gramlich argued, however, that there are important reasons why these previous estimates were too low. One reason is that the statistics used to estimate unemployment among teenagers resulting from minimum wages represent all teenagers, not just low-wage teenagers. Obviously, the impact of minimum wage increases on the employment of low-skilled teenagers would be greater than for the aggregate teenager category. Gramlich made allowance for this error and found that a 25 percent increase would actually reduce the employment of low-skilled teenagers by about 15 percent.[25]

Gramlich also investigated the effects of higher minimum wages on the overall wage bill. It was shown that the 1974 FLSA amendment raising the minimum from $1.60 to $2.00 per hour increased the overall wage bill by only 0.8 percent. However, if the increase were from $1.60 to $3.00 (an amount less than today's minimum), the direct impact on the wage bill would cause an increase of 6.0 percent and an indirect impact considerably greater.[26]

Many of the indirect wage bill effects of rising minimum wages occur in the unionized sector of the economy. Unions have been quick to recognize the bargaining advantage provided by higher minimum wages and, therefore, have become one of the strongest supporters of FLSA amendments. If, for example, the low end of the union wage scale has traditionally been 50 cents above the minimum wage and the minimum is increased by 50 cents, unions can bring substantial pressure on employers to increase collectively bargained wage rates by 50 cents per hour in order to preserve the historical differential.[27] A ratcheting effect of this kind indicates the potential impact of rising minimum wages beyond those workers directly affected by the legislation.[28] It is also true that a higher minimum wage raises the cost of unskilled relative to skilled workers. The result of this relative change is to induce firms to hire fewer unskilled workers, thus raising the relative demand for skilled workers who are mostly represented by labor unions.[29]

An important study by Mincer has shown that the unemployment effects of minimum wage increases underestimate the impact on the labor sector.[30] The major consequence, according to Mincer, is not unemployment, but a total withdrawal by workers from the labor force. In other words, the labor force does not remain constant during changes in the minimum wage; workers leave the industries that are covered and move into uncovered sectors or simply give up their job search entirely. Mincer pointed out that "no more than a third of the employment loss in the covered sector appears as unemployment, while the bulk withdraws from the labor force."[31] Therefore, Mincer's research suggests that, in order to determine the true impact of minimum wages on employment, one must take the estimated increase in unemployment resulting from legislated wage minima and multiply it by three.[32]

Two recent studies by Wessels and McKenzie have indicated that the adverse effects of the minimum wage are even greater than those discovered by Mincer.[33] According to these two researchers, previous investigations of the impact of minimum wages have incorrectly assumed that a firm's costs rise as a result of minimum wage hikes because the total wage bill increases and, also, that many workers who are retained by the firm will enjoy higher incomes. It is pointed out that, due to these assumptions, previous research has failed to take into account the negative effects a minimum wage increase can have on the nonwage costs of labor. Firms may react to an increase in the minimum wage by reducing nonwage benefits such as fringes, on-the-job training, vacations, and job safety. Lower expenditures on the nonwage aspects of work can easily offset the impact of rising minimum wages on the costs of the firm. Similarly, the corresponding reduction in workers' nonwage incomes can overcome any increase in their money incomes. Consequently, even workers who retain their jobs in the face of rising minimum wages may be made worse off.

Empirical research performed by Wessels, and consistent with Mincer, determined that minimum wage increases reduce the labor force participation of many worker groups. This result implies that minimum wages lower the welfare of job seekers and persons working in uncovered sectors of the economy. Wessels also found that minimum wages raised the quit rate of workers in several covered industries, thus suggesting that the value of the jobs in these firms fell relative to the value of searching for alternative employment. In his conclusion, Wessels pointed out that

> the expanded model suggests that the effect of minimum wages is far more severe than the standard model suggests. In effect, the minimum wage has created a "dual labor market" where those workers covered by the minimum wage may have to accept more dangerous jobs, less training, and poorer working conditions — even though they would be willing to accept lower wages in exchange for safer jobs, more training, and better working conditions.[34]

In the final analysis, the Fair Labor Standards Act and its amendments have been a costly failure. Not only have minimum wages failed to alleviate poverty and provide a better standard of living, but they have also managed to exacerbate both unemployment and inflation.

The impacts of minimum wage laws are so pervasive it is impossible to assess completely the consequences of such regulation on the labor market. Practically any attempt to measure quantitatively all the economic effects of minimum wage laws would be incomplete. However, an analysis of the existing studies of minimum wages reviewed herein can provide some idea of the relative magnitude and distribution of economic impacts.

According to Gramlich, a 25 percent increase in the minimum wage would cause teenage (ages 16-19) unemployment to rise by 15 percent. In 1974, the legal minimum wage was raised from $1.60 to $2.00 per hour, a 25 percent increase. Between 1973 and 1975 the unemployment rate for teenagers 16 to 19 years of age climbed from 14.5 percent to 19.9 percent of the teenage labor force. This change in the youth unemployment rate represented an additional .53 million jobless teenagers.[35] Assuming that 15 percent of the rise in teenage unemployment was due to the minimum wage, roughly 80,000 youths owed their unemployment to the 1974 wage hike. If the average work week for teenagers was about 30 hours, a conservative estimate of the lost income (at $1.60 per hour) to this group alone would amount to $200 million in 1975. Unfortunately, most of the financial burden created by this lost income will fall on business firms and taxpayers in the form of unemployment insurance contributions and government welfare payments, respectively.[36]

Linneman has pointed out that teenagers are not the only subminimum wage group. His research determined that 10 percent of U.S. adults are members of the subminimum wage population. Linneman also found that, on the average, a below-minimum adult lost $78 due to the 1974 increase in the minimum wage, representing a total income loss of $546 million. Again, the incidence of these lost earnings will be directed toward employers and the taxpaying public because they must financially support unemployment insurance and social welfare programs.

A previously neglected, but severe, economic effect of rising minimum wages is the propensity of labor force participants to drop out of the labor force entirely. Mincer showed that the number of persons who leave the labor force as a result of higher minimum wages may be three times the number estimated to be unemployed. In 1975, this finding would translate into 240,000 disemployed teenagers. If only one-half of these individuals or their families sought a minimum amount of government welfare assistance, the cost would have approached $432 million.[37]

The costs mentioned above represent only those figures that can be reasonably measured from information provided in recent empirical research. A number of extremely important costs of wage regulation by government cannot currently be measured. These nonquantifiable effects may well be the most significant impacts of FLSA amendments. As Wessels and McKenzie have pointed out, even low-skilled workers who retain their jobs when minimum wages are raised may suffer a loss in their effective income because employers reduce the nonwage benefits associated with the job. Wessels provided evidence that increases in the minimum wage caused workers to quit their jobs in 8 out of the 13 covered manufacturing industries that he studied.[38] Quite likely, the decline in effective income among job holders is the largest single cost associated with minimum wages.

The true but unmeasurable social cost attributable to minimum wages is the lost output that could have been produced by workers who were displaced by higher minimum wages. The magnitude of this cost depends on how fast displaced workers are reemployed and the time it takes for firms to substitute labor-saving machinery. There is no way of knowing just how much output is reduced, but there is no doubt that some reduction takes place. Further, even when displaced workers find new employment, they will not be utilized where they are most needed in the economy. In other words, labor is misallocated whenever wages are set at artificially high levels. Although again unmeasurable, there is some positive cost associated with the less desirable output mix created by misallocated labor.

It would be incorrect to suggest that there are no benefits whatsoever associated with minimum wages. As pointed out earlier, unions lobby politically to increase the legal minimum wage because a higher minimum pressures employers in organized sectors to increase the union wage scale. Empirical research conducted by Linneman found that the average union member gained $435 as a result of the 1974 minimum wage hike.[39] This gain in wages represented an increase in the income of union members totaling $7.5 billion. Because low-skilled labor has become more expensive due to minimum wage laws and because unions are often able to segment the labor market, the demand for union labor is relatively inelastic and, therefore, gains in union income do not result in any significant unemployment among this group. Also, employers are unable to make nonwage adjustments to the compensation package of union members because nonwage items are collectively bargained for in labor contracts and are not subject to change. Thus, union income increases resulting from rising minimum wages represent gains in both nominal pecuniary income and total effective income. Since employers are unable to adjust downward the nonwage components of union worker compensation, they must absorb a large portion of union wage gains in the form of higher production costs. To the extent that market demand for manufactured products is relatively inelastic, higher production costs will be passed on to consumers through higher prices. Therefore, the benefits resulting from minimum wages accrue to a rather narrowly focused interest group, namely, private sector labor unions. Unfortunately, these benefits represent costs (higher product prices) to a broader segment of society — private sector business firms and all consumers.

While it is impossible to quantify all of the costs and benefits associated with minimum wages, it is obvious, as mentioned previously, that the vast majority of unmeasurable values represent costs. In terms of what values can be measured, it was determined that the 1974 minimum wage hike produced benefits totaling $7.5 billion and costs amounting to approximately $8.3 billion.[40] Probably the most interesting fact about the costs and benefits of minimum wages is that the benefits do not accrue to those persons which the FLSA was designed to help while the costs are substantial and affect nearly everyone.

Davis-Bacon Act and Other Prevailing Wage Laws. Other types of wage regulation by government are the Davis-Bacon Act and similar prevailing wage laws such as the Walsh-Healy Act (Public Contracts Act) and the O'Hara-McNamara Services Act. The Davis-Bacon Act became law on March 31, 1931, for the purpose of protecting local wage rates on federal construction from competition with lower wage nonlocal labor. The Act requires that all workers on federal construction projects must be paid prevailing local wages. Numerous other laws incorporate the prevailing wage requirement of Davis-Bacon for projects that receive federal assistance such as housing, schools, and highways. Clearly, prevailing wage laws like Davis-Bacon cause labor market distortions in the determination of wages. Such legislation forces wages to be set at artificially high levels in order to restrict competition from low-wage firms. This restriction alone presents a case for deregulation in order to ensure a more efficient allocation of resources at lower costs. However, the inefficiencies that are created due to a divergence between market wages and prevailing local wages are only minor compared to the tremendous waste that actually arises through bureaucratic mismanagement and labor union pressure. Of course, this additional waste probably could not take place without the legislation itself.

In terms of prevailing wages, the construction industry labor market actually has two separate rates. One prevailing rate applies to open shop firms and is simply determined by supply and demand in the highly competitive nonunion labor market. The other rate is the union rate, which is much higher because construction unions hold a monopoly position against many local contractors who have large operations in metropolitan areas or are engaged in nonresidential construction.

The "prevailing" wage in any area is determined by the Department of Labor. As a result of the department's burdensome procedural rules and the influence of labor unions, prevailing wage calculations disproportionately represent the union wage level. Quite often, the union wage, which is certified as the prevailing rate, is taken from areas other than those in which construction is being done. Because of this wage determination process, open shop contractors must choose between either paying their employees much higher wages during construction of a federal project or not participating in the contract bidding. Therefore, prevailing wage laws such as Davis-Bacon cause construction costs to be much higher than they would in the absence of such regulation.

A recent study by Gould and Bittlingmayer summarized empirical research on prevailing wage laws and provided some original estimates of the costs associated with the Davis-Bacon Act.[41] Their evidence placed the cost of Davis-Bacon between $0.5 billion and $1.0 billion per year. This cost range is an estimate of the additional expense resulting from government wage regulation on federal projects. These extra costs were found to arise for a number of reasons: (1) union labor is used on construction projects instead of lower wage nonunion labor that would otherwise have performed the work, $228 million — $513 million; (2) union labor is actually paid higher wages while working on federal projects than it normally receives, $69.6 million — $284.6 million; (3) administrative costs to contractors resulting from Davis-Bacon regulation, $190 million; and, (4) taxpayer dollars to support Department of Labor administration of Davis-Bacon, $12.4 million. It appears, therefore, that repeal of the Davis-Bacon Act would produce not only savings in construction costs resulting from the difference between prevailing wages and market-determined wages but also cost savings due to the elimination of bureaucratic mismanagement and union monopoly power.[42]

Maximum Hour Regulation. In addition to minimum wages, the Fair Labor Standards Act also contains provisions for maximum hours of work. The Act places limitations on the use of child labor and requires that hourly wage workers in covered sectors be paid at the rate of time and a half for hours worked beyond 8 per day and 40 per week. The economic implications of this type of regulation are obvious: The labor cost of production of goods and services beyond some specified time limit increases by 50 percent and, therefore, discourages expanding output and encourages a shorter workweek than might otherwise exist.

Studies have shown that overtime pay provisions distort the average length of the workweek and that individuals who were free to vary hours of work at the same or lower wages actually chose longer workweeks than those persons who were constrained.[43] Overtime regulation has tended to compress the diversity of work schedules, so that there is very little variance around the 40-hour workweek.[44] Given current evidence on the labor supply decisions of workers, it would be safe to say that in the absence of maximum hour regulations a greater quantity of goods and services would be produced at a lower unit price and more labor would be demanded and supplied. The costs of such regulation are the output and employment foregone as a result of the conditions on hours worked. Unfortunately, these costs are very difficult to measure and, consequently, no empirical estimates are available.

Employer Payroll Taxes

Basically, there are two major taxes levied against the payrolls of business firms: unemployment insurance and social security. These payroll taxes produce undesirable economic effects in terms of the performance of both labor and business firms. Because unemployment insurance taxes are most directly concerned with labor relations, a brief summary of research findings on the costs created by this tax is undertaken below.[45]

Unemployment Insurance. Unemployment insurance (UI) compensation seeks to internalize to industry the social cost of unemployment and to subsidize the job search of unemployed workers. The first compulsory unemployment compensation law was enacted in January, 1932, in Wisconsin. The Social Security Act of 1935 mandated that every state adopt an unemployment insurance law, but each state, within certain limits, was allowed considerable discretion in both the financing of the contributions and in the benefits paid to claimants. This discretion has made a theoretically simple system extremely complex in practice because industry contributions and individual benefits vary markedly across states.

The federal UI tax is a payroll tax levied on employers in covered industries of 3.4 percent of all income up to some maximum limit per employee. In 1978, the maximum was set at $6,000. Federal law permits the employer to receive credit for payments into the state UI fund, which can potentially reduce the federal payments to as little as 0.7 percent of the tax base. Within states, tax rates are determined by some form of "experience rating" which relates a firm's contributions to the UI program to the benefits charged against that firm. A company with a very stable work force would have a better experience rating and, therefore, a lower tax rate than a firm that has had frequent layoffs.

In the economics literature, considerable attention has been devoted to the study of unemployment insurance. Most of this research has focused primarily on the impact of UI benefit payments on the job search of unemployed workers. Since unemployment insurance benefits reduce the cost to a worker of remaining unemployed, they may increase the duration of unemployment. Many economists believe that at least some unemployment is due to the incentives provided by UI rather than to a deficiency in the aggregate demand for goods and services. Strong evidence of this possibility can be found in the high levels of unemployment that have persisted even through periods of rapid inflation and high aggregate demand.

The economic argument that UI leads to increased unemployment is based on the simple concept that any income received by individuals while unemployed reduces the cost of consuming leisure or job search relative to work and, therefore, causes persons to choose more leisure or job search time. Table 4 contains a summary of the findings of fourteen investigators regarding the increase in the duration of unemployment due to the payment of UI benefits to workers. With only two exceptions, the length of job search is extended by the presence of UI benefits, although the magnitude of the extension varies from study to study. Overall, the findings, which are based on widely differing data sets in a variety of time periods, indicate that job search is extended by as much as 1.6 weeks because UI benefit payments lower the cost of search. It has been argued that this factor may not be so significant if the additional search time undertaken leads to a job with relatively higher earnings. Unfortunately, research conducted by Classen has shown that extra search time does not lead to higher-paying jobs. According to Classen, "the findings support the hypothesis that an increase in benefits leads to an increase in the duration of unemployment. There is no support, however, for the hypothesis that an increase in benefits leads to the generation and acceptance of more lucrative job offers."[46] This conclusion is reinforced by the fact that the typical adult unemployed worker is usually rehired by his former employer.[47] The cost associated with the prolonged unemployment due to UI is the social benefit produced by labor that would have been employed in the absence of UI benefits plus the added taxpayer dollars necessary to finance extended unemployment. If unemployment were, in fact, extended 1.6 weeks due to UI, and if those unemployed would have produced output valued at the minimum wage, the cost could amount to $2.2 billion.[48]

Recent research by Feldstein and Medoff has presented evidence to show that unemployment insurance substantially increases temporary layoff unemployment, particularly among unionized, i.e., larger firms.[49] According to Feldstein, "Our current UI program does impose an efficiency loss by the behavior of firms to lay off too many workers when demand falls rather than cutting prices or building inventories.

101

Table IV-4

*Summary of Selected Research Studies Estimating the
Incremental Weeks of Job Search Due to UI Benefits*

Research Study	Data Set	Incremental Weeks of Job Search
Liniger (1963)	Michigan, 1955	.06
Chapin (1971)	U.S., 1962-1967	.46
Burgess and Kingston (1974)	Boston, San Francisco, Phoenix, 1969-1970	.01 males − .04 females
Schmidt (1974)	U.S., 1966	1.6
Classen (1975)	Pennsylvania, 1967-1968	1.1
Crosslin (1975)	St. Louis, 1971-1973 Cleveland, 1970	− .09 − .05
Felder (1975)	Denver, 1970	1.4 males 1.4 females
Hanna, Butler, Steinman (1975)	Nevada, 1969-1972	1.0
Marston (1975)	Detroit, 1969	.23 to .62
Wandner (1975)	U.S. 1959-1972 1966-1969	.03 .53
Ehrenberg and Oaxaca (1976)	U.S. 1966-1979 1966-1967 1967-1970 1968-1971	.2 males 14-24 1.5 males 45-49 .5 females 14-24 .3 females 30-44
Holen (1976)	Boston, San Francisco, Phoenix, 1969-1970	.60
Classen (1977)	Arizona, 1968 Pennsylvania, 1967-1968	.10 .11
Holen (1977)	Boston, San Francisco, Phoenix, Seattle, St. Paul-Minneapolis, 1969-1970	.09

Source: See Appendix A to this chapter for a bibliography of the studies summarized in this table.

The substantial rate of temporary layoff unemployment suggests that this efficiency loss may be quite large.''[50] Empirical estimates show that UI is responsible for approximately one-half of all temporary layoff unemployment.[51] Firms which increase layoffs are rewarded under the operation of the current unemployment insurance system. Because of imperfect experience rating, a firm covered by collective bargaining can receive a higher per employee UI subsidy for greater use of layoffs.

Imperfect experience rating is due to the fact that there are maximum and minimum limits on UI tax rates. Therefore, if a firm has a particularly bad history of employee layoffs, the most it will have to pay for unemployment benefits is an amount equal to the maximum tax rate. In other words, the marginal UI cost of laying off an additional worker is zero once the maximum tax rate has been reached. Unfortunately, this experience rating system forces firms with stable employment histories to subsidize firms which practice excessive layoff.[52] Large unionized firms must use layoffs as a means of adjusting costs during periods of slack demand because unions impede the use of quits and reductions in wage rates while restraining the firms' ability to reduce average work time and discharge employees. In the face of these rigidities in the cost adjustment process, layoffs become the least expensive cost reduction procedure, especially when maximum UI tax rates are low. Unions much prefer this alternative because workers benefit from layoffs which are generally only temporary and workers know that they will return to their old job before unemployment benefits are exhausted. In many states, a typical unemployed worker can replace 85 to 90 percent of his lost net income through UI compensation.[53]

McLure has investigated the general incidence of UI taxes in the U.S. economy.[54] While many economists believe that the burden of a tax on business payrolls will ultimately be borne by labor through reduced real wages and employment, McLure contended that whether labor gains or loses depends upon whether substitution between capital and labor is easier in the industries that subsidize UI benefits relative to high layoff industries. If capital/labor substitution is easier, the real wage to labor will fall and vice versa. However, Bennett and Johnson produced evidence suggesting that real wages to labor may rise and thus redistribute income from business to labor when UI benefits increase.[55] Regardless of whether business or labor is harmed due to UI, such a payroll tax always interferes with the market allocation of resources. Where cross subsidies exist in the UI system, labor is transferred from its most productive uses.

Federal Manpower Programs

Prior to the 1960s, federal government employment programs focused on three basic issues: the direct creation of jobs, e.g., Works Progress Administration and the Public Works Administration; skill development, e.g., Area Redevelopment Act; and, job placement, e.g., employment services created by the Wagner-Peyser Act of 1933. The Great Society programs of the 1960s represented an extensive new federal involvement in the creation of jobs and skill development services. The Manpower Development and Training Act of 1962 (MDTA) was the first completely comprehensive federal manpower program and undertook such functions as classroom training, remedial education, on-the-job training, and job placement. Initially, MDTA emphasized retraining of workers who were displaced due to technological advance, but its focus eventually shifted to the provision of training for the economically disadvantaged, minorities, and unemployed youth. Although not explicitly stated, it appears that a major purpose of current manpower programs is to provide jobs and upgrade skills of those persons who were displaced as a result of other government regulatory policies, especially the minimum wage.

Since the passage of the MDTA, the federal government has initiated a number of programs specifically aimed at youth. The Economic Opportunity Act of 1964 established such youth programs as the Job Corps and the Neighborhood Youth Corps. Additional youth projects of the 1970s were the Youth Conservation Corps and the Youth Employment Demonstration Projects Act. A large number of these programs still exist, although some were terminated after initial experimentation. Many federal government employment and training functions are now largely concentrated in programs under various titles of the Comprehensive Employment and Training Act (CETA) of 1973.[56]

Unfortunately, these myriad federal manpower programs have succeeded in further distorting the allocation of resources in the labor sector. Figure 1 illustrates the impact of federal manpower policy. The equilibrium levels of wages and quantity of labor employed that would exist in an unconstrained labor market are designated by W^* and Q_L^*, respectively. The establishment of a minimum wage, W_m, above W^* causes a reduction in the quantity of labor demanded and an increase in the quantity of labor supplied so that unemployment results (the difference between Q_{L1} and Q_{L2}). The purpose of federal manpower policy is to create public sector jobs and training programs in order to absorb the unemployed labor into the public sector. This action reduces the supply of labor to the private sector (shifting the labor supply curve from S_L to S_L') and, thus, produces an equilibrium, E_2, at the minimum wage level.[57] Such a strategy eliminates private sector unemployment resulting from government wage floors; however, the outcome is a

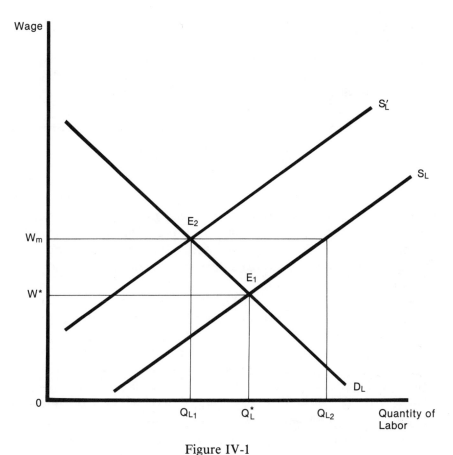

Figure IV-1

*The Impact of Federal Manpower Programs on the Allocation
of Labor Resources*

lower equilibrium level of employment, a higher equilibrium wage level, and reduced private sector output. Evidence has shown that most of the public sector jobs created to employ displaced and disadvantaged workers are of the "make work" type and do not lead to a significant increase in public services.[58] Therefore, federal manpower programs, in conjunction with minimum wages, have created a situation where labor has become more dependent upon the government for employment, causing an additional burden for taxpayers.

In fiscal year 1979, about $13 billion was expended on federal manpower programs. Of this total, $8.4 billion went to public service employment projects under Titles II and VI of CETA. Approximately

$1.9 billion was spent on employment and training services under Title I, and an additional $1.4 billion was devoted to youth programs under Title III. CETA consolidated the operations of many specialized programs under the general supervision of the Department of Labor and shifted control over their implementation from the federal government to state and local governments. Under CETA, state and local governments and private nonprofit organizations act as prime sponsors that are responsible for the planning, development, provision, and evaluation of manpower services programs.

Even if one were to accept the federal government's "band aid" approach to curing an unemployment due largely to its own regulatory actions, the performance of government in providing permanent employment and useful occupational training has been poor. One primary reason for this poor performance is the displacement effect that occurs when federal grants are made to state and local governments for the purpose of job creation.

Several studies have examined the employment impact of federal grant dollars provided to state and local governments. In general, the findings showed that only a fraction of the federal dollars allocated ended up in employment budgets. Gramlich estimated that just 45 percent of annual federal grant dollars went for employment purposes.[59] Ehrenberg has shown that, for the years 1958-1963 and 1965-1969, 22 percent of incremental federal monies filtered into employment budgets.[60] Ashenfelter found that, for the period 1929-1965, 24 to 47 percent of federal budget allocations went for employment purposes.[61] More recent studies that analyzed the permanent employment effects of federal grant allocations are much more pessimistic.[62] These studies show that only between 6 and 9 percent of federal grant dollars end up in the wage bill.[63] If these studies are, in fact, correct, the short-run employment impact of the federal government's $13 billion 1979 manpower program was the creation of about 448,500 new public sector jobs at a cost of $28,986 per employee. The long-run employment effect of this program was the provision of 97,500 permanent public sector jobs at a cost of $133,330 per worker.[64] Clearly, such results are unacceptable by almost any set of performance criteria.

Another important side effect of federal manpower programs and minimum wage laws is the increased utilization of illegal aliens in the private sector. Because minimum wage regulations have priced much domestic labor out of the secondary labor market and manpower programs have absorbed large quantities of unskilled job seekers, there is a large demand for low-wage labor in the private sector. Presently, the major source of low-wage labor is the illegal alien. A subcommittee of the U.S. House of Representatives estimated the illegal population at between one and two million and estimates by the Immigration and Naturalization Service have ranged as high as four to five million.[65] Recent studies by Piore and by Bennett and Johnson presented evidence that supports the thesis that there is a shortage of workers in U.S. secondary labor markets and that illegal aliens are filling these jobs.[66]

Occupational Safety and Health

In 1970, Congress passed the Occupational Safety and Health Act (OSHA) establishing the principle of federal authority over practices in the workplace. The enactment of OSHA resulted from growing concern about industrial practices which may have a deleterious effect on the health of American workers. Three new federal agencies were originated under OSHA: the Occupational Safety and Health Administration in the Department of Labor; National Institute of Occupational Safety and Health in the Department of Health, Education and Welfare (now the Department of Health and Human Services); and the Occupational Safety and Health Review Commission, an independent agency. The first two agencies conduct inspections and investigations under the authority of federal law, while the third agency deals with employer appeals regarding actions by the inspection agencies.

When OSHA became law in 1971, plant safety standards were set based on equipment specifications determined over past decades by health associations and nonprofit safety organizations. The regulations contained extremely detailed requirements for the physical conditions of production. An example of the extent of OSHA regulations is provided in the specifications for wooden ladder safety. The standard required that "the general slope of grain shall not be steeper than 1 in 15 rungs and cleats. For all ladders cross-grain not steeper than 1 in 12 are permitted."[67]

Federal control of equipment and production processes of private firms has impacted both industry costs and prices. In terms of equipment, safety regulations have escalated costs and limited options available to firms. Such actions have increased both short-run and long-run costs of production and, ultimately, produced higher product prices. Evidence has shown that firms have had to undertake large increases in investment simply for the purpose of dealing with OSHA requirements. As a result of OSHA regulations, private industry spent $4 billion in 1975 for equipment to increase safety in the workplace.[68] The major incidence of these regulations fell on five basic industries: chemicals, metals, wood products, paper, and automobile manufacturing.

Given the amount of additional equipment expenditures required by OSHA, the industries most affected must have experienced increases in production costs. In the short-run, cost increases from operation of required equipment should have resulted in higher prices and, therefore, reduced output growth. In the long-run, the substitution of safety investments for output-enhancing investments should have caused a lower rate of capacity growth and, thus, higher prices and lower production also. Evidence suggests that these effects have, indeed, occurred among OSHA-regulated industries. McAvoy has demonstrated that over the period 1969-1973, prices in these industries increased by 1.7 percent more than other industries and during the period 1973-1977, prices increased by 1.6 percent more than elsewhere.[69] Although inflation may have contributed to higher relative prices, its effect was probably small since production in the most regulated industries grew at lower rates than in other industries.[70]

Another important cost of OSHA regulation consists of the opportunity losses from the long-run reduction in goods and services resulting from reduced investments and growth. As prices rise and demand is depressed in regulated industries, production or investment there is replaced by that in occupational safety equipment industries. Total GNP should thus be about the same with or without controls, given that monetary and fiscal policies eliminate any unemployment involved in transferring resources to the new safety equipment industries. However, there would still be some long-run substitution of safety equipment for capital investment which would reduce the growth of GNP generated from capital. To the extent that this occurs, full-capacity GNP will increase at a lower rate. According to Denison, such opportunity costs of safety regulation would result in a level of GNP (by the mid-1980s) — 5 percent lower than would otherwise exist.[71] At 1979 prices, such opportunity costs would amount to approximately $115 billion of foregone GNP.

Considering the fact that occupational safety and health regulation has failed to produce any significant reduction in work-related accidents and illness (as documented in Chapter II), one must conclude that the costs associated with such intervention in the labor sector are staggering. Weidenbaum has estimated that the administration of OSHA alone amounted to $483 million in 1976.[72] Therefore, the total cost of occupational safety and health regulation is at least $119.5 billion ($.483 billion in administrative costs, $4.0 billion in additional equipment costs, and $115 billion in foregone GNP). What is so unfortunate about this situation is that everything OSHA has attempted but failed to achieve at this point could have easily been accomplished through compensating wage differentials for jobs with higher risks — something a free market in labor is completely equipped to do. In an unregulated labor market, employers must offer higher wages in order to attract workers to higher-risk occupations. Individuals will choose to accept a job offer only when they feel that the benefits received from wages exceed the costs that they attribute to a particular job. Such a system would not eliminate accidents and illnesses in the workplace (a goal OSHA has failed to achieve at substantial cost), but it would compensate persons for the risks they take without destroying thousands of job opportunities.

Employment and Earnings Discrimination

The foundation of federal regulatory policy regarding employment discrimination is the Civil Rights Act of 1964. Title VII of the Act declares it illegal for an employer to discriminate against any individual on the basis of race, color, religion, sex, or national origin in any way that would deprive that person of employment opportunities or equal pay for equal work. The Civil Rights Act was originally aimed at private business, labor organizations, employment agencies, and apprenticeship programs, but was extended to include state and local governments in 1972. Coverage of the law applies to organizations with a minimum of fifteen employees. Title VII of the Act is administered by the Equal Employment Opportunity Commission (EEOC), a five-member board appointed by the President. Headquarters for the Commission are located in Washington, D.C., with branch offices distributed throughout the country. The EEOC's role in preventing employment discrimination is twofold: to seek on a case-by-case basis voluntary compliance by employers with the letter and spirit of the law and to pursue court actions on the behalf of complainants. Voluntary compliance is achieved through a consent agreement between an employer and the EEOC (labeled "affirmative action"). A consent agreement involves the establishment, by the Commission, of numerical goals for the employment and wage rates of minorities and women and a timetable for meeting them.

Several studies have been conducted to evaluate the effectiveness of federal government efforts to regulate employment and earnings discrimination. Only one piece of scholarly research has found that attempts to regulate discrimination have been successful, but others have shown the study to be seriously flawed. Based on time series analysis for the period 1948-1972, Freeman concluded that blacks had significantly improved their income and occupational position relative to that of whites due to EEOC efforts, particularly in the 1960s.[73] This finding has been challenged by other investigators. Flanagan has pointed out that Freeman's results were simply the consequence of favorable economic circumstances rather than government policy.[74] He also showed that Freeman's finding of an improved income and occupational position for black males disappears when relative education is considered. Butler and Heckman reported that if relative participation in the labor force is considered, federal antidiscrimination policy has had no impact on the wage rates of black men or black women.[75] In addition, Butler and Heckman asserted that the upward trend in the relative status of blacks began to occur in the late 1950s, or well before any attempt by government to regulate discrimination.[76]

Adams has examined conciliation efforts by the EEOC for the period 1966-1971.[77] Changes in the relative employment and job titles of minority workers in 26 firms which had signed consent agreements were compared with similar firms in the same industry and metropolitan area which had not signed agreements. Adams found that there were no significant differences in the progress of minorities in these two sets of firms. A similar conclusion was also reached by Wolkinson in an examination of 75 discrimination cases involving unions and minority workers.[78] He found that the consent agreements negotiated by the EEOC were not effective in reducing discrimination because they tended to be violated by the unions in question. A study of Carolina textile industries by Kidder determined that there was a negative relationship between charges of discrimination brought by the EEOC against employers and subsequent increases in the employment of blacks.[79] It was also concluded that employment of blacks in the textile industry increased most dramatically in the period preceding the establishment of the EEOC. Recent research by Beller attempted to isolate the wage and employment effects of enforcement of Title VII.[80] Findings from 1970 census data and EEOC reports showed that enforcement of equal wage regulations produced a negative effect on the employment of blacks.

An unregulated labor market is perfectly capable of dealing with discrimination. Most people believe that employer bias is the major cause of discrimination; however, it is pressure from the community, majority employees, or unions which most often leads to discriminatory practices. Competition in the labor market makes it very costly for employers to discriminate in their hiring and pay practices. If employers can hire equally productive minority workers at lower wages than, say, white males, the profit motive creates a strong incentive to do so. If an employer continues to hire high-wage white workers when similar minority employees are available at lower wages, the costs of the firm will be higher than those of nondiscriminating competitors. Higher costs of production will obviously reduce profits; therefore, it does not pay to be a racist or sexist employer. Nondiscriminating employers will refuse to offer whites higher wage rates than equally productive minority workers. Whenever it is less costly to hire minority rather than majority employees, the unbiased employer will take advantage of the situation. An equal opportunity policy will reduce relative costs and give nondiscriminating employers an advantage over a competitor who discriminates.[81] The relationship between costs of production and employer discrimination has been well articulated by Sowell:

> In general, job discrimination has a cost, not only to those dis-
> criminated against and to society, but also to the person who is
> discriminating. He must forego hiring some employees he needs,
> or must interview more applicants in order to get the number of
> qualified workers required, or perhaps offer higher wages in order
> to attract a larger pool of applicants than necessary if hiring on
> merit alone. These costs do not necessarily eliminate discrimina-
> tion, but discrimination — like everything else — tends to be more
> in demand at a low price than at a high price.[82]

EEOC regulations such as the "equal pay for equal work" rule actually lower the costs of discrimination in employment. If, for instance, an employer is forced to pay the same wage to men and women, discriminatory hiring practices become less expensive. An employer's profits are no longer lowered by passing over equally qualified women to hire men. If it becomes difficult for women or minorities to accept employment at lower wages, their ability to make employers absorb the costs of discrimination is reduced. Therefore, the strict enforcement of an equal pay for equal work regulation will, more likely, lead to more employment discrimination rather than less.

Because equal pay rules have probably caused more employment discrimination, the use of employment quotas has gained popularity among regulators. Under a system of quotas, employers who react to legally mandated higher wages for women and minorities by reducing their employment of such persons will be found guilty of employment discrimination. A policy of employment quotas in conjunction with equal pay rules might reduce discrimination but the costs of such a program relative to the market solution are huge.

Quotas do not make a distinction between workers with real productivity differences. If less productive women and minorities replace more qualified men, economic efficiency will decline, producing a general welfare loss to society. In addition, hiring quotas eliminate the link between employment and productivity by requiring firms to employ a certain percentage of minorities and females regardless of their performance or credentials. Workers hired under such a system will be less motivated to produce; a decline in total productivity thus occurs; and total output, income, and employment are therefore lower. It is impossible to guess the overall welfare loss of such a regulatory program, but it could easily fall into the billion dollar category. The administrative costs of the EEOC alone amounted to $217 million in 1979.[83]

Collective Bargaining and Union Organizing

Chapter III has discussed in some detail the various ways in which the federal government has regulated the bargaining activities of unions and employers and the organizing practices of unions. The evidence clearly shows that government intervention in these areas has aided union organizing efforts and enhanced their bargaining power over employers. Unfortunately, the legal immunities and protective regulations granted to unions have produced massive negative externalities for society in general. The primary effect of such protective regulation has been the ability of unions to drive a wedge between union and nonunion wages, aggravate inflation and general macroeconomic instability, and create spillover costs through strike activity.

Considerable attention has been given in the economics literature to the effects of unions on relative wages. A seminal work by Lewis concluded that the average proportionate wage advantages of union members over the wages of nonunion workers ranged between 10 and 15 percent depending upon the time span of the analysis.[84] Table 5 summarizes the results of six major studies (including Lewis') that examined union-nonunion wage differentials. All of the findings indicated that rather large, positive, and statistically significant wage differentials (ranging from a low of 10 percent to a high of 52 percent) existed between union and nonunion workers.[85] The source of a significant portion of these wage gains, however, is nonunion labor. In other words,

Table IV-5

A Summary of Studies Estimating the Extent of
Union Wage Advantage Over Nonunion Workers

Empirical Study	Type of Sample	Union Wage Effect
H.G. Lewis (1963)	Aggregate time series data on non-union workers by industry and for the economy as a whole.	10-15 per cent for all workers (1955-1958).
L.W. Weiss (1966)	1960 Census, industry-wide unionisation data taking into account degrees of industry concentration.	20 per cent for male operatives and craftsmen in unregulated firms.
F.P. Stafford (1968)	1966 Consumer Finances Data on individual union membership for all wage and salary workers.	18-52 per cent for all wage and salary workers.
A. Throop (1968)	Aggregate industry data with information on skill levels and average city size of residence.	25 per cent in 1950 30 per cent in 1960.
S. Rosen (1969)	1958 Census of Manufactures and 1960 Census data with controls for education, race, age, urban areas, proportion of production workers, hours worked, and firm size.	38 per cent in highly unionized industries; 10 per cent in lightly organized industries.
P. Ryscavage (1974)	1973 Current Population Survey data controlling for age, occupation, education, and region.	12 per cent for all workers.

Source: See Appendix B to this chapter for a bibliography of the studies summarized in this table.

some of the union wage increases ensuing from regulated bargaining advantages are obtained at the expense of nonunion workers. A number of studies have shown that union wage gains have not resulted in a redistribution of income from capital to labor, but rather a redistribution from nonunion to unionized labor.[86]

Greater bargaining power has also allowed unions to maintain wages above the level of industry productivity. Normally, productivity increases are distributed to labor as higher wages, to firms as higher profits, and to consumers as lower prices, although unions have been successful in negotiating incomes that capture more than 100 percent of these increases. Table 6 shows that between 1971 and 1977 union wage increases were greater in every year than productivity. Obviously, since union wages have exceeded productivity, business firms and consumers have not shared in any of the gains in economic efficiency. Whenever wage increases exceed productivity increases, profit margins must fall or be maintained by higher product prices. If the latter occurs, consumers are twice made worse off: first, by not benefiting from increased productivity; and second, by paying higher prices. Therefore, in their efforts to gain a larger portion of income, unions have managed to influence rising prices and thus reduce the welfare of consumers.

Table IV-6

Union Wages Increases and Productivity Gains
in Manufacturing, 1971-1977

Year	Wage Increase	Productivity Increase	Difference
1971	9.0%	1.46%	7.54
1972	5.8	2.06	3.74
1973	5.9	3.02	2.88
1974	8.2	2.88	5.32
1975	9.5	1.54	7.96
1976	9.1	2.24	6.86
1977	8.1	2.48	5.62

Source: Bureau of Labor Statistics, *Chartbook on Prices, Wages and Productivity*, U.S. Department of Labor, various years.

Economists generally recognize that recent inflation has consisted of both demand-pull and cost-push phases. Demand-pull inflation occurs when governments pursue expansionary fiscal and monetary policies that increase aggregate demand relative to the economy's productive capacity. In this case, demand pressures tend to bid up prices. Cost-push inflation, however, arises on the supply side of the market and occurs when firms raise prices to cover increased costs.

The cost-push market power exerted by unions through collective bargaining has been identified by some investigators as a major contributor to inflation. By negotiating wage increases that exceed productivity gains, unions force firms to pass on increased labor costs as higher prices. Humphrey asserted that

> . . . although rises in material costs and profit margins may exert significant upward pressure on prices in the short run, empirical studies have indicated that increases in unit labor costs are the predominant price-raising factors in the long run and often the paramount factor in the short run.[87]

Recent studies have identified unions as the source of significantly increasing labor costs and, therefore, as a source of inflation. Hammermesh found that short-run discretionary power over wage increases is a positive function of industry concentration and unionization.[88] That is, firms in concentrated, highly unionized industries have short-run options to set wages and prices above competitive levels. In a related study, Greer substantiated this conclusion and, in addition, contended that highly unionized, highly concentrated industries establish inflationary wage and price reference patterns that are transferred, in the long-run, to more competitive industries in the economy.[89] These reference patterns can move from sectors with high market power to those with low market power through either price effects or labor market interdependencies.

Some economists, namely strict monetarists, hold a rigid demand-fueled view of inflation. According to the monetarists, expansionary monetary policy initially expands the demand for goods and services. A by-product of the first-round impact is an increase in the derived demand for labor as employers seek to produce those goods and services. A combination of rising prices and growing excess demand for labor leads to wage increases. But the wage increases are seen as a result of inflation, not as a cause. Others argue, however, that the monetarist view of inflation is not incompatible with the position that unions are the major cause of a rising general price level. Lee has pointed out that in order to protect its favored position, organized labor vigorously lobbies for government-initiated income maintenance legislation and manpower programs.[90] A common characteristic of these policies is an expansion of the government deficit which applies enormous pressure on the Federal Reserve to increase the money supply. Lee concluded that

> . . . organized labor has a major demand side inflationary impact through its political activities. It has effectively pressured for a wide range of specific federal spending programs (programs which comprise the fastest growing portion of the federal budget), resisted all efforts to place a general limitation on government spending, and consistently worked to insure that a large percentage of the resulting federal budget deficit is monetized.[91]

Definitive work by Mitchell contended that an excess-demand theory is crucial in explaining the initiating cause of the U.S. inflation, but, he argued, this approach alone does not provide a complete justification for the current rate of increase in the price level.[92] Experiences during the mid-1970s indicated that exogenous price shocks such as crop shortages, dollar devaluation, and oil cartels could, in fact, raise overall prices. Mitchell asserted that researchers who relied on models of demand-induced inflation alone greatly underestimated the acceleration of inflation that began in 1973, when exogenous price elements came into play.[93]

Union labor market power has had a profound affect on the allocation of resources in the U.S. economy. As a result of the large relative wage gains by unions, firms in the unionized sector have chosen to substitute other factors of production for labor. This behavior has, obviously, increased the marginal product of union labor but at the cost of reduced employment. To the extent that unionized firms possess market power, the increased cost of labor will be passed on as higher prices. Consumers will, therefore, substitute less expensive goods for union-produced goods causing a decrease in quantity demanded so that even fewer workers will be employed in this sector than before.

Since the high wage rate of union workers decreases the demand for labor in unionized firms, the supply of labor to nonunionized firms and industries increases. Therefore, the marginal productivity of labor in the nonunion sector decreases, wage rates fall, and firms substitute labor for other factors of production. A decline in GNP occurs as a result of this displacement because unionized workers who are forced to shift to

116

the nonunion sector generally cannot find full employment for their specialized skills. Reduced output results from lower production in the unionized sector and underemployment of labor in the nonunion sector.[94] The welfare loss from displacement effects due to the increased cost of union benefits was estimated by Rees to be at least $600 million for the year 1957.[95] In a more recent study, Johnson and Mieszkowski found that the loss in aggregate welfare in 1970 due to resource misallocation caused by unionism was .33 percent of GNP, or about $6.6 billion annually for a $2 trillion economy.[96] Reynolds has pointed out, however, that this traditional measure of welfare loss underestimates the cost of collective bargaining.[97] In fact, additional union earnings from collective bargaining require the consumption of real resources. Reynolds estimated that the annual union wage advantage was at least $30 billion and that if only one-half of this earnings differential represented real costs, the loss in GNP would approach $22 billion at an annual rate.

Excessive labor union power also contributes to general macroeconomic instability. The traditional Phillips curve shows the relationship between the rate of wage and price changes and the rate of unemployment. The slope of this curve represents the inflation/unemployment tradeoffs attainable through macro-stabilization policies. Attempts to achieve a lower rate of unemployment can only be pursued at the cost of a higher rate of inflation. Structural impediments in the economy such as labor unions frustrate macroeconomic policy efforts designed to attain desired combinations of unemployment and inflation. Through the exercise of their labor market power, unions aggravate the inflation/unemployment tradeoff. In times of recession unions are willing to accept increased unemployment rather than wage cuts (the advantages union members obtain from unemployment compensation were discussed above). During the expansionary phase of the business cycle, trade unions' bargaining power increases, and unions press for money wage increases to offset inflation and maintain real wages. Thus, the unions' sensitivity to fluctuations in the economy will tend to shift the Phillips curve upward, worsening inflation/unemployment tradeoffs.

At the level of the firm, unions inhibit competitive responses to market forces. By reducing labor market mobility, unions prevent interdependent labor markets from adjusting to changes in demand. Further, strong unions in particular sectors will react to increases in demand by pushing wages above the level necessary for an adequate supply response. Therefore, unions may also act to shift the Phillips curve upwards by increasing wage adjustments at a given level of unemployment causing inflation/unemployment combinations to be unnecessarily more costly.

Another important effect of the bargaining power of unions is the social cost imposed by strikes. Although it is difficult to aggregate the total social cost of strikes, Table 7 shows a significant percentage of days idle due to economic causes. On average, economic strikes accounted for 71 percent of the total number of days idle, with a high of 84.3 percent in 1974. The total number of man-days idle between 1967 and 1975 due to economic strikes was 266.6 million. Welfare losses resulting from these strikes include the loss of wages, general disruption of production, inconvenience to the community, and, possibly, higher prices to consumers.

The costs to society of labor market power being exercised in our current industrial relations system are extremely high relative to the benefits accruing to union members. By transferring the bargaining

Table IV-7

Work Stoppages and Days Idle from Economic Issues

Year	General Wage (Percent)	Supplementary Benefits and Wage Adjustments (Percent)	Total Economic Causes (Percent)	Total Days Idle (Thousands)	Days Idle From Economic Causes (Thousands)
1975	71.1	2.1	73.2	31,237	22,865
1974	81.1	3.2	84.3	47,990	40,456
1973	59.8	5.2	65.0	24,948	16,216
1972	63.2	3.3	66.5	27,066	17,999
1971	66.7	7.1	78.8	47,589	35,120
1970	54.4	2.4	56.8	66,413	37,723
1969	64.1	3.6	67.7	42,869	29,022
1968	73.1	2.0	75.1	49,018	36,812
1967	71.9	2.6	74.5	42,100	31,364

Source: Bureau of Labor Statistics, *Handbook of Labor Statistics 1977.* Department of Labor Bulletin 1966.

function to the private market system, the externality problem that currently exists would disappear and fiscal and monetary policies would become more effective. The Needless to say, the deregulation of collective bargaining would not require an oversight agency such as the National Labor Relations Board. Therefore, the administrative costs of this agency would no longer be required. Savings to taxpayers for this function alone would amount to almost $117 million annually.[98]

Occupational Licensing

The licensing of various professions has generally been considered to be a necessary practice in order to protect persons from incompetent and dishonest service by businessmen, professionals, and laborers. However, researchers and policymakers are beginning to realize that licensing restricts freedom of entry into various fields of work thus creating occupational cartels.

Any government policy that restricts the supply of labor will eventually lead to increased equilibrium wage rates. Therefore, occupational licensing requirements, regardless of their intention, have the effect of reducing entry into a profession and limiting the labor supply. Although there are numerous studies of the impact of unions on the supply of labor and the determination of wages (unions are simply licensing institutions), very little research has been undertaken to document the effects of licensing in other areas. Most studies have concentrated on the legal and medical professions.[99] For example, Holen has shown that there is little movement between states among dentists and lawyers due to licensing practices within states and the lack of reciprocity agreements.[100] In addition, Holen demonstrated that there is a significant relationship between licensing-exam failure rates and the average incomes in dentistry and law.

A recent study by Pashigian also provided evidence of the adverse effects of licensing.[101] According to Pashigian,

> if reciprocity was practiced in the dental and legal professions, the interstate migration rate would rise from .105 to .155-.163 in the legal profession and from .098 to .129-.142 in the dental profession. Elimination of all licensing raises the migration rate to .259-.281 for the legal profession and to .218-.261 for the dental profession. . . . Licensing does not merely reduce the total number of members or certify quality, effects which are frequently

119

mentioned by economists, but reduces the interstate flow of human capital.[102]

Williams has pointed out that occupational licensing is another form of labor market restriction that produces ill effects for minorities and other disadvantaged persons.[103] As an example, he mentioned the taxicab business where there are low skill requirements and no major capital requirements for entry (only an automobile is needed). This profession could provide minorities and youth self-employment and the potential for earning a lucrative income. However, because there are high cost licensing requirements in most cities, many would-be entrants are prevented from participating. Williams indicated that some cities grant monopolies to a single taxicab company while others require the purchase of license medallions which are extremely expensive. Los Angeles awarded Yellow Cab Company an exclusive franchise to operate within its city limits. New York City issued medallions at a cost of $26,000 and $28,000 in 1975, and Chicago and Baltimore charged as much as $18,000 in the same year.[104]

There is a large number of licensed occupations which have unjustified restrictions that reduce employment opportunities that would otherwise be available for minorities, youth, and other disadvantaged members of society.[105]

Summary

This chapter has attempted to assess the social costs of regulation in the labor sector. Since the deregulation of labor relations would eliminate the social costs documented herein, clearly, the gross benefits of such a policy would be approximated by the dollar value of these costs. As pointed out earlier, it is impossible to estimate accurately in dollar terms the benefits gained from deregulation of the labor sector. However, it is possible to make some statement about the magnitude of the potential gains from such action. From the analysis of regulatory impacts and survey of research studies undertaken above, a very rough estimate of the gross benefits from deregulation can be obtained. Table 8 shows the dollar value of benefits that would be generated by eliminating various governmentally-induced distortions in the labor sector. These estimates should be viewed with caution for two reasons: any losses that might be inflicted through deregulation are not considered and many additional gains that cannot be quantified are excluded. Given the large number of unmeasurable benefits, there is little doubt that more accurate estimates of the gains from deregulation would produce much higher figures.

Table IV-8

Estimated Gross Benefits from the
Elimination of Labor Sector Regulation

Regulation or Regulatory Agency	Estimated Benefits Billions of 1979 dollars
Fair Labor Standards Act	$12.4
Davis-Bacon Act	1.0
Unemployment Insurance	2.2
Comprehensive Employment and Training Act (federal budget only)	13.0
Occupational Safety and Health Act	119.5
Equal Employment Opportunity Commission (administrative cost savings only)	.2
National Labor Relations Act	22.0
TOTAL	$170.3

Appendix A
REFERENCES ON EMPIRICAL STUDIES OF JOB SEARCH AND UI BENEFITS

Burgess, Paul L. and Jerry L. Kingston, "The Impact of Unemployment Benefits on Reemployment Success," *Industrial and Labor Relations Review* (October 1976), pp. 25-31.

Chapin, G., "Unemployment Insurance, Job Search and the Demand for Leisure," *Western Economic Journal* (March 1971), pp. 102-107.

Classen, Kathleen P., "The Effects of Unemployment Insurance: Evidence from Pennsylvania," mimeo. Washington, DC: ASPER, U.S. Department of Labor, 1975.

_____, "The Effects of Unemployment Insurance on the Duration of Unemployment and Subsequent Earnings," *Industrial and Labor Relations Review* (July 1977), pp. 438-444.

Crosslin, Robert L., "Unemployment Insurance and Job Search," mimeo, Department of Economics, Mississippi State University, 1975.

Ehrenberg, Ronald G. and Ronald L. Oaxaca, "Unemployment Insurance, Duration of Unemployment, and Subsequent Wage Gain," *American Economic Review* (December 1976), pp. 754-766.

Felder, Henry, "Job Search: An Empirical Analysis of the Search Behavior of Low-Income Workers," mimeo, Stanford Research Institute, 1975.

Hanna, James S., Robert T. Butler, and John Steinman, "The Socioeconomic Impact of Extended Benefits," mimeo, Nevada Employment Security Department, 1975.

Holen, Arlene, "Effects of Unemployment Insurance Entitlement on Duration and Job Search Outcome," *Industrial and Labor Relations Review* (July 1977), pp. 445-450.

Liniger, Charles A., *Unemployment Benefits and Duration* (Ann Arbor, MI: University of Michigan Institute for Social Research, 1963).

Marston, S., "The Impact of Unemployment Insurance on Job Search," *Brookings Papers* (1975), pp. 13-60.

Schmidt, Ronald M., "The Determinants of Search Behavior and the Value of Additional Unemployment," mimeo, School of Management, University of Rochester, 1974.

Wandner, Stephen, "Unemployment Insurance and the Duration of Unemployment in Periods of Low and High Unemployment," mimeo, Unemployment Insurance Service, U.S. Department of Labor, 1975.

Appendix B
REFERENCES ON EMPIRICAL STUDIES OF UNION-NONUNION WAGE DIFFERENTIALS

Lewis, H. Gregg, *Unionism and Relative Wages in the United States* (Chicago: University of Chicago Press,1962).

Rosen, Sherwin, "Trade Union Power, Threat Effects and the Extent of Economic Organization," *Review of Economic Studies* (April 1969), pp. 185-194.

Ryscavage, Paul, "Measuring Union-Nonunion Earnings Differences," *Monthly Labor Review* (December 1974), pp. 3-9.

Stafford, Frank P., "Concentration and Labor Earnings: Comment," *American Economic Review* (March 1968), pp. 174-181.

Throop, Adrian, "The Union-Nonunion Wage Differential and Cost-Push Inflation," *American Economic Review* (March 1968), pp. 79-99.

Weiss, Leonard W., "Concentration and Labor Earnings," *American Economic Review* (March 1966), pp. 96-177.

NOTES TO CHAPTER IV

¹The Act also required employers to pay one-and-one-half times the worker's regular wage rate for all hours worked beyond forty. Originally, only a small proportion of the labor force was covered; very few workers in wholesale and retail trade and the service industry were covered. For a thorough background discussion on minimum wages see *Minimum Wage Legislation, Legislative Analysis* (Washington, DC: American Enterprise Institute for Public Policy Research, 1977), pp. 1-3.

²Other motivations behind political support of minimum wage laws may have nothing to do with the desire to reduce poverty. Studies have shown that the primary reason why politicians in northern states support minimum wage legislation is to force up the wages of southern workers so that they cannot effectively compete for the jobs of northern workers. For a complete treatment of this topic see Jonathan Silberman and Gary Durden, "Determining Legislative Preferences on the Minimum Wage: An Economic Approach," *Journal of Political Economy* (April 1976), pp. 317-330; and Farrell Bloch, "Political Support for Minimum Wage Legislation," *Journal of Labor Research* (Fall 1980), pp. 245-254.

³U.S. Department of Labor, Wage and Hour and Public Contracts Division, *Minimum Wage and Maximum Hour Standards Under the Fair Labor Standards Act, 1969,* 1969, pp. 3-4.

⁴For a complete discussion on the marginal productivity theory of labor see Charles E. Ferguson, *Microeconomic Theory,* third edition (Homewood, IL: Richard D. Irwin, Inc., 1972), pp. 393-425.

⁵In some cases, marginal low-skilled workers may remain employed when minimum wages rise because nonwage compensation items are reduced so that the cost to the firm does not change. This point is discussed in more detail later in this chapter. Also, Walter Williams ["Government Sanctioned Restraints that Reduce Economic Opportunities for Minorities," *Policy Review* (Fall 1977), p. 11] has pointed out that many young workers are initially paid below the value of their productivity so that they might receive on-the-job training. Minimum wages make it impossible for low-skilled young workers to pay for job training in the form of lower beginning wages.

⁶A survey of results reported in Jacob J. Kaufman and Terry G. Foran, "The Minimum Wage and Poverty," *Readings in Labor Market Analysis,* ed. J. F. Burton, Jr., et al. (New York: Holt, Rinehart & Winston, Inc., 1971), showed that, even though 88 percent of academic economists supported the "war on poverty," 61 percent of those same economists opposed minimum wage laws (p. 508).

⁷Walter Williams, "Government Sanctioned Restraints," p. 10.

⁸U.S. Bureau of Labor Statistics, *Hours and Earnings of Employees of Independent Tobacco Stemmeries,* (Washington, DC: U.S. Government Printing Office, 1941).

⁹Gordon Bloom and Herbert Northrup, *Economics of Labor Relations,* seventh edition (Homewood, IL: Richard D. Irwin, Inc., 1973), p. 503.

¹⁰A. F. Hinrichs, "Efffects of the 25 Cent Minimum Wage on Employment in the Seamless Hosiery Industry," *Journal of the American Statistical Association* (March 1940), pp. 13-23; and H. M. Douty, "Minimum Wage Regulation in the Seamless Hosiery Industry," *Southern Economic Journal* (October 1948), pp. 176-189.

¹¹H. M. Douty, "Minimum Wage Regulation," p. 504.

¹²U.S. Department of Labor, *Report Submitted to the Congress in Accordance with the Requirements of Section 4 (d) of the Fair Labor Standards Act* (Washington, DC: U.S. Government Printing Office, January 1963), pp. 35-40.

[13]U.S. Department of Labor, *Effects of Minimum Wage Rates Established under the Fair Labor Standards Act in Retail Trade in the United States and Puerto Rico: A Study of Changes in Wage Structure of a Matched Sample of Retail Establishments, 1961-1962* (Washington, DC: U.S. Government Printing Office, November 1963), p. 5.

[14]George Macesich and Charles Stewart, "Recent Department of Labor Studies of Minimum Wage Effects," *Southern Economic Journal* (July 1960), pp. 281-290.

[15]John Peterson, "Employment Effects of Minimum Wages, 1938-1950," *Journal of Political Economy* (May 1957), pp. 412-430.

[16]John Peterson, "Employment Effects of State Minimum Wages for Women: Three Historical Cases Re-examined," *Industrial and Labor Relations Review* (July 1959), pp. 406-422. Also see O. Ashenfelter and R. Smith, "Compliance With Minimum Wage Laws," *Journal of Political Economy* (April 1979), pp. 333-350.

[17]Yale Brozen, "Minimum Wage Rates and Household Workers," *Journal of Law and Economics* (October 1962), pp. 103-109.

[18]Yale Brozen, "The Effect of Statutory Minimum Wages on Teenage Employment," *Journal of Law and Economics* (April 1969), pp. 109-122.

[19]T. G. Moore, "The Effect of Minimum Wages on Teenage Unemployment Rates," *Journal of Political Economy* (July/August 1971), pp. 897-902.

[20]Marvin Kosters and Finis Welch, "The Effects of Minimum Wages on the Distribution of Changes in Aggregate Employment," *American Economic Review* (June 1972), pp. 323-332.

[21]Finis Welch, "Minimum Wage Legislation in the United States," *Economic Inquiry* (September 1974), pp. 285-318.

[22]Ibid., p. 314.

[23]Robert Goldfarb, "The Policy Content of Minimum Wage Research," *Proceedings of the Industrial Relations Research Association* (December 1974), pp. 261-268.

[24]Edward Gramlich, "The Impact of Minimum Wages on Other Wages, Employment, and Family Incomes," *Brookings Papers on Economic Activity* (1976), pp. 409-451.

[25]Finis Welch and James Cunningham, "Effects of Minimum Wages on the Level and Age Composition of Youth Employment," *Review of Economics and Statistics* (February 1978), pp. 140-145.

[26]It has been shown, however, that firms may well adjust the nonwage items of compensation so that the effective wage bill is not changed. For a thorough discussion of this effect see Walter Wessels, "The Effect of Minimum Wages in the Presence of Fringe Benefits: An Expanded Model," *Economic Inquiry* (April 1980), pp. 293-313; and Richard McKenzie, "The Labor Market Effects of Minimum Wage Laws: A New Perspective," *Journal of Labor Research* (Fall 1980), pp. 255-264.

[27]Peter Linneman ["The Economic Impact of Minimum Wage Laws: A New Look at an Old Question," Working paper No. 014, Center for the Study of the Economy and the State, University of Chicago, April 1980, pp. 1-31] has shown that the average union member gained $435 as a result of the 1974 minimum wage hike.

[28]See, for example, Neil Chamberlain, Donald Cullen, and David Lewin, *The Labor Sector,* third edition (New York: McGraw-Hill Book Co., 1980), pp. 507-508; David Meiselman, *Welfare Reform and the Carter Public Service Employment Program: A Critique,* Occasional Paper, Law and Economics Center, University of Miami School of Law, 1978, pp. 8-9; and Walter Williams, "Government Sanctioned Restraints," pp. 6-7.

[29]Jack Hirshleifer, *Price Theory and Applications,* second edition (Englewood Cliffs, NJ: Prentice-Hall, Inc., 1980), p. 441.

[30]Jacob Mincer, "Unemployment Effects of Minimum Wages," *Journal of Political Economy* (August 1976, part 2), pp. 87-104.

[31]Ibid., p. 103.

[32]Evidence in support of Mincer's conclusions can be found in J. Peter Mattlia, "Youth Labor Markets, Enrollments, and Minimum Wages," *Proceedings of the Industrial Relations Research Association* (August 1978), p. 137.

[33]Walter Wessels, "The Effect of Minimum Wages," pp. 293-313; and Richard McKenzie, "The Labor Market Effects of Minimum Wage Laws," pp. 255-264.

[34]Walter Wessels, "The Effect of Minimum Wages," p. 312.

[35]Unemployment statistics were taken from *Economic Indicators,* prepared for the Joint Economic Committee by the Council of Economic Advisers, 95th Congress, 2d Session (Washington, DC: U.S. Government Printing Office, 1980), pp. 11-12.

[36]Surveys of unemployed youth indicate that many working teenagers come from families with no other working member. See, for example, the discussion in *Minimum Wage Legislation, Legislative Analyses,* p. 19.

[37]Statistics on federal government welfare expenditures were taken from Martin Anderson, *Welfare* (Stanford, CA: Hoover Institution Press, 1978), p. 56.

[38]Walter Wessels, "The Effect of Minimum Wages," p. 308. The 13 industries (classified by SIC code) examined by Wessels were: 232-Men's and Boy's Furnishings, 2252-Hosiery, 212-Cigars, 244-Wooden Container, 314-Footwear, 394-Toys and Sporting Goods, 2017-Confectionery Products, 3251-Brick and Structural Clay Tile, 229-Miscellaneous Textile Products, 213-Men's and Boy's Suits, 243-Millwork, Plywood, and Related Products, 311-Leather Tanning and Furnishings, and 211-Cigarettes.

[39]Peter Linneman, "The Economic Impacts of Minimum Wage Laws," p. 24. Exactly what portion of the $435 received by union members which is net of all direct and indirect costs is not known. Union members must also incur the added costs of higher prices and unemployment resulting from their wage gains.

[40]The $7.5 billion increase in union wages may also be viewed as a cost. The $16.8 billion cost estimate only takes into account the loss in producer surplus due to higher labor costs; however, it does not include any loss in consumer surplus resulting from higher factor prices. The dead-weight loss to society is the difference between consumer surplus and the wage gains to unions.

[41]John P. Gould and George Bittlingmayer, *The Economics of the Davis-Bacon Act: An Analysis of Prevailing Wage Laws* (Washington, DC: American Enterprise Institute for Public Policy Research, 1980). Other empirical studies of the economic impact of Davis-Bacon which were summarized by Gould and Bittlingmayer are: U.S. General Accounting Office, *The Davis-Bacon Act Should Be Repealed,* 1979; Armand J. Thieblot, Jr., *The Davis-Bacon Act,* Labor Relations and Public Policy Series, Report No. 10 (Philadelphia: University of Pennsylvania Press, 1975); D.R. Gujarati, "The Economics of the Davis-Bacon Act," *Journal of Business* (July 1967), pp. 303-316.

[42]John P. Gould and George Bittlingmayer, *The Economics of the Davis-Bacon Act,* p. 68.

[43]Institute for Social Research, University of Michigan, *A Panel Study of Income Dynamics,* Ann Arbor, 1970.

⁴⁴Edward Kalachek, *Workers and the Hours Decision,* Center for the Study of American Business, Washington University, St. Louis, MO, October, 1979.

⁴⁵Social security taxes have very complicated long-term impacts which produce wide-ranging effects. Therefore, a discussion of the costs associated with social security has been relegated to this note.

Before the Social Security program came into effect, individuals usually insured themselves against loss of income after retirement by saving part of the income earned during their working years. Individual saving out of current income could consist of investments in stocks and bonds, bank deposits, annuities, or real estate. Personal saving served the purpose of financing private sector investments that led to an expansion in the real capital stock of the entire economy.

When Social Security was introduced, however, continued income was guaranteed to retired workers, thus reducing the propensity to save during their working years. In addition, Social Security taxes on earnings of workers reduced the take home income of individuals which, in turn, reduced the funds available for personal saving. Because of the incentives created by Social Security, aggregate private saving might be expected to decline over time as tax rates and benefits increased. Of course, the federal government was receiving a huge amount of Social Security tax receipts with which it could fund retirement income commitments by investing them in financial securities, and, therefore, balance the reduction in saving by individual contributors.

Unfortunately, the federal government chose not to fund Social Security by holding invested reserves sufficient to generate income for future commitments. Instead, tax revenues were used to support general expenditures by government. This behavior has led economists to conclude that there has been a severe adverse effect on aggregate saving in the U.S. economy and a corresponding decline in aggregate real investment. Martin Feldstein ["Social Security, Induced Retirement, and Aggregate Capital Accumulation," *Journal of Political Economy* (September/October 1974), p. 922] has estimated that the Social Security program has caused an overall reduction in private saving while the federal government has failed to provide any compensating increase in collective saving. The resulting lower level of real investment over the years has led to a smaller stock of real capital in the U.S. than would otherwise have existed. In the words of Feldstein,

> because individuals substitute social security for . . . private saving, total private saving and capital formation is reduced. . . . There is no real investment of social security benefits to offset the planned reduction in private savings and investment. The result is a fall in our nation's rate of saving and in our capital stock . . . With less capital there is a lower level of productivity, lower wages and fewer good jobs. By reducing private saving through social security, we deny ourselves the opportunity to invest with a rate of return to the nation of 15 percent and limit ourselves to the implicit return of only 2 percent that social security will provide in the future. (Joint Economic Committee, Congress of the United States, *The Social Security System,* 94th Congress, 2d session, May 26 and 27, 1976, p. 119.)

Since real capital contributes to production by raising the average productivity of labor and other resources, wages and, thus, national income become affected by social security. Feldstein estimated that by 1972 the Social Security program had caused a reduction in GNP of between 11 and 15 percent, or, in dollar terms, a loss of between $127 and $175 billion.

The most important implication of reduced saving due to Social Security, however, is not the decline in income or wages but the fact that there is the substitution of an asset having a very low implicit rate of return for real capital which has a much higher social rate of return. While the real rate of return on social security taxes of 2 percent is not that bad relative to the return on risk-free fixed-income investments, it is considerably less than what individuals or employers could earn through investments in the private sector. Although the stock market has experienced a relatively poor performance over the past decade, the long-run rate of return on equity capital investments has maintained an average of at least 6 percent over the rate of inflation. Because individuals are forced to provide more and more of their retirement income through Social Security, they are also being coerced into investing in a program whose real rate of return is vastly lower than the earnings from contributions into a private retirement program.

⁴⁶Kathleen P. Classen, "The Effect of Unemployment Insurance Entitlement on Duration and Job Search Outcome, "*Industrial and Labor Relations Review* (July 1977), pp. 438-444. Findings by Ronald Ehrenberg and Ronald Oaxaca ["Unemployment Insurance, Duration of Unemployment, and Subsequent Wage Gains," *American Economic Review* (December 1976), pp. 754-766] lend some weak support to the theory that increased UI benefits lead to better jobs after unemployment.

⁴⁷Evidence to this effect is provided in Martin Feldstein, "Temporary Layoffs in the Theory of Unemployment," *Journal of Political Economy* (October 1967), pp. 937-957.

⁴⁸The minimum wage is currently $3.35 per hour. Assuming a 40 hour work week, 1.6 additional weeks of work would produce output valued at $1.2 billion. Feldstein and others have shown that the average manufacturing worker is able to receive 85 percent of his net income through unemployment compensation. Therefore, the cost to taxpayers of providing UI benefits an additional 1.6 weeks is about $1.0 billion — assuming workers earn only the minimum wage.

⁴⁹Martin Feldstein, "The Effect of Unemployment Insurance on Temporary Layoff Unemployment," *American Economic Review* (December 1978), pp. 834-846; and James L. Medoff, "Layoffs and Alternatives under Trade Unions in U.S. Manufacturing," *American Economic Review* (June 1979), pp. 380-395.

⁵⁰Martin Feldstein, "The Effect of Unemployment Insurance," p. 844.

⁵¹Ibid., p. 834.

⁵²The potential for cross-subsidies can easily be understood by examining the maximum and minimum tax rates across states. A sample of tax rates in 8 states is presented below

State	Maximum Rate	Minimum Rate
California	3.9%	0.4%
Idaho	4.4	0.2
New Mexico	4.2	0.6
North Carolina	4.7	0.5
Ohio	4.8	1.1
Oregon	4.0	2.6
Texas	4.0	0.1
Wisconsin	6.5	0.0

Clearly, given the low level of maximum tax rates among states, there is little incentive for firms with unstable employment histories to try to correct this problem.

⁵³See Martin Feldstein, "Unemployment Compensation: Adverse Incentives and Distributional Anomalies," *National Tax Journal* (June 1974), pp. 231-244.

⁵⁴Charles E. McLure, Jr., "The Incidence of the Financing of Unemployment Insurance," *Industrial and Labor Relations Review* (July 1977), pp. 469-479.

⁵⁵James T. Bennett and Manuel H. Johnson, "The Economic Impact of Unemployment Insurance on Small U.S. Firms," mimeo., Institute for Economic Policy Research, George Mason University, 1980.

⁵⁶*Youth Employment Legislation: The Youth Act of 1980, Legislative Analyses* (Washington, DC: American Enterprise Institute for Public Policy Research, 1980), p. 3.

[57]Although the purpose of many manpower programs is ultimately to return unemployed workers to jobs in the private sector, the short-term result is simply a reduction in labor supply. Also, there is substantial evidence indicating that these programs create worker dependence so that many persons never return to the private market.

[58]Alan Fechter, *Public Employment Programs,* Evaluative Studies (Washington, DC: American Enterprise Institute for Public Policy Research, 1975), p. 11.

[59]Edward M. Gramlich, "The Effect of Federal Grants on State and Local Expenditures: A Review of the Econometric Literature," National Tax Association, *Proceedings of the Sixty-second Conference on Taxation,* 1969, pp. 569-593.

[60]Ronald Ehrenberg, "The Demand for State and Local Government Employees," *American Economic Review* (June 1973), pp. 366-379.

[61]Orley Ashenfelter, "Demand and Supply Functions for State and Local Employment: Implications for Public Employment Programs," Princeton University Discussion Paper, mimeo., n.d.

[62]George E. Johnson and James D. Tomola, *An Impact Evaluation of the Public Employment Program,* Technical Analysis Paper No. 17 (Washington, DC: U.S. Department of Labor, Office of the Assistant Secretary for Policy Evaluation and Research, Office of Evaluation, April 1974), pp. 8, ff; Orley Ashenfelter and Ronald Ehrenberg, "The Demand for Labor in the Public Sector," in *Labor in the Public and Non-Profit Sectors,* ed. Daniel S. Hamermesh (Princeton: Princeton University Press, 1976).

[63]This takes place because once state and local government bureaucrats are able to anticipate continued funding for a program they become more sophisticated in ways of sidetracking federal dollars.

[64]These figures assume a short-run displacement effect of 65 percent and a long-run displacement effect of 92.5 percent. It is also assumed that the average annual earnings of workers employed in public sector job programs is $10,000.

[65]James T. Bennett and Manuel H. Johnson, "Illegal Aliens: Economic and Social Issues," *Akron Business and Economic Review* (Fall 1978), p. 11.

[66]Michael J. Piore, "Impact of Immigration on the Labor Force," *Monthly Labor Review* (May 1975), pp. 41-43; James T. Bennett and Manuel H. Johnson, "Illegal Aliens," pp. 11-16.

[67]*U.S. Code of Regulations,*Title 29, Section 1910.25(b)(3)(ii).

[68]See The McGraw-Hill Publications Company Economics Department, "5th Annual McGraw-Hill Survey of Investment in Employee Safety and Health," (May 1977). Evidence supporting this figure can also be found in Murray L. Weidenbaum, *The Future of Business Regulation* (New York: Amacom, 1979), p. 22, Table 2.

[69]Paul W. MacAvoy, *The Regulated Industries and the Economy* (New York: W.W. Norton & Co., 1979), p. 89 and p. 139, n.9.

[70]Ibid., pp. 90-91, Table 3.1.

[71]Edward Denison, "Effects of Selected Changes in the Institutional and Human Environment upon Output per Unit of Input," *Survey of Current Business* (January 1978), pp. 24-44.

[72]Murray L. Weidenbaum, *The Future of Business Regulation*, p. 22, Table 2.

[73]Richard B. Freeman, "Changes in the Labor Market for Black Americans, 1948-72," *Brookings Papers on Economic Activity* (1973), pp. 67-120.

[74]Robert J. Flanagan, "Actual Versus Potential Impact of Government Antidiscrimination Programs," *Industrial and Labor Relations Review* (July 1976), pp. 486-507.

[75]Richard Butler and James J. Heckman, "The Government's Impact on the Labor Market Status of Black Americans: A Critical Review," in *Equal Rights and Industrial Relations,* Leonard Housman, et al., eds., (Madison, Wisconsin: Industrial Relations Research Association, 1977), pp. 255-256.

[76]Ibid.

[77]Arvil V. Adams, *Toward Fair Employment and the EEOC: A Study of Compliance Under Title VII of the Civil Rights Act of 1974,* Washington, D.C., Equal Opportunity Commission, August, 1972.

[78]Benjamin W. Wolkinson, *Blacks, Unions and the EEOC* (Lexington, MA: D.C. Heath, Inc., 1973).

[79]Alice Kidder, "Federal Compliance Efforts in the Carolina Textile Industry: A Summary Report," *Proceedings of the Twenty-fifth Annual Meeting of the Industrial Relations Research Association,* Madison, Wisconsin, 1973, pp. 353-361.

[80]Andrea Beller, "The Effects of Title VII of the Civil Rights Act of 1964 on the Economic Position of Minorities," Ph.D. dissertation, Columbia University, New York, 1974.

[81]James D. Gwartney and Richard Stroup, *Economics: Private and Public Choice,* 2nd ed. (New York: Academic Press, Inc., 1980), p. 637.

[82]Thomas Sowell, *Race and Economics* (New York: David McKay, 1975), p. 168.

[83]Michael E. Simon, "Counting the Costs: What We Did," *Regulation* (May 1979), p. 21.

[84]H. Gregg Lewis, *Unionism and Relative Wages in the United States* (Chicago: University of Chicago Press, 1962).

[85]Some recent literature has criticized the failure of earlier studies to treat unionization as an endogenous variable in the determination of wages. Several empirical studies attempted to account for this fact; however, the results to date are ambiguous. Studies which find no union impact on wages are: Orley Ashenfelter and George E. Johnson, "Unionism, Relative Wages, and Labor Quality in U.S. Manufacturing Industries," *International Economic Review* (October 1972), pp. 488-508; Peter Schmidt and Robert P. Strauss, "The Effect of Unions on Earnings and Earnings on Unions," *International Economic Review* (February 1976), pp. 204-212; and Harlan David Pratt, "A Simultaneous Equations Model of Wage Determination Under Collective Bargaining," Ph.D. dissertation, Department of Economics, University of Michigan, 1976. Studies that endogenize unionization and also find a positive union impact on wages include: John M. Abowd and Henry S. Farber, "An Analysis of Relative Wages and Union Membership: Econometric Evidence Based on Panel Data," paper presented at the December, 1977, meeting of the Econometric Society; Lung-Fei Lee, "Unionism and Wage Rates: A Simultaneous Equations Model with Qualitative and Limited Dependent Variables," *International Economic Review* (June 1978), pp. 415-433; Peter Schmidt, "Estimation of a Simultaneous Model with Jointly Dependent Continuous and Qualitative Variables: The Union-Earnings Question Revisited," *International Economic Review* (June 1978), pp. 453-465.

[86]Studies of the compensation of employees as a percentage of national income have been conducted by the following: Edward F. Denison, "Income Types and the Size Distribution," *American Economic Review* (May 1954), pp. 254-269; Harold M. Levinson, "Collective Bargaining and Income Distribution," *American Economic Review* (May 1954), pp. 308-316; Joseph D. Phillips, "Labor's Share and Wage Parity," *Review of Economics and Statistics* (May 1970), pp. 164-174; N.J. Simler, "Unionism and Labor's Share in Manufacturing Industries," *Review of Economics and Statistics* (November 1961), pp. 369-378; Martin Bronfenbrenner, *Income Distribution Theory* (Chicago: Aldine-Atherton Press, 1971), pp. 85-90; James T. Bennett and Manuel H. Johnson, "Free Riders in U.S. Labour Unions: Artifice or

Affliction?" *British Journal of Industrial Relations* (July 1979), pp. 158-172. In general, all of these investigations find that labor's share of income has not changed significantly over the decades since the 1920s.

[87]Thomas Humphrey, "Changing Views of the Phillips Curve," *Federal Reserve Board of Richmond Monthly Review* (July 1973), p. 4.

[88]Daniel Hammermesh, "Market Power and Wage Inflation," *Southern Economic Journal* (October 1972), pp. 204-212.

[89]Douglas Greer, "Market Power and Wage Inflation: A Further Analysis," *Southern Economic Journal* (January 1975), pp. 466-478.

[90]Dwight R. Lee, *The Inflationary Impact of Labor Unions,* Research Monograph Series, No. 5 (College Station, TX: Texas A & M University, 1980).

[91]Ibid., p. 19.

[92]Daniel J. B. Mitchell, *Unions, Wages, and Inflation* (Washington, DC: The Brookings Institution, 1980). Also see Daniel J. B. Mitchell, "Some Empirical Observation of Relevance to the Analysis of Union Wage Determination," *Journal of Labor Research* (Fall 1980), pp. 193-216.

[93]Daniel J. B. Mitchell, *Unions, Wages, and Inflation,* p. 219.

[94]A detailed discussion of resource misallocation due to union/nonunion wage differentials and worker displacement can be found in Albert Rees, *The Economics of Work and Pay* (New York: Harper & Row, Publishers, 1973), pp. 159-161.

[95]Albert Rees, "The Effects of Unions on Resource Allocation," *Journal of Law and Economics* (October 1963), pp. 69-78.

[96]Harry G. Johnson and Peter Mieszkowski, "The Effects of Unionization on the Distribution of Income: A General Equilibrium Approach," *Quarterly Journal of Economics* (November 1970), pp. 539-561.

[97]Morgan O. Reynolds, "The Free Rider Argument for Compulsory Union Dues," *Journal of Labor Research* (Fall 1980), pp. 295-313.

[98]National Labor Relations Board, *Forty-Fourth Annual Report,* Washington, DC: U.S. Government Printing Office, 1979, p. 29.

[99]Selected studies of interest which cover several occupations and deal with theoretical issues include Milton Friedman and Simon Kuznets, *Income from Independent Professional Practice* (New York: National Bureau of Economic Research, 1954); Simon Rottenberg, "The Economics of Occupational Licensing," in *Aspects of Labor Economics,* H. Gregg Lewis, ed., (Princeton, NJ: Princeton University Press, 1962), pp. 3-30; Thomas Moore, "The Purpose of Licensing," *Journal of Law and Economics* (October 1961), pp. 93-104; Benjamin Shimberg, et al., *Occupational Licensing: Practices and Policies* (Washington, DC: Public Affairs Press, 1973); *Occupational Licensing and the Supply of Nonprofessional Manpower,* U.S. Department of Labor, Manpower Administration, Monograph No. 11 (Washington, DC: U.S. Government Printing Office, 1969).

[100]Arlene Holen, "Effects of Professional Arrangements on Interstate Labor Mobility and Resource Allocation," *Journal of Political Economy* (October 1965), pp. 492-498.

[101]B. Peter Pashigian, "Occupational Licensing and the Interstate Mobility of Professionals," *Journal of Law and Economics* (April 1979), pp. 1-25.

[102]Ibid., pp. 15-16.

[103]Walter Williams, *Youth and Minority Unemployment* (Stanford, CA: Hoover Institution Press, 1977), pp. 25-26.

[104]Ibid., p. 26.

[105]See Stuart Dorsey, "The Occupational Licensing Queue," *Journal of Human Resources* (Summer 1980), pp. 424-433.

Chapter V

Deregulating Labor Relations: Alternative Approaches

The preceding chapters have presented evidence which clearly shows that relationships between employers and employees are heavily regulated by government and that the economic costs of this regulation are enormous. Further, there is an ample and growing volume of literature which indicates that the actual results produced by much of the regulation often are very different from the expressed intent of the goals of the regulatory activity. As examples, it is now generally accepted that minimum wage legislation excludes many unskilled workers from the labor market rather than guaranteeing such workers a minimum income and there is no evidence that the costly regulations enforced by OSHA have measurably increased the safety of workers. There is, therefore, a compelling economic argument in support of the deregulation of labor relations. Such a course of action would reduce unemployment, increase productivity, ease inflationary pressures in the economy, make American-made products more competitive in world markets, and greatly increase the efficient utilization of resources which are now distorted by government regulation.

Given the fact that the regulation of labor relations has produced substantial costs and few, if any, recognizable benefits to the economy, an important question must be addressed: why have these regulations persisted — in some cases, for decades? The next section answers this question by addressing the "political economy" of the regulation of labor relations, i.e., those groups that benefit and those that lose from the government restraints on labor exchanges. Having shown that much of the conventional wisdom about the costs and benefits of regulation is inaccurate, we briefly explore the effects of repeal of the National Labor Relations Act (as later amended by the Taft-Hartley and Landrum-Griffin Acts) on dispute resolution, the level of conflict in industrial relations, collective bargaining, the role of unions, and strikes. The deregulation of wages and hours is then considered along with some proposals for partial deregulation and the decentralization of control of labor exchanges.

At the outset, it is essential to recognize that the topics considered are complex, extremely broad in scope, and that the very concept of deregulating labor relations is completely novel. Our objective is not to provide a definitive analysis of every issue because, given the nature of the subject matter, such a task would be impossible in this limited space. Instead, we hope to stimulate others to do research relating to these issues so that more detailed insights can be gained into the numerous topics that the deregulation of labor relations entails.

Winners and Losers from the Deregulation of Labor Relations

The benefits from the regulation of labor relations are concentrated among a relatively small number of individuals while the associated costs are widely dispersed among all consumers and taxpayers. Those who directly benefit from the regulation of labor relations have a powerful vested interest in maintaining and broadening the scope of regulations. Those who bear the costs in the form of higher taxes, higher prices paid for products, lower incomes, etc., are, relative to the beneficiaries, unorganized and do not as individuals have the incentives to lobby and form pressure groups advocating the deregulation of labor-management relations. In short, those who benefit from government regulations are convinced that they have far more to lose as individuals from a policy of deregulation than individuals who would benefit from deregulation stand to gain.

By conventional wisdom, four groups can be identified as the principal beneficiaries of the regulation of labor relations: labor union officials, labor union members, officials and staffs of regulatory agencies, and politicians. Bureaucrats involved in the enactment and enforcement of regulations clearly benefit from the perpetuation and proliferation of regulations, for if the government's involvement in employer-employee transactions were to cease, their jobs and sources of income would presumably disappear as well. Workers in the union sector and their leaders have been thought to benefit from the regulatory environment which encourages unionization and collective bargaining because the pay of unionized workers is higher than that of their nonunion counterparts. Furthermore, labor union officials enjoy salaries and perquisites rivalling the officers of major corporations. The politician, whose goal is to remain in office, benefits from the continuation of regulations because unions are politically active, powerful, and well-financed. Any politician who advocates deregulation of labor relations would incur the strong displeasure of labor unions and, as a result, would jeopardize his chances for reelection. Thus, as long as labor union officials and the bureaucrats associated with regulatory programs are strongly opposed to deregulation of labor relations, politicians are unlikely to support a wide departure from practices of long standing.

As is often true, conventional wisdom may be incorrect. There are convincing arguments to suggest that unionized workers may not benefit measurably from the regulation of labor relations. As pointed out earlier, the wage differential of union workers relative to nonunion workers is obtained at the expense of workers in the nonunion sector. To the extent that regulation encourages collective bargaining, a transfer of income from nonunion to union workers occurs. In 1976, approximately 25 percent of the nonagricultural work force was unionized — a small minority of workers. The regulation of labor relations, therefore, benefits a special minority interest group within the economy at the expense of others whenever an income transfer to unionized workers is produced because of government involvement in employer-employee relations. Although there have been increasingly vocal negative sentiments expressed that condemn special interest groups which obtain benefits for a minority at the expense of the majority, labor unions have, for the most part, escaped widespread criticism. If for no other reason, the entire spectrum of labor relations regulation should be carefully examined because of the special interest nature of the gains that accrue to the unionized sector at the expense of the majority of American workers.

Even though regulation may benefit unionized employees as a group, it does not by any means follow that all individual union members are better off because of the transfer of income from the nonunion to the union sector, for important income transfers occur *within* the unionized sector itself. A central tenet of unionism has always been the standardization of wage rates across workers; such a system permits little differentiation among workers on the basis of performance or productivity. Without standardization of wages, economic theory indicates that employers would pay more to attract and retain highly productive workers. When all workers are paid at the same rate, a more productive worker must forego a higher wage; in essence, an income transfer occurs in which less capable employees are subsidized by more capable workers. Stated simply, an efficient worker can be penalized by the standardization of wages even if the average wage paid to all workers in an organization is higher. There are no estimates of the size of the transfers within the union sector from more to less productive employees, but a reasonable guess would indicate that the potential magnitude is enormous. If one assumes that performance among workers is approximately "normally" distributed, that is, about one-half of the unionized workers are more efficient than the average worker and the other half are less efficient, then approximately one-half the unionized work force is paid less than would be the case without the standardization of wage rates while the other half is paid more.

A second reason that regulations which encourage collective bargaining may not benefit the unionized worker may be found in recent research indicating that the higher average wages paid to the union sector may not be due to unionization at all.[1] The logic of this statement is based upon the notion of cause and effect: Are the wages of unionized workers higher because of the presence of unions or do unions simply have greater success in organizing high wage industries (or, alternatively, do unions simply choose as a matter of strategy to concentrate their organizing efforts upon high wage industries)? A survey of this literature which raises serious doubt about the efficacy of unions in increasing wage rates has been provided by Parsely, who concluded:

> . . . it appears that wages affect unionization to a greater degree than unionism influences wages, but paradoxically workers presumably become union members because they believe that the latter causal direction predominates.[2]

One point, however, should be stressed: All studies of the union wage effect overstate the union-nonunion wage differential because all assume that the differential is obtained at zero cost. As every union member is all too well aware, unions collect dues, fines, fees, and assessments from their members which, in total, amount to billions of dollars each year. If these costs alone were taken into account, the union wage differential would unquestionably be smaller. The differential would be reduced still further if, rather than wage *rates*, research were conducted on employee income. At the very least, strikes have a negative effect upon the latter while leaving the former unchanged. Of what value is an artificially inflated wage rate if, in order to obtain it, the employee through his union was on strike for a sufficiently long period of time that his income remained at or near the pre-raise level over the life of the contract?[3]

Even if unionization does produce higher wages, there is a third reason that at least some individual workers will suffer. The employer's response to higher wages is both predictable and immediate: The employer responds to higher wages by reducing the size of the work force. Those employees who lose jobs and are displaced receive none of the benefits.

There is increasing evidence that workers in the private sector are questioning the benefits of membership in unions and, by implication, the government regulations which foster collective bargaining. Private sector unions are experiencing a secular decline in membership and the origins of this decline can be traced back at least as far as the 1950s. In the private sector, union membership has fallen as a percentage of the number in the nonagricultural labor force, i.e., in relative terms, as well as in absolute numbers. As a percentage of nonfarm employment, *total* union membership declined from about 1 worker in 3 in 1955 to about 1 in 4 in 1976.[4] Because total membership data include the flourishing public sector membership (which increased by 75 percent between 1968 and 1974), it is clear that membership in the private sector has declined dramatically.

There is little to be gained from speculation about an accurate count of union members in the private sector. At least six sets of figures exist which give conflicting estimates[5]; one investigator has convincingly argued that reported data overestimate membership by at least 10 percent.[6] In addition, thousands of workers in industries such as autos and steel are still members, even though they are on indefinite layoff and have little prospect of ever returning to work. For the purposes here, it is sufficient to note that membership in the private sector has fallen steadily over a long period of time so that the relative importance of unionized labor in the economy has deteriorated: on this point, there is wide agreement.

Membership has declined because labor unions are failing to attract new members and to retain old members. Data from the *Annual Reports* of the National Labor Relations Board indicate that unions are now winning a smaller proportion of certification elections and are losing a larger proportion of the decertification elections than previously. In 1956, unions won almost two-thirds (65.3%) of all certification elections; by 1966, however, the victory rate had diminished to 60 percent and, by 1976, less than half (48.2%) of the certification elections produced a union victory. A similar trend is also apparent in the data on decertification elections. By 1977, labor unions were losing three-fourths of all decertification elections — the highest loss percentage ever reported. To make matters worse for the unions, the number of decertification elections has also increased substantially. Between 1977 and 1979, a total of 2,433 decertification elections were held; between 1967 and 1969, only 766 were conducted. More decertification elections were lost by unions in the three-year period 1977-1979 (a total of 1822) than in the entire decade 1960-1969, when only 1628 union defeats were recorded. The record shows that employees are much less inclined to join unions or to remain unionized now than only a few years earlier.

Stated simply, it is reasonable to question the continuation of regulations which, directly or indirectly, encourage the continuation of collective bargaining when the American worker (who, by conventional wisdom, is the prime beneficiary of collective bargaining) has, over a long period of time, shown increasing disenchantment with unionization in the private sector. It is questionable for union officials, bureaucrats, and politicians to insist that the regulation of employer-employee relations in general, and collective bargaining in particular, is in the best interest of the worker when workers have clearly demonstrated by their actions in rejecting unionization that they think otherwise.

On close inspection, even labor union leaders might come to the conclusion that the regulation of labor relations is, at best, a mixed blessing, if not a positive detriment to the economic progress of the American worker and even the union member. As discussed in detail in earlier chapters, the net result of regulation in the labor area is to limit options by legislative action or by the interpretation and administration of labor law by government agencies. One consequence of such actions is to reduce the need for unions to bargain for the worker. Although labor union officials have, virtually without exception, always supported more restrictive legislation dealing with employer-employee relations, the passage of these laws may have greatly reduced the bargaining role of unions in representing and protecting workers. The federal government has, through regulatory action, reduced the need for union representation and the value of union services to the worker has been greatly diminished.

Consider the following. Traditionally, unions have bargained with employers about "wages, hours, and working conditions." With the establishment of the Occupational Safety and Health Administration, every aspect of the work environment has come under federal control. Nothing seems to have escaped the attention of the regulation-oriented bureaucrat: There are even explicit mandates specifying the number and placement of toilet facilities. Adverse working conditions (in the extreme, the sweatshop) are no longer within the purview of union-management bargaining because the federal government now has juris-diction. As abhorrent as the sweatshop may have been to workers and others concerned with the conditions of work, it was also undoubtedly a strong selling point for the union organizer. Other regulations may also have had the effect of reducing the workers' perceived need for union representation. If, for example, the minimum wage law applied to the agricultural sector, one might wonder whether the union movement in this area would have ever developed at all. Ironically, it seems that the regulations that labor union leaders have nurtured and fostered for years have contributed to a reduction in the importance of collective bargaining and in the value of union representation to workers. Why should any worker pay dues to a union to bargain for benefits made mandatory by law?

It should also be noted that unions have supported other types of legislation that have, in the long run, been detrimental to the interests of their members and the unions themselves. Environmental regulations are a case in point. Labor unions actively supported very stringent air and water quality standards to reduce pollution. Much of the pollution is generated by firms in manufacturing, the traditional bastion of union strength in the private sector. As resources were diverted to pollution control equipment, fewer funds were available for plant expansion and the creation of new jobs in the very sector that is most heavily unionized. To maintain profit margins, firms raised prices which contributed to inflation and gave a competitive edge to foreign firms not subject to stringent environmental controls. Domestic output in such industries as automobiles and steel has fallen dramatically as imports of foreign products have soared. The result has been massive retrenchments, plants closings, and substantial unemployment, especially among unionized workers.

Labor union officials have been unable to make a positive response to counteract the economic dislocations which inevitably occur in industries and communities where plants are closed and workers are terminated or placed on indefinite layoff. The perceived impotence of labor unions in these circumstances has not escaped the American worker, whether unionized or not. One explanation that can be offered for the decline of unions in the private sector noted earlier is that employees now view labor unions as a "fair weather" phenomenon; that is, when economic conditions are sound, unions may be effective, but in severe economic conditions ("foul weather"), they are largely powerless. If workers also perceive that the actions of labor unions can contribute to economic adversity and the loss of jobs, the labor union movement will, indeed, experience an uncertain future.

Conventional wisdom among labor union leaders has also long held that the primary strategy for achieving union goals has been to restrict competition as much as possible between union and nonunion labor. As discussed earlier, the minimum wage and Davis-Bacon regulations are prime examples of restricting competition in the labor market. Although in the short run such tactics may seem effective, they are, in the long run, at best a mixed blessing. Far more is involved than merely the transfer of income from the nonunion to the union sector. The regulations which implement restrictions on labor market competition result in a misallocation of labor resources, a lower level of aggregate income, a lower rate of economic growth and capital formation, a transfer of resources from the private to the public sector, greater foreign competition in the market for goods, and increased inflationary pressures. By encouraging increases in the scope of labor regulations, union leaders have, over time, reduced employment in the economy and have therefore reduced the potential membership in labor unions.

In sum, if conventional wisdom is questioned, a strong case can be made that the regulation of labor relations reduces the need for and role of unions. After all, regulation is nothing more than the imposition of government restraints on the relationships between employees and employers; regulation reduces the number of issues subject to collective bargaining. Yet, collective bargaining in the interest of employees is, at least in theory, the essential justification for the existence of labor unions. Every regulation that constrains labor relations reduces the benefits to workers of labor union membership. Labor union leaders may, in fact, have more to gain from deregulation than is commonly believed. This point is explored in greater detail below.

There is little doubt that union officials would strongly oppose the relaxation of most existing regulations on labor relations. Although it may be recognized that certain restraints do not foster the goals of unions, there is obviously a strong belief that, overall, the regulatory environment favors collective bargaining and the union position. If any part of the total regulatory structure were dismantled, the entire edifice might be threatened. A less charitable view is that union officials are convinced that their organizations could not even survive deregulation. If deregulation threatens their very survival, then labor unions are indeed frail institutions that will find their prospects increasingly difficult as economic conditions and the structure and composition of the

work force change over time. As mentioned earlier, worker disenchantment with unions is indicated by an increasing rate of union losses in
both certification and decertification elections: Unions must adapt to
changing circumstances.

Deregulation: The Repeal of NLRA

The most comprehensive regulation of labor relations is embodied
in the National Labor Relations Act, i.e., the Wagner Act of 1935, Taft-
Hartley, and the Landrum-Griffin Act of 1959. Repeal of the strictures
contained in these laws would most dramatically alter the existing relationships among employers, employees, and the agents of employees
(labor unions). In addition, the National Labor Relations Board[7] would
lose its statutory authority to exist and would have no labor law to apply
in any case.[8] Numerous adjustments would have to occur as the authority for practices of long standing were swept away; we survey briefly some
of the changes that would take place and their implications. By necessity, our discussion must be suggestive rather than exhaustive in content.

Dispute Resolution. With the removal of the NLRB, alternative
approaches would have to be developed or expanded to carry out the
dispute resolution function currently vested in the Board. For the individual employee, repeal of NLRA should open up additional avenues of
redress to protect rights of individual workers endangered by either
employers or unions. As administered by the Board, the law now severely
restricts the appeals process of workers. Controversies between unions
and employers are inevitable and would not disappear even if the
dispute resolution function of the Board were to vanish. Further, it is
not certain whether the volume of disputes would increase or decrease.

It could be argued that repeal of NLRA would produce an increase
in the number of disputes between unions and employers, because the
mere presence of a dispute-resolving mechanism (together with a massive body of precedent) encourages parties to come to terms if both are
convinced that the solution is clearcut under existing precedents. In the
absence of the Board and its precedents, it might be argued, parties
would pursue their conflicting claims much more aggressively. Such a
conclusion, however, implicitly assumes that no alternative mechanism
would be able to perform the dispute-resolving function, an assumption
which runs counter to all experience with market responses to perceived
needs. There are, after all, the existing courts and an existing body of

141

law, applied over centuries, regarding contracts. Given the number of NLRB decisions that already are challenged in the courts, it may be that any net increase in the demand for formal judicial resolution of labor exchange disputes would be moderate at most. Moreover, the disappearance of the NLRB would produce a tremendous expansion in private agencies which already exist to reduce industrial conflict. Labor arbitration even today is a thriving industry, indicating that the dispute-resolution function of the NLRB is costly and untimely for many conflicts in the work place.

An equally strong argument can be made that repeal of NLRA would reduce the volume of disputes. To the extent current labor law *creates* causes of disputes which might not otherwise exist, the repeal of those laws would eliminate the formal, and some might claim artificial, causes of many cases now being handled. Furthermore, because the Board is widely recognized as an adjudicating rather than a rule-making regulatory body,[9] its actions produce a body of precedent that is so large, complicated, and contradictory that its very complexity stimulates cases where none might ordinarily exist.

There is merit in both sides of the argument briefly discussed above, and various influences will affect the volume of controversies requiring formal external resolution. It is also likely that controversies will be affected differentially according to subject. Duty of fair representation cases, for example, would virtually disappear, because this duty was an artificiality devised by the courts to make constitutional the unions' privilege of exclusivity as created by statute. Similarly, in the absence of exclusivity, cases involving unit elections would not arise, for if the privilege of representing all employees in a unit does not exist, there is no need for either unit determinations or elections. There would likely be, however, some increase in the number of controversies regarding the interpretation of contract language.

The important point is that there is no reason to expect the termination of the dispute-resolution function of the NLRB to produce automatically a marked increase in the number of disputes in the labor relations area. Moreover, alternative mechanisms for dispute resolution already exist, are widely used, and could perform this function in the Board's place.

Conflict. Repeal of the NLRA raises also the somewhat different issue as to whether the volume of conflict would be changed. Conflict is part and parcel of a labor exchange, as it is in every economic exchange, in the sense that each party has different goals that conceivably are not simultaneously achievable. As sellers and buyers of a commodity (labor), the parties differ on their valuations of cost, price, terms, and conditions. At the extreme, each seeks a maximum of return for a minimum of outlay. Yet each needs the other for, without an exchange, neither can achieve goals which are presumably even more important than the exchange terms. Thus, employers need labor and employees need persons to hire their labor else the former cannot produce and the latter cannot obtain the resources to buy the products of others.[10] Although this general incentive to come to terms undergirds the conflict, the question is, what happens to the level of conflict should the regulatory framework provided by federal labor laws be eliminated?

One thing is clear, the repeal of NLRA is no more likely to produce *more* industrial conflict, in and of itself, than the passage of the Wagner Act originally was said to produce industrial peace. By any measure, including controls for a larger work force, industrialization, or unionization, a reduction in conflict did not follow from the enactment of any piece of labor regulation — even though the enhancement of industrial peace was one of the stated objectives in the preamble to the NLRA. If anything, industrial conflict as measured by number of strikes, length of strikes, number of employees involved, or a combination of these (e.g., man-days lost) has seen a steady rise throughout this century, overlaid by a long-term cycle of several decades plus a short cycle of no more than several years' duration.[11] On these terms alone, one might conclude that industrial conflict has in part been *caused* by increasing political intervention.

Whether NLRA has or has not caused, in whole or in part, the observed increase in private sector strikes is problematical and beyond the scope of the analysis here. If it has, the chances are good that repeal could halt or reverse that trend. If the existence of NLRA is totally independent of strike behavior (a proposition which seems untenable), it is still possible that the elimination of NLRA regulation, together with the effects of whatever system replaced it, could influence future patterns of strikes. This point deserves careful consideration, because it involves the essential phenomenon of regulation.

Regulation, to repeat once more the basic definition, consists of a foreclosure of options imposed externally upon a market by political authorities. This indicates that exchanges in a regulated market are fewer, less flexible, less mutually satisfactory to the principal exchange parties, and the result of a lengthier bargaining process. This strongly suggests, in turn, that exchange agreements in a regulated market are preceeded by greater levels of conflict as the parties attempt to achieve a bargain under conditions which are more hostile, *net*, to the exchange than would be the case in an unregulated market. In effect, the exchange is being forced by politically inspired constraints into a format which the parties would not have chosen were they negotiating freely: That, after all, is the avowed purpose of regulation in the first place. What must be stressed is the reduced satisfaction occasioned by regulation. As parties in the pre-exchange stage attempt to find a single set of terms which will be mutually acceptable relative to the costs and benefits of the alternatives, they will explore particular conditions which, given regulatory constraints, are no longer feasible. The consequences of choosing a constrained set of terms have been altered through the political process so that it is more costly to one party or more beneficial to another party — depending upon the regulatory objectives. For example, criminal law sanctions add the possibility (a possibility which criminals may inexactly calculate) of fines, jail sentences, or both to the usual cost/benefit ratio for, say, engaging in a burglary. An employer may decide not to bargain with a certified union but, under current conditions, the choice must include the costs associated with committing an "unfair labor practice" of this sort. A union officer may decide to rig the election process to ensure his retention, but account must be taken of the chance that a member may challenge the outcome under Landrum-Griffin provisions.

Clearly, one party to a regulated exchange may experience greater satisfaction from the bargain than if the bargain had been reached in an unregulated market. A requirement that employers may not permanently replace striking employees (where the strike is over an alleged "unfair labor practice")[12] makes the strike a more effective element in the bargaining process and this accordingly tends to push any bargain attained as a result of such a strike closer to the most preferred set of union terms. An employer whose business has become unprofitable partly or wholly as a result of a union contract is less able to sell the business on satisfactory terms because the successor owner must assume responsibility for the same contract.[13] The fact than an employer may commit an "unfair labor practice" by refusing to make a counter-offer during negotiations means that employers generally must modify their positions toward the union proposals. To the extent unions are under similar constraints (and, as argued in Chapter III, they are *not* constrained in this regard to the same degree as are employers), their counter-offers must do likewise. The result is a set of terms which is less satisfactory to both parties than would otherwise be the case but relatively *more* satisfactory to one party than to the other.

Overall, then, one can argue that labor exchanges, as currently regulated, feature more conflict precisely because they are regulated and that this is inherently true from the very nature of the regulatory framework. It seems more than likely that a policy of deregulation would reduce not only the number of formal disputes but also the general level of conflict. With the elimination of politically-induced costs and benefits which restrain the choice of some exchange terms while favoring the choice of other terms, the parties would be more free to achieve a mutually satisfactory set of employment terms according to costs and benefits which derive from market conditions themselves rather than from conditions, objectives, or circumstances which are chiefly political in nature. Further, the total number of agreements would increase and the average amount of time it takes to reach an agreement would decrease.[14]

Collective Bargaining. The impact of the repeal of NLRA on collective bargaining is also an issue of critical importance. Those opposed to deregulation are likely to contend that repeal would mean the end of collective bargaining and the doom of labor unions. Such a position implies that collective bargaining is sustained only by the altered schedule of costs and benefits imposed by NLRA (as administered and enforced). If this is true, as mentioned earlier, collective bargaining is a frail reed indeed. Collective bargaining is a fairly widespread phenomenon which antedates every instance of labor market regulation, and there is every reason to suspect that its vitality would easily withstand even the total repeal of those political constraints. Every case of parties voluntarily combining to achieve a common end for themselves is predicated on the axiomatic presumption that the end sought collectively is more satisfactory to each and every member of the group than could likely be achieved by any group member individually. In practice, a collectivity will form even if the visible group result is thought to be no better or possibly marginally worse for some than the outcome achievable by their individual efforts because they will calculate into the balancing of costs and benefits a variety of imponderables which only individuals can evaluate. The simplest market exchange is surrounded by these imponderables to the extent that, with all notion of collective behavior absent, it is difficult for anyone not party to the exchange to list all the factors which went into the decision. For collective exchanges, the calculations become impossible for the outside observer. Yet, when collectivities form freely, it is known *a priori* that the principle holds. It is also known, of course, that individuals often possess incomplete or inaccurate information so that their calculations may be wrong. Further, individuals have varying degrees of skill or luck in predicting a future course of events. For these reasons, a group may form on the basis of *belief* that the product of its collective labor will be more satisfactory to every individual member but, in fact, this may turn out not to be true due to the sorts of problems noted.

When frontier families cooperated to raise a neighbor's barn, it stemmed from an expectation that they would have similar help from their neighbors in a similar situation. Moreover, each barn, schoolhouse, or church could be raised faster (hence more quickly benefit the community) if a large number of people participated. A collective buying group forms when individuals discover that large orders receive preferential prices, and the preferential price is granted because the seller realizes savings from a reduction in order processing costs (together with an increased confidence that larger portions of what he has produced will in fact be sold). Car pools form when commuters realize a reduction in passenger mile costs (plus such nonpecuniary benefits as relief from driving/parking tensions, from which must be deducted the nonpecuniary cost of less flexibility in scheduling travel). All these examples are much more complex than as stated here, but they serve to indicate the very strong impulses to collective behavior in the achievement of goals.

There is no reason to believe that such impulses are absent or inoperative in the labor market. It is accurate to say, as pointed out in Chapter III, that one principal consequence of procedural regulation in the labor market (of which NLRA is a prime source) has been the collectivizing of employment relationships, but the more specific meaning of the statement should be well understood. There has been produced a level of collectivization which exceeds the degree of voluntary grouping which would occur in the absence of regulation. Repeal of NLRA would certainly not eliminate collective action; at most, the level might possibly be reduced, but the amount of reduction is unknown. Any analysis of deregulation would have to take into account the fact that labor exchanges have been occurring in a regulated market for nearly fifty years. To the extent a limiting factor in joining a collective endeavor is the availability to the individual of information regarding the potential benefits of such a choice, it may be argued that literally millions of employees today possess at first hand this sort of information. We would therefore expect that the level of collective action in a post-deregulation labor market might be less than currently exists, but more than would exist if the market had never been forcibly collectivized through regulation.

With respect to the labor market, what are the factors which might influence individuals to act collectively? The answer to this is more analogous to collective buying than to frontier barn-raising, i.e., the favorable consequences derive from economies of scale. Employees need a variety of data in order to evaluate their commodity (labor). They must know what value their labor adds to the production process, how many others of comparable ability and experience would queue for their jobs, the costs they would incur to provide the labor for which they would contract, the probable long-term demand for the commodity they would participate in producing (one indicator of employment stability), the number and quality of alternative employments (in the same or different industry or geographic area), the reputation of the employer and his staff in resolving intra-company personnel disputes, the amount of time probably available to decide to accept or continue employment, the value in real terms of the compensation package, one's employability elsewhere following the acquisition of company-specific training, and, literally, a host of similar matters.

If there is one characteristic of information relevant to the issue addressed here, it is that the cost of obtaining any specific item of knowledge varies little no matter how many people need to know it. It follows that the more people need to know something and are willing to participate in some fashion in the acquisition of information, the lower will be the cost to each person who joins in a collective effort. Conceptually, starting from one, the addition of no more than one other person would make the information acquisition process more cost-effective, but in practice there is probably some minimum limit on numbers.[15] At some point, then, the number of employees who need to have certain information, who are aware of similar needs possessed by others, and who know that savings will be produced if the acquisition of the information were collectivized will be sufficient to sustain a group effort. A smaller group within, or a single individual, will be appointed to find out what group members need to know. Later, the same or another person or group will distribute the information to the larger group's members. The longer the group exists (i.e., maintains self-awareness, mutual contact, continuing joint activity), the more cost effective its operations become as experience is gained, information is stockpiled, confidence is

147

built, and lines of communication are institutionalized. Over time, each member will develop interests in retaining group association beyond those which initially caused it to be formed.

Apart from the acquisition of information, there is a further purpose which might be pursued more efficiently and at lower cost collectively as opposed to individually. Once having formulated a preferred set of employment terms on the basis of all available information, a labor exchange must still await the presentation of that offer to an employer, the transmission of the employer's preferred set of terms, the comparison of these two sets of terms,[16] the process of modifying the offers over a succession of communications until either only a single set remains or one party determines that no further modifications are possible, and, if the former, finalization of an agreement with whatever formalities are needed to ensure mutual adherence. Each of these actions could be, frequently is, and historically has been accomplished by individuals. At the same time, each is characteristically susceptible to collectivization under the right conditions. As above, the larger the number of employees who must engage in the activity on roughly the same basis, the lower will be the unit costs because, with few and generally insignificant exceptions, the total cost of performing each activity is roughly constant whether it is performed on behalf of one person or many.[17] It is of more than passing interest that, for several if not all these activities, employee collectivization carries with it the potential of producing economies of scale for the employer as well. Assuming the employer agrees with the self-perception of the group's members that they are in fact roughly comparable among themselves as regards their role in the production process, their terms and conditions of employment, and so forth, then as far as the employer is concerned there is no particular reason to differentiate among them except along lines the group itself may propose (i.e., skill, education, experience, seniority, training, etc.). Under these circumstances, it is to the employer's cost advantage to bargain with a collectivity since this option reduces duplicative effort.

We have stated and explained our belief that collective bargaining would continue were NLRA to be repealed: The pressures which impel a collectivization of bargaining are independent of the NLRA and are, to a certain extent, shared by employees and employers alike. The resulting level of collective behavior is difficult to estimate, though we suggested earlier that it might be less than currently exists but greater than had the labor market never become regulated. On the one hand, some amount of collective behavior is forced by the regulatory framework and that would disappear with deregulation. On the other hand, information is now widespread regarding the "natural" benefits of collective action; also, one could argue that both employers and employees would be less resistant to the phenomenon were its currently coercive nature transformed into a voluntary action predicated upon rational self-interest. Finally, as discussed earlier, deregulation would provide a greater justification for collective action. Regulation not only forecloses options, but also reduces the amount of information available to make decisions because, as the number of options increases, so does the need for information about the available options. In short, deregulation might well increase the benefits of collective action for employees. These statements merit a more detailed explanation.

Effects on Unions. Unions are institutions which have organizational interests apart from those of their members or those of the somewhat larger number of employees for whom unions are the certified exclusive representative. As such, their leaderships may pursue objectives which are unrelated to the bargaining function discussed here. Yet one objective traditionally associated with the union movement stands out as eminently relevant to the sort of collective bargaining which would permit unions not only to survive, but also to thrive following procedural deregulation of the labor market. That objective embodies the notion of agency.

Simply put, collective action by employees, applied to the bargaining process, involves as a matter of practice some delegation of authority. Unless one envisions the entire group gathering information, meeting *en masse* with an employer, affixing their individual signatures to a contract, and so forth, it follows that the group must appoint some significantly smaller portion of itself to engage in these actions on the group's behalf. Such a smaller group (which may be simply a single person) thereby becomes the "agent" of the group. Generally comparable results may be achieved if the group appoints someone not from within but, rather, outside to serve as agent. While some degree of risk is involved in this alternative arrangement (it may be assumed that an agent who is from within is better able to understand and identify with the group's aims, needs, and preferences), the benefits might overcome these risks. After all, the appointment of an agent/representative from within the group could entail a sufficiently large workload as to justify the agent's full-time attention. Consequently, the agent appointed initially from within would diverge over time from the rest of the group and its common experiences. Furthermore, though the particular abilities required in serving as an agent may not be rare, employee groups would not always be fortunate enough to find within themselves individuals who possess the requisite combination of skills. Thus, as with most tasks in a highly specialized society, there would undoubtedly develop a separate market of persons and organizations offering themselves as skilled, experienced, and knowledgeable employee agents.

It is obvious that union leaders and even existing unions would have a preeminently rational basis for arguing that this was a function for which they were uniquely qualified in any post-deregulation environment. Others would undoubtedly seek to enter the employee agent market, some would probably be successful, but those who have already served in such a capacity would dominate this new profession. Equally clear, however, is the fact that current union leaders and union organizations would need to adapt themselves to a substantially different environment where previously protected practices had become impermissible and where a number of options had become feasible.

There is no reason to believe that unions, as employee agents, would not continue to specialize (as they do now) in particular industries, companies, or geographic areas. Nor would their federation necessarily disappear as there could remain a need for some sort of "trade association" for sharing information, developing professional expertise, publicizing the services of its members, administering training programs, and resolving disputes arising either among its members or between a member and the employee group which that member is representing. Organizing would continue, though its character would be altered somewhat as employee agents sought to bring into their represented groups as many employees as would qualify. Organizing appeals, however, would need to incorporate a combination of three arguments — the cost savings which derive from collectivizing employee participation in bargaining over labor exchanges, the value of contracting with an outside agent, and evidence of past or predicted success.

Lacking exclusivity, an employee agent could bargain only on behalf of his "principals," i.e., those prospective or current employees who had affirmatively appointed the agent to act in this capacity. As an adjunct to the elimination of exclusivity, issues of "unit determination" and "bargaining agent election" would not arise because "units" would be self-determined (or constructed by the agent with the voluntary cooperation of the employees involved) and "elections" would not be held since agents could represent only those who had appointed them. Equally unnecessary would be the so-called "duty of fair representation." This duty was created solely to provide a constitutional justification for exclusivity. Employees who did not wish a particular form of representation would not need to accept it in the first place (if NLRA were repealed) or, if they did and became dissatisfied later, employees could withdraw from the collectivity as freely as they joined it.[19]

The "duty to bargain in good faith" is a major issue, if for no reason other than its having become a union device of broad proportions. How can anyone say there ought not to be such a duty? Good faith bargaining should be a commitment of all negotiators, all agents, all people in fact, for the logical obverse is "bad faith bargaining." Yet there is a universe of difference between a moral purpose and, alternately, a legal principle which must be monitored, administered, and judged on purportedly objective bases. In Chapter III it was argued that, in practice, the good faith bargaining concept has been defined in terms of its outcome, i.e., bargaining has occurred in good faith if it has led to an agreement or if, in the process, the parties (notably the employer) have made meaningful concessions. Thus, the formal repeal of NLRA provisions embodying this duty would do little more than end decades of regulatory charades. This is not to endorse "bad faith": It is merely a recognition that bargaining will occur when the parties desire to reach an agreement (in other words, when the costs of not agreeing are greater than the costs of the likely bargain). Failure to agree would carry a variety of consequences for all parties. Once the contract terminates, employees are free to leave their jobs but the employer has also lost his work force. There is no reason why the contract could not contain provisions involving temporary extensions of employment and/or payments to employees who are replaced following termination of the relationship.

Thus, in a post-deregulation environment, unions would continue to exist[20] and would in fact be the organizations to which employees would most likely turn for experienced agents. The principle underlying the new relationship between employees and unions would be voluntary association, hence voluntary non-association as well. This must be seen as a major transformation, one which justifies the elimination of virtually all special government intrusions into the internal workings of such organizations. No longer would it be thought necessary to regulate their constitutions, leadership selection processes, or financial operations. It need hardly be added that the repeal of these measures would produce as yet unmeasured budgetary savings stemming from the severe reduction or elimination of those units of government which administer the measures. Unions would legally be defined as businesses which specialize in providing a service. They could incorporate or not and be subject to precisely the same regulations as affect all businesses. Those unions which chose to retain their historical tradition as membership groups could do so, while other unions might choose different arrangements. In any event, there is no reason to believe that membership unions would not function as do countless other similar cooperatives. Membership apathy will always be a problem but, with voluntary association and voluntary exit,[21] members would possess effective means of voicing their objections to policies and would, through normal legal processes, be able to challenge alleged misconduct. It would follow that the union's political, ideological, and other lawful activities would not be subject to challenge except from within, that the only limits on the sorts of activities in which unions could engage would be limits placed originally in stating the purposes of incorporation or detailed in the union's own constitution or imposed from time to time by the membership. With such a transformation, there would be no need to unravel the tangle of where collective bargaining stops and political/ideological activities begin. Further, to the extent that this is a problem,[22] the infiltration of organized crime into unions could well become considerably more difficult. For much the same reasons, the level of fraud and corruption would be reduced.

Strikes. A post-deregulation labor market would be governed considerably more by formal contracts than is the case today. Not surprisingly, this would extend to the subject of work stoppages. As before, it is not our intention to develop in minute detail solutions to the multiple issues raised by strikes, but only to suggest that the solutions are achievable. First, of course, it will be necessary to realize that a job is simply a shorthand term for a complex of relationships and mutual duties. No one has a property right in any specific job. If no contract exists, employment is at will (subject to implied duties, oral agreements, and other statutory responsibilities covering, e.g., payment for work already done, sufficiency of notice, or minimum health conditions); however, if there is a contract, employers and employees are obligated to provide certain things to each other over the life of the contract. One of these is labor, and it should be provided according to contract terms. The conditions under which a party may refuse to perform an agreed obligation are often covered by the contract itself and are also the subject of established legal precedents. In short, strikes as commonly defined would not occur. Employees could withdraw their labor from an employer, individually or collectively, under four conditions: no contract at all; contract ended and no new or replacement agreement; contract exists but the employer has allegedly acted in derogation of his responsibilities; and, last, contract exists, but there is no alleged employer fault and the withdrawal is not in accordance with any contract terms dealing with this matter. The first two of these situations present no serious problems. If the employer is thought to have breached some contract term which justified employee withdrawal, there are remedies at law. Nonperformance by one party can not only dissolve the obligations of others, but also can trigger a variety of penalties which aggrieved parties may pursue under the contract (if such provisions are included) or under established judicial precedents. As for the last situation, one would ask first of all why employees might withdraw their labor under the posited circumstances. Individual withdrawals are not the issue. People change jobs, move, decide to retire, come to dislike their jobs, and so forth: Within limits established by mutual agreement, individuals may freely decide to quit without penalty, with minor impairments, or at most with an employment record which might make job applications more difficult in the future. The only problem of any real dimension which arises is when a number of employees concertedly withdraw their labor. Given that no employer breach of contract is claimed, such a course of action is doubtful. The only purpose which might conceivably be served is to pressure the employer for more favorable contract terms; yet this sort of pressure already exists as the current contract comes to a close and negotiations begin on its renewal. If the parties fail to reach agreement, the employer knows that covered employees will be free to quit. Furthermore, if the withdrawal occurs during the contract, in a manner not consistent with provisions for individual resignations, each employee would be hazarding the same sorts of penalties which are available were the issue one of an employer breach of contract.

Other Effects. The scope of regulation under the NLRA is so extensive that it would be all but impossible to discuss every conceivable change that would occur with repeal. There are, for example, such issues as the handling of grievances, the implications of a more varied pattern of personnel relations within companies, the use of boycotts as a bargaining tactic, the locus of responsibility for the management of trust funds, picketing, and so forth. In the case of the NLRA, partial deregulation would be very difficult to achieve, because of the marked degree of interaction and mutual dependence among the main elements of federal labor relations statutes. The regulation of internal union affairs is closely linked to compulsory representation and membership provisions, the duty of fair representation is meaningless unless read in conjunction with exclusivity, the notion of a unit election depends as well upon exclusivity, and the good faith bargaining duty derives strictly from the NLRA's fundamental discrimination against either individual bargaining or collective negotiations outside a union context.

Partial deregulation is feasible in other instances of the regulation of labor relations where the constraints are more substantive than procedural and are far less comprehensive in scope. Though less desirable than total deregulation, partial approaches at least reduce the costs incurred to some extent. Examples of regulations which might be reduced by degrees or phased out over time are the constraints on wages and hours.

Deregulation of Wages and Hours

As noted in Chapter III and elsewhere, the establishment of a wage floor effectively removes from lawful employment those workers subject to the minimum whose marginal productivity is valued below the limit, i.e., typically the young, unskilled, and inexperienced worker. The minimum wage precludes such workers from obtaining on-the-job training, skills, and experience because the minimum wage makes employers unwilling to hire workers with low productivity, unless the government provides adequate subsidies in the form of grants or tax credits. When the employment of workers is subsidized, the taxpayer in one form or another bears the costs.

There are two ways to partially deregulate minimum wage restraints on labor exchanges: (1) the coverage of the law could be reduced by exempting certain industries or by exempting certain workers, e.g., a youth subminimum has been proposed to alleviate the persistently high unemployment rates of teenagers; and, (2) the legislated minimum rate of pay could be lowered or, given current rates of inflation, simply left unchanged so that the nominal minimum rate would be eroded in terms of real purchasing power. Obviously, some combination of the two approaches could be employed as well. Regardless of the specific mechanism employed to relax the minimum wage constraints, employment opportunities would be developed for workers now excluded from the labor market and a number of government programs which subsidize uneconomic employment could be phased out. Not only would this save the cost of the subsidy itself, but administrative, paperwork, and compliance costs would also be eliminated.

Another form of minimum wage regulation is Davis-Bacon restrictions on wages in federal construction contracts. The economic effects of Davis-Bacon derive not only from the requirements specified in the legislation, but also from the administration of these requirements by the U.S. Department of Labor. As the General Accounting Office has documented, the economy must contend not only with the direct regulation of wage levels, which are sufficiently onerous to increase the cost of federal construction by hundreds of millions of dollars, but also with paperwork compliance costs that have been estimated at nearly $200 million annually.[23] The cost of compliance is incorporated into the costs of construction so that the taxpayer ultimately bears the burden of the paperwork and administration of the Act as well.

Although it is difficult to estimate the lower levels of productivity of construction labor which result from Davis-Bacon regulation, these costs are by no means insignificant. In addition to wage classification and wagesetting, the U.S. Department of Labor also *defines* the construction techniques and technologies that can be used on federal projects. Generally, the work rules established by local union organizations are accepted as the standard. For example, if local unions have restrictions against spray guns for painting or power-driven concrete fasteners, the Davis-Bacon Section of the Labor Department will enforce these rules by refusing to certify wage rates for anyone to use these or comparable techniques. Not infrequently, unusual work classifications or wage rate standards are taken from the labor contracts in distant and unrelated areas.

Without doubt, the Davis-Bacon Act severely distorts the federal contract construction industry. Further, these distortions also apply, at least in part, to much of the construction undertaken by state governments because the GAO has found that many states have adopted similar provisions concerning their contracting. The distortion extends far beyond the higher costs due to high wage rates, lower productivity, and compliance. The construction industry itself is distorted by Davis-Bacon-type regulations.[24] For example, mandating wage costs stabilizes the most significant element of a construction contract or a repair project budget. With a major cost factor standardized by law, competition among potential contractors is greatly reduced and project bid costs tend to rise overall. The same reduction in competition tends also to favor bidders who are large, multi-state enterprises. Thus, the federal construction business increasingly is concentrated in the hands of a few providers. Needless to say, the effect of these developments in turn is a freezing out of the smaller, independent, and (notably) nonunion contractor.

The total effects of Davis-Bacon extend far beyond the construction industry itself. Given a finite amount of federal funds for construction, a cost increase overall for this activity implies a proportionate reduction in the amount of the activity itself which can be funded. Emergency appropriations and budget supplements aside, if X dollars will build Y housing units for low income families and if those units increase in cost, it follows that fewer than Y housing units will be built. Quite apart from questions as to the intrinsic wisdom of government-subsidized housing, government-subsidized hospitals, government-subsidized schools, and so forth, it is still true that a multitude of programs involving construction are vitally affected by Davis-Bacon. In responding to pressures for such programs, pressures which do not scale back simply because construction costs are rising, Congress is forced to appropriate more just to keep even and these higher budgets contribute to higher taxes or a higher inflation rate. Finally, though it is less certain and more difficult to isolate, higher federal construction costs (combined with political pressures which prevent the natural consequence, after an appropriate time lag, of less construction activity) may well tend to pull up the costs of private sector construction: Higher wage rates in public building programs will draw workers away from the private sector and, until balance is restored in the labor market, the smaller pool of workers available to construct homes, offices, and stores, will pull those private sector construction wage rates upward. Thus, one component of the higher price being paid today for housing (due to mounting wage rates and fewer housing "starts") can be attributed to federal construction under Davis-Bacon.

With regard to deregulation, Davis-Bacon differs from the minimum wage in at least two important respects. First, the benefits of the Davis-Bacon Act are concentrated primarily among unionized workers in the construction industry, whereas the minimum wage is generally believed to reduce competition with unionized workers in virtually every sector of economy. Thus, the group that would lose most from deregulation under Davis-Bacon is much smaller than the number of those who would lose under the deregulation of the minimum wage. Opposition, then, would likely be less to removal of the strictures of Davis-Bacon than to elimination of the minimum wage — unless labor union officials interpreted repeal of Davis-Bacon as a threat to the privileged position of unionized workers in general and an omen of further deregulation in other sectors. Second, unlike the minimum wage, the strictures of Davis-Bacon can be suspended by presidential directive. For a very short period in 1971, President Nixon did suspend the Act as part of his program on wage-price controls. Thus, Davis-Bacon regulations may be significantly mitigated without the involvement of Congress, provided the chief executive desired to do so. Moreover, it would take little more than an appropriate order from the Secretary of Labor to produce major changes in how the "prevailing wage" standards are set and administered.

There are also similarities between the minimum wage and Davis-Bacon in terms of opportunities for partial or "phased" deregulation. For example, the Davis-Bacon provisions could be nullified for certain types of construction, e.g., low income housing, schools, or hospitals. Alternatively, to encourage competition in the construction industry, Davis-Bacon could be made applicable only to projects with total costs above a certain level. The level could be raised over a set period of time to produce a phased deregulation of the industry. Phased or partial deregulation should produce less political opposition than total deregulation at some fixed point in time, for it permits to those who are protected by the regulatory provisions the time to adjust to the altered economic environment.

In order to consider seriously the removal of ceiling limits on labor activity, i.e., maximum hours, it is first essential to dispense with the "slave labor" notion, for in contemplating the removal of the hours ceiling, along with elimination of the attendant rules regarding premium pay, the charge might well be leveled that the necessary result would be a return to some presumed nineteenth century practice of forcing workers to labor untold hours. Economic historians are not so sure that such practices were in fact all that commonplace. And the objection, even where the 60 or 70 hour week did exist, was not so much to the sheer *volume* of work since, during this country's entire push westward, the typical frontier family labored over a far larger number of hours per week than did the typical factory worker. The objection, rather, though this did not always come through in the simplified slogans of the day, was really to the *conditions* of work. In comparison with the frontier family, the industrial factory worker was under qualitatively different conditions, separated from family, with unfamiliar stresses and strains, performing tasks which lacked immediate or observable gratifications, and with considerably reduced opportunities for individual initiative.

It is not true that most factory workers of the time were really forced to labor longer hours than they may have wished. In most cases it was a matter of choice. Where the employer specified the hours to be worked, there were usually other or different employment options. We do not seek to paint a rosy picture of circumstances during the industrial revolution. Far from it, but the country was faced with a period in which technological progress was outstripping the immediate adaptabilities of the labor force. Moreover, many citizens and immigrants perceived such labor as the key to personal or family advancement. The very fact that "overtime" today normally is tied to some premium payment as opposed to being merely strictly limited is an indication that the hours ceiling did not develop entirely from an objection to volume of work. It was based more on the thought that, as a matter of social policy, people should be free to advance their family interests, engage in recuperative recreation, consume what others had produced, develop an awareness of themselves as citizens, and so forth. There was, of course, the powerful additional thought (discussed in Chapter III) that more people would have work available to them if the amount of work any particular person could do were limited.

Seen in this light, the elimination of an hours ceiling and of overtime premiums carries a considerably revised set of implications. It must be emphasized that only a proposal to eliminate a statutory requirement is being considered: Any labor exchange could, and many undoubtedly would, continue to carry some mutually imposed limit (minimum and/or maximum) — together with a potentially more complex, sophisticated, and beneficial schedule of exchange rates at different levels of labor provided. Does this mean that some individuals might wind up working 45, 50, or 60 hours per week? Yes, if they wished to and if their employer were willing to compensate them for it. Assume an employer, for some reason, required a lengthy work week (i.e., employees had to work, say, 48 hours per week as a condition of employment). The reaction of the labor market to such an event would be no different than its reaction to a distasteful wage level. Those who wished to work under these conditions would do so; others would not. If the number of those in the first category were insufficient to meet the employer's needs, the wage rate (or some other term of employment) would have to be revised upward to provide inducement, the requirement would need to be loosened, or a combination of the two would occur. The elimination of statutory premium rates would permit far greater flexibility in fitting pay schedules to the preferences of each party to the exchange. While "overtime" itself could well remain as a viable concept, there would be a nearly infinite variety of arrangements possible to compensate employees who work "extra" hours (including options regarding regular pay for those who might wish to be guaranteed no additional work altogether).

It should be stressed, in this as in other topics discussed here, that the shape of American society has changed over the past hundred years. Industrial relations, like religious practices, the family, political relationships, and so much else, is supported by and congruent with the general values, beliefs, and norms which exist at the time. It would be foolish in the extreme, not to mention an obvious propaganda tactic, to argue that removing an hours ceiling, a wage floor, or anything else of this nature would somehow reverse decades of practice to the contrary. The work experience common to the late nineteenth or early twentieth century in the United States was inextricably bound up with an entire range of social, cultural, and other economic practices. So is the work experience in the 1980s. In many important respects, the original imposition of hours limits merely confirmed and regularized the beliefs which had become politically dominant.

It is consequently most unlikely that, given contemporary work norms, either employees or employers would be comfortable with or find agreeable any significant shift upward in the average number of hours worked per week. The main difference would be that, with deregulation, hours limits could be developed according to the mutual interests of all parties.

At the same time, current limits force all labor exchanges into a common mold and, it must be honestly recognized, reduce to some unknown degree the information costs of seeking or maintaining employment. Thus, potential employees know generally that the subject of hours is one which does not need to be bargained: They, and employers, know that a certain constraint operates throughout the economy and that neither party has to expend any resources searching for a different option. None exists.

Because this standardization is a potential benefit deriving from regulation, the issue is worth a closer look. Throughout this book, emphasis is given to *federal* regulation, but much of the analysis applies to political constraints on labor exchanges regardless of the level of government which imposes them. It can be argued that a regulation such as an hours ceiling is least desirable when imposed at the most comprehensive level of government. If nothing else, state or local hours ceilings reduce the negative economic consequences simply because they aren't nationwide; further, a state or local regulation permits experimentation among political units across the nation with the negative (or positive) effects more readily measured by the flow of capital, entrepreneurs, and labor. Finally, as a general political observation, state or local regulations are more likely responsive to community demands and more easily altered as demands or conditions change. This is not a brief for merely localizing all federal regulations; it suggests only that, as a less preferred but arguable alternative to deregulation, policy makers should consider decentralization of labor regulation. A strategy of the sort implicit in auto emission standards, is totally artificial, because decentralization would not include the imposition of federal "minimum standards" backed by thinly disguised budgetary strings.

Would the information costs be all that much greater if "maximum hours worked" were deregulated or at least decentralized? While such a question cannot be answered in concrete terms, it is doubtful that these costs would change much. If there is one generalization which has been made most commonly about the United States in the last part of this century, it is that information costs have declined — often in spectacular fashion. Labor market information would be available and would be transmitted both rapidly and at low cost to a sufficient number of employees who would be aware of a wide variety of alternative employer arrangements as to "hours worked" and premium payments. Furthermore, the cost of transportation is sufficiently low (certainly compared to any earlier period in our history) that these opportunities would be accessible. In fact, based on data regarding labor mobility today, it would seem that opportunity costs are already well within the means of most employees. These costs would be even lower were the situation one of deregulation rather than simple decentralization since any particular locality would evidence greater variation within itself.

In short, dropping the legislated hours ceiling and its attendant premium rate requirements is likely to produce no great change overall in what has come to be considered the "standard work week." What *would* likely happen is that the variation around the average would increase. In other words, though the mean would change very little, individual employees would be less clustered at the mean with more above or below the standard. It would not be unreasonable to describe this greater variation as functionally equivalent to an increased flexibility which, in turn, would evidence itself as a higher level of satisfaction regarding the work situation. Further, a policy of decentralization would have beneficial consequences, for productivity would increase. Since an hours ceiling tends to increase the number of employees required for any given task, it follows that deregulation would increase the ratio of output per employee.[25] Finally, the information costs in labor exchanges would not increase significantly under conditions of greater variation in work requirements because of modern communication and transportation technologies.

These two procedural regulations (minimum wage and maximum hours) have been discussed at some length because they are archetypical examples of limitations on work: One constrains prices, the other constrains volume, but both are closely related to each other and to a host of lesser forms of regulation discussed in other chapters. By and large the impact of removing regulations regarding work rules and licensing is analytically comparable. Clearly, eliminating or reducing licensing requirements would tend to expand greatly employment opportunities. This is particularly true when the specific license criteria have little to do directly with competence. Very often licensing criteria are claimed to be nothing more than convenient stand-ins for competence, the imposition of which turns out to benefit the special interests of some group other than consumers. No one doubts that educational or apprenticeship requirements *can* indicate competence, but the relationship is neither necessary nor sufficient. Meanwhile, the schools, organizations, or unions whose programs are defined as adequate providers of the requirement reap the benefits of having a captive clientele. The payment of registration fees, beyond compensating for administrative costs, serves only to restrict entry (as sources of government revenue, their portion of the overall budget is generally miniscule). A classic case is the taxi "medallion" charge in many large cities: in New York it is extremely high ($50,000 plus) and there are far fewer taxis per capita than in Washington, D.C., where the medallion charge is much lower.[26] The inevitable counterclaim is that the actual purpose is to assure the consumer some minimum level of competency and that most licensing criteria are administratively convenient indications. As a practical matter, there is a rationale for state-imposed minimum qualifications in those professions where the practitioner's actions may lead to irreversible or particularly dangerous consequences (professions in the health field, for example). In other fields, however, market mechanisms are quite adequate to weed out those whose services are inferior, to inform consumers of which practitioners are both able and priceworthy, and (through accessible dispute resolution agencies — courts, arbitrators, and the like) to rectify any harm which incompetence or fraud may produce. The market mechanisms may well include voluntary certification agencies, capable of making a commercial profit, as an aid to consumers who desire to reduce their information costs. It is well-established that, under conditions of greater entry opportunities, consumers are better served through lower prices, higher quality, greater availability, or some combination of these.[27]

Conclusions

The regulation of labor relations is so extensive that enormous costs are imposed upon the economy by government intervention in labor markets. The benefits from these regulations accrue mostly to government employees who promulgate and enforce the regulations and, it is generally believed, to special interest groups, primarily union officials and members. Although the regulations are often justified on the basis of aiding disadvantaged workers, there is a considerable body of evidence which shows that there is a wide divergence between the actual and intended effects — stated directly, the unskilled worker bears the brunt of the regulations rather than reaping the benefits.

Throughout this chapter, conventional wisdom has been repeatedly questioned. It is not certain that unionized workers and even union officials would lose more than they might gain from the deregulation of labor relations. Indeed, a strong case can be made that government regulation of labor markets has greatly reduced the bargaining role of unions and that ever-increasing restrictions on labor markets may be one of the root causes of the sagging fortunes of labor unions in the private sector. The role of these organizations in representing workers has, to a degree, been preempted by the government: Congressionally-mandated working conditions and wages cannot be the subject of bargaining. Deregulation would greatly broaden the scope of labor unions in representing employees, if unions could adapt to the changed circumstances of a deregulated environment.

Several deregulation scenarios have been briefly outlined. The most comprehensive strictures are found in the National Labor Relations Act and its amendments so that repeal of this legislation would be required, simply because partial approaches would be very difficult in practice. Partial approaches, though less desirable, could be undertaken for the regulations dealing with wages and hours; gradual deregulation could be accomplished by exemptions based on some measure of firm size, on various worker characteristics (e.g., age in the case of minimum wages), or on certain economic activities such as the exemption of federally-subsidized housing construction from the provisions of the Davis-Bacon Act. The exemptions could then be broadened in scope over a specified period of time. The greatest benefits would accrue to taxpayers and consumers if deregulation of labor markets were comprehensive and immediate; more gradual approaches, including decentralization from the federal to the state and local level of government would, however, allow a transition period for adjustments which would be more palatable politically.

In our view, a total deregulation of labor relations would not produce such dramatic changes that the market would become unrecognizable, even though the environment in which labor exchanges occur would be greatly altered. Deregulation would not transform the economic actors in the labor exchange process or even their primary modes of interaction but, rather, their relative standing. A fundamental shift in focus would occur toward the individual and toward small groups of individuals who have voluntarily allied themselves to accomplish more efficiently a variety of economic objectives. Things would never be the same; nor would things be like they were in the nineteenth century, or 1910, or 1932, or whenever — even were this desirable, which we do not argue is the case. Labor relations would be less centralized, less authoritarian, less political, less complicated by the intrusion of third parties, and potentially more satisfying to the parties whose interests are most directly involved.

The transition would not be easy. So far, every instance of deregulation has been partial, hesitant, and quite narrow in the number of people whose lives are directly affected. In the case of labor relations, the change would affect almost half the population of the United States.

NOTES TO CHAPTER V

[1]This literature is surveyed briefly in James T. Bennett and Manuel H. Johnson, "Free Riders in U.S. Labour Unions: Artifice or Affliction?" *British Journal of Industrial Relations* (July 1979), pp. 158-172.

[2]C. J. Parsley, "Labor Unions and Wages: A Survey," *Journal of Economic Literature* (March 1980), p. 29.

[3]Consider an employee whose wage rate is $10 per hour: Over a forty hour week his pay is $400 per week. Suppose, to win a wage rate hike to $12.50 per hour, his union went on strike for six weeks. Aside from such offsetting income as, for example, unemployment compensation and food stamps (which unions have pushed for precisely because they have the effect of mitigating the impact of strikes), this employee would have to work *24 weeks* at the higher rate before he merely made up the income loss from the strike. On the impact of welfare payments, see Armand Thieblot and Ronald Cowin, *Welfare and Strikers: The Use of Public Funds to Support Strikes* (Philadelphia: University of Pennsylvania, Wharton School, 1972).

[4]Daniel J. B. Mitchell, "Some Empirical Observations of Relevance to the Analysis of Union Wage Determination," *Journal of Labor Research* (Fall 1980), p. 3.

[5]Dan C. Heldman, "Making Policy in a Vacuum: The Case of Labor Relations," *Policy Review* (Fall 1979), pp. 75-88.

[6]Armand J. Thieblot, "An Analysis of Data on Union Membership," (St. Louis: Center for The Study of American Business, 1978).

[7]In addition to the NLRB *per se*, we also include the National Mediation Board as created by the Railway Labor Act which covers employment in the railway and airline industries.

[8]For practical purposes, the Board could be maintained so long as it and its staff were considering cases arising from the prederegulation laws. Given bureaucratic proclivities, it might be advisable to put a time limit on this (2-3 years), with the Board therefore being phased out of existence.

[9]For a definition and analysis of these terms, as applied to the NLRB, see Note, "NLRB Rulemaking: Political Reality Versus Procedural Fairness," 89 *Yale Law Review* 982 (1980).

[10]We note, of course, the limiting case of employers who may be faced by such large labor costs that the choice is made not to produce (e.g., to close down) and employees who may be faced with such low demands (or low prices) for their labor that the choice is made not to work (e.g., to "go on welfare"). Nevertheless, we choose to suggest that these "limiting cases" are generally rare (relative to the total body of employers and employees).

[11]Bruce E. Kaufman (Georgia State University), "Strikes in the United States: What Is the Correct Explanation?," paper presented at the Southern Economic Association Meeting, Washington (DC), November, 1980.

[12]See, among many examples, *NLRB v. Mackay Radio,* 304 U.S. 333 (1938) or *NLRB v. Fotochrome,* 343 F2d 631 (1965); also note, "Replacement of Workers During Strikes," 75 *Yale L. Rev.* 630 (1966). Following an "economic strike," an employer must rehire workers whose jobs have not been permanently filled and must reinstate them (if they so desire) when their "permanent replacements" depart: *NLRB v. Fleetwood Trailer,* 389 U.S. 375 (1967) and *Laidlaw Corp.,* 171 NLRB No. 175 (1968).

[13]*William J. Burns Agency,* 183 NLRB No. 50 (1970).

[14]While the markets are not entirely analogous, we would tend to support this conclusion on the evidence supplied by the experience of the airlines: fare rates changed less often and only after far longer processes during the period of regulation than was the case either before or after that period (i.e., pre-regulatory and post-deregulatory).

[15]For example, with one person the "unit cost" is 100% of the actual cost and, with two people, unit costs for each drop to 50% (plus a slight additional cost to cover dissemination among group members, a factor which also enjoys an economy of scale as group membership increases). We speculate, however, that even such a dramatic drop in unit costs may not be sufficient to impel the formation of a collective (with a size of only two) to share these costs because, if nothing else, there is a certain amount of inertia to be overcome. In addition to sheer resistance to change, it may also be necessary to overcome suspicion or a concern for accuracy and to compensate for the fact that each group member must expend some effort to monitor the actions of the group (e.g., participate in group decisions, oversee its behavior, etc.).

[16]Closely related to this comparison is the need to evaluate the employer's offered terms in an attempt to estimate how closely they reflect what are believed to be the employer's "true" intentions and how distant is the offer from what is believed to be the employer's maximum terms. Of course, the employer must do likewise.

[17]One possible exception to this assumption of constant cost is the stage of successive communications during which offers may be incrementally modified. Here, it may well be that collectivizing leads to no savings (indeed, it may increase costs) in comparison with individual actions. The main difference is time and, secondarily, the expenditure of resources. The individual need only consult with himself, he has already internalized a schedule of ranked preferences and it requires only minimal time to determine whether and how much he will modify his own position in an effort to reach agreement. A group, however, must allocate sufficient response time during each communication cycle to allow information to be disseminated and considered, individual opinions to be formed and transmitted, and a single response aggregated from these various inputs. The principal device by which this problem is partially, though probably insufficiently, overcome is "delegation of authority": This is accomplished first by the appointment of one or more representatives of the group (taking the place of a New England town meeting sort of approach) and, second, by granting the representative some measure of independence to modify the group's position within limits (which may be broadly or narrowly set) without having to return to the group for approval. This will be discussed later.

[18]See Dan C. Heldman and Deborah L. Knight, *Unions and Lobbying: The Representation Function* (Washington, DC: Foundation for the Advancement of the Public Trust, 1980), especially Chapters 1, 3.

[19]A number of subsidiary questions are raised by this which we do not have the space to answer. They are, however, answerable. For example, having joined the group, authorized an agent to act for him, and become convinced he was being treated unfairly, to what degree is an employee bound to an agent? That depends upon what obligations are created by the employment contract, the agent's contract, or both. The point is, simply, that these matters can be governed by written agreements which, in turn, have centuries of legal tradition behind them.

[20]Though not predicting the "end of unions," one NLRB member has warned that "those who seek to abolish or weaken the agency [i.e., NLRB] risk a return to the conditions of economic chaos of the 1930s." Remarks of Howard Jenkins to Southwestern Legal Foundation conference, October 17, 1980, as reported in *Daily Labor Reports*, No. 208 (October 24, 1980), p. A-15.

[21]Exit would, of course, be subject to the fulfillment of preexisting obligations: It is not believed that *any* organization can bind a member permanently, i.e., prevent him from exiting under any but the most reasonable of conditions.

[22]See, for example, *U.S. News & World Report* (September 8, 1980), pp. 33-36; *Miami Herald* (July 6, 1980).

[23]Government Accounting Office, *Report to the Congress: The Davis-Bacon Act Should Be Repealed* (Washington, DC: GAO, HRD-79-18, April 27, 1979), pp. iii-iv.

[24]The scope of Davis-Bacon-type legislation is impressive. The GAO identified some 77 different statutes which set minimum wages in federal contracts according to a formula patterned after that pioneered by Davis-Bacon, and many states have created similar provisions governing their contracting.

[25]There is the added possibility that increased general satisfaction could also positively affect individual productivity. We note here the argument that unemployment might also rise in the short term: To the extent limits on hours worked is a "spread the work" policy, their elimination might decrease employment opportunities. We are not convinced, however, that this tentative consequence, if it exists at all, would hold in the long term because there is the counter-balancing likelihood that enhanced flexibility in hours (together with a minimum wage deregulation) would tap some portion of the unemployed pool whose predicament stems directly from this statutory standardization of wages and hours.

[26]Interestingly, there is a higher proportion of minority drivers in D.C. as compared to New York. The high medallion charge not only restricts entry but restricts it disproportionately against those most in need of employment opportunities.

[27]As in the case of taxi medallions, above, we also postulate more employment opportunities for minorities and others who are shut out by direct discrimination or by the greater likelihood their professional competence would be achieved by alternate, nontraditional means.

Chapter VI
Summary and Conclusions

At the risk of appearing repetitious, it is critical in this final chapter to stress once again the central purpose of our analysis of the deregulation of labor relations. In essence, four basic themes have been developed throughout this book. First, there is no functional difference between government intervention in the labor market and government intervention in other markets, e.g., transportation, drugs, energy, communications, banking, dairy, real estate, insurance, and medical services. Second, it is reasonable to believe — at least in terms of a working hypothesis — that the "perils of regulation" which have been increasingly detailed in other economic exchanges possess counterparts in the labor market. Third, if deregulation is an effective remedy for the ills of the trucking, broadcast, or energy industry, then the same therapy should be considered in the case of labor relations. Fourth and finally, our evaluation of the effects of a deregulated labor market suggests that the resulting changes would be substantial, diverse, and extensive, but not unmanageable. Each of these related propositions is reviewed briefly below.

An economic exchange consists of two transferrals of something from one party to another. No voluntary exchange will take place unless the principle of relative benefit obtains: Each party values what he will receive higher than what he gives.[1] This obviously means that each of the items exchanged carries two potentially different valuations, a most likely possibility since the values arise from the preference schedules of two different individuals. When the exchanges involve a particular commodity or pair of commodities, when they occur in sufficient number and with a certain regularity, there is a "market." Bargaining or negotiations occur as each party attempts to widen the spread between these two values for himself and to influence the other party's evaluation of the items so that the pressure to participate in the exchange is increased. Governments, in response to well-organized pressure groups, intervene in market exchanges to limit the type or quantity of a commodity which can be traded or, through the imposition of conditional costs, to alter the values of a commodity as perceived by one or both of the exchange parties. As a consequence of this intervention, some exchanges become so costly that they do not occur at all (producing relative dissatisfaction for those parties which would have preferred them to occur) whereas other exchanges become more frequent because the value of the benefit received has been artificially raised (again producing relative dissatisfaction for those who would have preferred the exchange *not* to occur under those terms and for those who must pay for the benefits the government has now introduced into the exchange). Of course, while relative dissatisfaction is created through regulation, so is relative satisfaction: The question becomes *who* experiences *which* and what is their influence upon the governmental processes through which regulations are created and administered. Needless to say, the same question is raised by the issue of deregulation.

The most common, frequent, and fundamental exchange in any economy is that of labor. Although there are those who would object for philosophical, ideological, propagandistic, or other reasons, the fact remains that labor is a commodity; it has a value for buyer and seller, and the terms of its exchange are constrained at every turn by government rules. These rules, just as in other markets, alter the shape of the exchange by prohibiting prices outside a certain range, by prohibiting the exchange beyond certain quantities, and by attaching extraneous conditions to the exchange which alter the values each party assigns to costs and benefits. In short, regulation of labor exchanges is essentially the same as regulations imposed upon any other market.

Furthermore, we see at work in the labor market counterparts to virtually every consequence of regulation which analysts have discovered in their studies of other markets. Regulations produce disproportionately higher prices, reduced entry, inflexibility, discrimination (racial, age, sex, etc.), capture by special interests, high administrative costs, burdensome paperwork, reduced quantities of the commodity, economic inefficiency, misallocation of resources, and so on and so forth. Even Sen. Kennedy (D., Mass.) has recognized that, when regulation fails, the perverse result is often *more* government intervention with a further aggravation of the economic difficulties.[2] And Professor Kirzner has added a hitherto unremarked peril: Drawing from the Mises-Hayek criticisms of economic calculations under socialism, Kirzner has pointed to the stultifying effect of regulation upon what he calls the "spontaneous discovery process" which unregulated markets tend to generate.[3]

Almost every case study of regulation[4] has made it clear that the intervention by government has been justified either by expressly political standards or by political considerations overlaid with an economic veneer. Thus, for example, one finds the so-called "market failure" proposition used to justify regulatory interventions; yet, if regulation were truly a matter of curbing the predatory powers of big business cartels against the interests of consumers, one is entitled to wonder why it is that consumers have been the principal backers of airline deregulation while their opponents (i.e., those in favor of retaining regulation) have been the airlines and the airline industry unions (plus the AFL-CIO). It requires no particularly innovative political theory to suggest that the identity of those who gain or lose from a policy decision may be deduced in part from the roster of those who lobby for or against a measure. We posit, therefore, a working hypothesis: If the ills of regulation are essentially the same whether the market is for labor or for some other commodity and if deregulation is an effective remedy for those ills in other markets, then the possibility is at least worth further investigation that the parallel ills in the labor market might benefit from a policy of deregulating labor relations.

Deregulation would not radically alter the current structure of labor relations. Neither unions nor collective bargaining would disappear. Of course there would be differences — else why deregulate? — but we believe there is ample evidence to suggest that the changes would be beneficial overall. We propose, for example, that a deregulated system of labor relations would probably experience less corruption, more satisfaction, greater flexibility, more individualism, a measure of decentralization or localism, a decrease in industry-wide bargaining, a resurgence of personal liberty, more formal contracts, higher productivity, fewer strikes, less infiltration by organized crime, freedom of union internal affairs from government controls, greater competition within the labor representation industry, and less paperwork. This is not to say that deregulation of labor relations would be a panacea. Any change of this magnitude and extent produces net costs for some.

Government intervention in markets, at least on a large and continuing scale, can be traced back almost a century to the enactment of the Interstate Commerce Act in 1887 and the establishment of an Interstate Commerce Commission to regulate a railroad industry which, at that time, enjoyed monopoly powers over shippers. Since then, the regulatory powers of the federal and state government have expanded and the consequent market intervention has broadened rapidly in scope. In many cases, government regulation was justified on the basis of perceived imbalances in economic strength in the market. This was the case for the shippers and the railroad in the late nineteenth century and for employees and employers in the 1930s. A practice of such lengthy duration is not easily overturned, even in the face of increasingly critical academic and public opinion. Social and political inertia is an extremely difficult force to overcome.

While the regulatory Leviathan is now ponderously being forced to give back some of what it has possessed for so long, there has developed the very real danger that the reasons for rescuing our economic lives from its coils may be lost in the struggle of the moment.

Deregulation has been accomplished or is in process for airlines, trucking, advertising in the professions, railroads, and oil and natural gas pricing (among others). According to economic theory, regulation can be justified only in industries where there are natural monopolies or situations where substantial external costs result. However, much of the regulation that has taken place from the 1930s to the present has been justified by proponents on the basis of social rather than economic arguments. Regulations initiated for the sole purpose of social change carry with them a high price tag that taxpayers are no longer committed to finance. Marginal effective tax rates are now over 30 percent of income and industrial productivity has stagnated. Further, it has been shown that, regardless of the rationale, regulation has failed to accomplish its intended objectives. Practically every study of government regulation has demonstrated that controls have been ineffective in fulfilling their intended purpose. In fact, the regulatory process had been characterized more by government failure than by market failure. In other words, the effect of regulation has been to transfer wealth to those groups which were to be regulated and to the regulating authorities themselves at the expense of consumers and taxpayers. Such a result is made possible through lobbying by special interest groups and through bureaucratic manipulation, while voters remain unorganized as a counterforce.

It is important that deregulating the drug industry would likely achieve the availability of new life-saving preparations at a lower cost. It is important that deregulating taxicabs results in more entrepreneurs of all races and colors providing better and less expensive service to the public. It is important that deregulating the energy industry would increase the likelihood of developing more of our traditional energy sources while also increasing the possibility of discovering new sources of power. However, most important of all is the personal economic freedom that results from the reduction of political intervention in markets. Characterizing the Supreme Court's original emphasis on this issue, Siegan stated that "freedom is the rule and restraint the exception."[5] He quoted approvingly from Justice Sutherland's 1923 majority decision in *Adkins v. Children's Hospital* (261 U.S. 525):

> To sustain the individual freedom of action contemplated by the Constitution is not to strike down the common good but to exalt it; for surely the good of society as a whole cannot be better served than by the preservation against arbitrary restraint of the liberties of its constituent members (p. 561).

Ironically, *Adkins* held unconstitutional minimum wage legislation in the District of Columbia and was explicitly reversed fourteen years later in *West Coast Hotel v. Parrish* (300 U.S. 379; 1937). Thus began the U.S. judiciary's "formal termination of economic due process."[6]

We cannot overemphasize the danger regulation poses for economic freedom. The regulation of labor relations is arguably the most extreme case of government failure. Those persons who are harmed by such regulation, e.g., employees, consumers, and competitive businessmen, are notoriously ineffective at presenting their interests to government authorities. However, the parties who are favorably affected are highly organized, politically potent, and heavily activist. Because those benefited by labor regulation are politically more influential and because most persons find it difficult to view labor as a marketable commodity, government intervention in labor relations has proceeded almost unaffected by the current atmosphere of deregulation.

Labor sector regulation impacts more sectors of the U.S. economy than all other forms of regulation combined. It has been pointed out that minimum wage and maximum hour laws cover about 65 percent of the nonagricultural work force. Unemployment compensation payments are required from firms that employ roughly 97 percent of all private sector workers. The regulatory activities of the National Labor Relations Board can potentially control the employer-employee relations of almost every private firm in the economy. According to the Davis-Bacon Act, all firms accepting work on federal government projects must agree to pay the prevailing wages in the region where work is to be performed. Occupational safety and health regulation heavily impacts firms in the mining, manufacturing, and construction industries. Manpower programs, occupational licensing, and affirmative action regulation also have a substantial effect on labor relations.

A policy of deregulation simply will not work if attention is diverted to particular cases. For every specific market deregulated, two new ones will appear if we fail to recognize that it is not the specific market which is important. As with government subsidies generally, we risk the hypocrisy of eagerly deregulating the other person's market while leaving our own special privileges intact. The value of turning our attention and energies to the labor market is that everyone is potentially involved: The number of those who stand to gain is so great that no amount of effective organization by the considerably smaller number of opponents will suffice to block an active, measured, and steadfast policy of labor relations deregulation.

We have conservatively estimated the social costs of labor sector regulation to be at least $170 billion annually. That works out to about $2000 for each civilian employee in the U.S. economy. We have occasionally wondered how swift might be the public reaction and how direct might be its effect if every product carried a price tag which showed graphically the components of that price — so much for raw materials, so much for labor, taxes, paperwork, compliance with regulations, retained profit, capital investment, return paid to stockholders, and so forth. Similarly, employees might more readily appreciate the costs of labor market regulation if there were some equally graphic way to show that the compensation they receive is, on average, lower by some $2,000 annually because of government instrusions into their freedom to contract for employment on individually advantageous terms.

To many, even the idea that the deregulation of labor relations is possible or desirable will be viewed as a radical departure from a national policy that has existed for almost half a century. The concept may seem so revolutionary that a natural tendency is to dismiss the arguments in favor of deregulation out of hand rather than consider them on the basis of their merits. The status quo is known and predictable, whereas sudden or even gradual, but dramatic, shifts in policy inevitably create doubts and uncertainties about the future course of events. It is, therefore, important to place the deregulation of labor relations in a context with the deregulation initiatives in other sectors of the economy. From such a perspective, the end of government intervention in labor exchanges is not such an inconceivable action.

Over the nearly fifty years since the passage of NLRA, dramatic changes have occurred in the labor market. The average American worker (and manager) is much better educated, more knowledgeable about employment opportunities, and more mobile than was the case even twenty years ago. To attract and retain such workers, firms have had to develop positive industrial relations because turnover of dissatisfied employees is costly. Brains have in many cases replaced brawn in the workplace as industry has mechanized and automated on a large scale and workers have developed firm-specific skills in operating equipment. Computerization has vastly altered the world of work and the white-collar component of the labor force is growing much more rapidly than the blue-collar. In fact, the service sector of the economy has grown far more rapidly than the manufacturing sector and is now, in terms of total employment, dominant. In short, there have been enormous changes in the working environment, in workers and their attitudes, and in labor relations practices by firms. The labor market is substantially different from that which existed in the depths of the Great Depression when the NLRA and later regulatory legislation were enacted.

Much new research and innovative thinking are called for to deal with the inhibitions of those who live in the past. Even where past conditions may have been sufficient justification for the intrusions of NLRA upon the freedom of workers, there can be little doubt that new modes of thinking are now appropriate. Yet, we are led to suspect that "there is nothing new under the sun." The Constitutional Convention which replaced the Articles of Confederation with the 1787 Constitution (the latter a document whose 200th anniversary we shall soon celebrate) was called in large measure because the state legislatures had been serving as political arbiters of vital economic issues and had, on the evidence presented by the authors of the Federalist papers, seriously harmed the interests of both individuals and the economy overall. The 1787 Constitution was intended to limit the role of *government* in these matters — not simply to replace the power of states with that of a national bureaucracy. It is not easy, as Siegan notes, "to stop a political experiment."[7] The possibility that we cannot or will not is what we should fear.

NOTES TO CHAPTER VI

[1]Exchanges in which this principle does not hold are either nonvoluntary (coerced) or infrequent (usually symbolic gestures).

[2]124 *Congressional Record: Senate* (Daily edition), March 1, 1978, pp. 52663-64.

[3]Israel M. Kirzner, *The Perils of Regulation: A Market-Process Approach* (Coral Gables, FL: Law and Economics Center Occasional Paper, 1978), Chapter IV.

[4]See references throughout previous chapters, *infra*. A recent sketch by commodity market may be found in Chapter 13 of Bernard Siegan, *Economic Liberties and the Constitution* (Chicago: Universitiy of Chicago Press, 1980).

[5]Siegan, p. 303.

[6]Ibid., p. 145.

[7]Ibid., p. 327.

Author Index

Aaron, Benjamin, 81
Abowd, John M., 130
Adams, Avril V., 110, 130
Addison, John T., 77, 79
Anderson, Martin, 126
Aptheker, Herbert, 12
Annable, James E., Jr., 12
Ashenfelter, Orley, 106, 125, 129, 130

Barker, C. P., 81
Bator, Francis, 36
Bednarzik, Robert M., 77
Beller, Andrea, 110, 130
Bennett, James T., 12, 37, 38, 77, 78, 82, 103, 107, 128, 129, 130, 164
Bittlingmayer, George, 99, 126
Bloch, Farrell, 124
Bloom, Gordon F., 45, 77, 124
Bradley, Philip D., 12
Bronfenbrenner, Martin, 130
Brooks, George, 77
Brozen, Yale, 89, 90, 81, 125
Buchanan, James, 36, 37, 38
Burgess, Paul L., 102, 122
Butler, Richard, 110, 130
Butler, Robert T., 102, 122

Chamberlain, Edward H., 12
Chamberlain, Neil W., 36, 125
Chapin, G., 102, 122
Classen, Kathleen P., 101, 102, 122, 128
Coase, Ronald, 20, 36
Cowin, Ronald, 164
Cox, Archibald, 81
Craypo, Charles, 82
Crosslin, Robert L., 102, 122
Cullen, Donald E., 36, 125
Cunningham, James 93, 125

Denison, Edward, 108, 129, 130
Dorsey, Stuart, 132

Douty, H. M., 88, 89, 124

Ehrenberg, Ronald, 102, 106, 122, 128, 129

Farber, Henry S., 130
Farmer, Don Erik, 12
Fechter, Alan, 129
Felder, Henry, 102, 122
Feldstein, Martin, 101, 127, 128
Fiorina, Morris P., 38
Flanagan, Robert J., 110
Frankel, Carl, 83
Freeman, Richard B., 110
Friedman, Milton, 131

Getman, Julius, 78
Goldfarb, Robert, 93, 125
Gomberg, William, 79
Gould, John P., 99, 126
Grabowski, Henry, 27, 36
Gramlich, Edward, 93, 95, 106, 125, 129
Greer, Douglas, 115, 131
Gujarati, D. R., 126
Gwartney, James D., 130

Hammermesh, Daniel, 115, 131
Hanna, James S., 102, 122
Harper, F. A., 12
Hayek, F. A., 168
Hazlitt, Henry, 12
Heckman, James J., 110, 130
Heldman, Dan C., 80, 82, 164, 165
Hill, Herbert, 79
Hinrichs, A. F., 88, 124
Hirschleifer, Jack, 36, 126
Hobbes, Thomas, 2
Holen, Arlene, 102, 119, 122, 131
Humphrey, Thomas, 115, 131
Hutt, W. H., 12

Johnson, George E., 129, 130
Johnson, Harry G., 117, 131
Johnson, Haynes, 81
Johnson, James C., 33, 38
Johnson, Manuel H., 12, 77, 78, 82, 103, 107, 128, 129, 130, 164

Kalachek, Edward, 127
Kaufman, Bruce E., 164
Kaufman, Jacob J., 124
Kidder, Alice, 110, 130
Kingston, Jerry L., 102, 122
Kirzner, Israel, 168, 174
Knight, Deborah L., 80, 165
Kosters, Marvin, 77, 92, 125
Kotz, Nick, 81
Kreuger, Ann O., 38
Kuznets, Simon, 131

Landau, Richard, 37
Langwehr, M. L., 81
Lee, Dwight R., 36, 116, 131
Lee, Lung-Fei, 130
Leiter, Robert D., 79
Levine, M. J., 80
Levinson, Harold M., 130
Lewin, David, 125
Lewis, H. G., 112, 113, 123, 130, 131
Lindbloom, Charles E., 12
Liniger, Charles A., 102, 122
Linnemann, Peter, 96, 97, 125, 126

MacAvoy, Paul W., 26, 36, 38, 108, 129
Macesich, George, 90, 125
Marston, S., 102, 122
Mattlia, J. Peter, 126
McKenzie, Richard B., 78, 94, 96, 125
McLure, Charles E., 103, 128
Medoff, James L., 101, 128
Mieszkowski, Peter, 117, 131
Mincer, Jacob, 94, 95, 126
Mises, Ludwig von, 168
Mishan, E. J., 36
Mitchell, Daniel J. B., 116, 131, 164
Moore, Thomas G., 12, 91, 92, 125, 131

Morris, Charles A., 78, 79

Niskanen, William A., 38
Noll, Roger, 38
Northrup, Herbert R., 45, 77, 124

Oaxaca, Ronald L., 102, 122, 128

Panzar, John C., 38
Parsely, C. J., 136, 164
Pashigian, B. Peter, 119, 131
Peltzman, Sam, 27, 37
Peterson, John, 90, 125
Petro, Sylvester, 12
Phillips, Joseph D., 130
Piore, Michael, 107, 129
Posner, Richard A., 38
Pratt, Harlan D., 130

Rakowski, James P., 33, 38
Rees, Albert, 117, 131
Reynolds, Morgan O., 117, 131
Roberts, P. C., 37
Rose-Ackerman, Susan, 38
Rosen, Sherwin, 113, 123
Rottenberg, Simon, 131
Ryscavage, Paul, 113, 123

Scherer, Frank M., 36
Scherer, Joseph, 28, 37
Schmidt, Peter, 130
Schmidt, Ronald M., 102, 122
Seneca, Joseph J., 36
Shimberg, Benjamin, 77, 131
Siebert, W. Stanley, 77, 79
Silberman, Jonathan, 124
Simler, N. J., 130
Simon, Michael E., 130
Simons, Henry C., 12
Singer, Ezra, 82
Slichter, Sumner H., 79
Smith, R., 125
Snow, John, 38
Sowell, Thomas, 111, 130
Stafford, F. P., 113, 123
Steinman, John, 102, 122
Stewart, Charles, 90, 91, 125

Stigler, George, 37, 77
Strauss, Robert P., 130
Strickland, Allyn D., 36
Stroup, Richard, 130
Stubblebine, W. C., 36

Taussig, Michael K., 36
Thieblot, Armand, 126, 164
Throop, A., 113, 123
Tobias, Paul H., 80, 81
Tomola, James D., 129
Tullock, Gordon, 37, 38

Viscusi, W. Kip, 27, 28, 37

Wagner, Richard E., 38

Wandner, Stephen, 102, 122
Wardell, William, 27, 37
Webb, Sydney and Beatrice, 6, 7, 12
Weidenbaum, Murray, 28, 29, 37, 77,
   109, 129
Weiss, Leonard, 36, 113, 123
Welch, Finis, 77, 92, 93, 125
Wessels, Walter, 94, 95, 96, 125, 126
Wilcox, Clair, 36
Williams, Walter E., 77, 88, 120,
   124, 132
Wilson, James Q., 32, 38
Wolkinson, Benjamin W., 110, 130
Woll, Peter, 38
Wright, David McCord, 12

Subject Index

Abood v. Detroit Board of Education, 82
Adkins·v. Children's Hospital, 171
Aeronautical Lodge 727 v. Campbell, 80
AFL-CIO, 42, 45, 77-78, 169
AFTRA (*See* American Federation of Television and Radio Artists)
Agricultural Marketing Service, 22
Airlines, 4, 5, 11, 22, 33, 49, 169
Alienation, 9
Allis-Charlmers (NLRB v.), 78
Alvey v. GE and IUE, 82
American Federation of Television and Radio Artists (AFTRA), 81
American Newspaper Publishers' Association v. NLRB, 78
Animal and Plant Health Inspection Service, 23
Appropriate Unit (*See* Unit determination)
Area Redevelopment Act, 104
Automotive Plating Corp., 80
Auto Workers Union, 5, 72

Bargaining, 41, 149-152
Beck v. CWA, 82
Booster Lodge (See IAM v. NLRB)
Boycotts, 153
Broadcasting, 3, 81
Buckley v. NLRB, 81

Capital replacement, 46
Cartel (*See* monopoly)
Certification, 137
Civil Aeronautics Board (CAB), 22, 23, 33
Civil Rights Act, 109
Class, 7
Clayton Act, 7
Collective bargaining, 41, 112-118, 145-149, 152

Commodity Futures Trading Commission, 24
Communications Workers Union (CWA), 7, 82
.Comprehensive Employment and Training Act (CETA), 104-106
Compulsory unionism (also Union shop, Union security), 68, 70, 71, 73-74, 81, 82
Concessions (*Also* Counterproposals), 60-62
Conflict (*See* Dispute resolution, Strikes), 142-145
Consolidated Edison Co. v. NLRB, 79
Consumer Product Safety Commission, 24
Cooper Thermometer Co., 78
Copyright Royalty Tribunal, 24
Council on Environmental Quality, 26
Criminal Code, 3
Crises, 30-31

Davis-Bacon Act, 23, 43, 48, 86, 98-99, 140, 155-157, 163, 166, 171
Decertification, 65-66, 137-138
Dehumanization, 9
Department of Agriculture, 3
Department of Energy, 22
Department of Labor, 42, 85, 88, 98, 107
Deregulation, Social benefits of, 121, 172
Discrimination, 66-67, 80, 109-112
Displaced workers, 91, 96-97, 117
Dispute resolution (*See* also Strikes), 141-142
Drugs, 4
Drug Enforcement Administration, 24
Duty of fair representation, 64-68, 80, 142, 150-151, 154
Duty to bargain (*See* Good faith bargaining)

Economic Opportunity Act, 104
Efficiency, 46, 16-21
Elections, 137-138, 150
Ellis v. Railway Clerks, 82
Employee rights, 50, 81
Energy Regulatory Administration, 24
Environmental Protection Agency,
   23-24, 26
Equal opportunity, 49, 109-112
Equal Opportunity Employment
   Commission (EEOC), 119-121
Erhardt Construction (*See* United
   Construction Workers)
European guild system, 6
Exclusive agent (*See* Exclusivity)
Exclusivity (*Also* Exclusive agent) 53,
   55-57, 62-64, 66, 68-69, 79, 142,
   150, 154
Externalities, 14-21, 26

Fair Labor Standards Act (FLSA), 23,
   43-44, 88-89, 93, 96, 98-99
Fair representation (*See* Duty of fair
   representation)
Federal Aviation Administration
   (FAA), 23
Federal Communications Commission
   (FCC), 3, 22
Federal Highway Administration,
   23, 27
Federal Maritime Commission, 22
Federal Railroad Administration, 24
Financial core membership, 69-71
Fleetwood Trailer (NLRB v.), 164
Food and Drug Administration
   (FDA), 3, 22
Ford Motor Co. v. Huffman, 80
Fotochrome (NLRB v.), 164
Free rider, 73-74

Gabauer v. Woodcock, 81
General Accounting Office, 155
General Electric Co. (NLRB v.), 79
General Knit of California, 78
General Motors (NLRB v.), 81
Gissel Packing (NLRB v.), 78
GNP, 23, 108-109, 116-117

Good faith bargaining (*Also* Duty to
   bargain), 57-62, 64, 79, 151
Government analogy, 54, 55-56, 66
Government failure, 29-32
Granite State (NLRB v.), 82
Grievances, 41, 73, 153

Hines v. Anchor Freight, 81
Houde Engineering Corp., 79
Hours ceiling (*See* maximum hours)

IAM v. NLRB, 82
IBEW v. Foust, 81
Inflation, 25, 115-116, 133-140
Interstate Commerce Act, 169
Interstate Commerce Commission
   (ICC), 3, 136, 169

J. I. Case, 62-63, 67, 76
Job Corps, 104

Labor as a commodity, 5, 6-9
Labor unions (*See* also specific
   unions), 4, 42, 47, 49-74, 93, 97,
   119, 134-141, 149-152
Laidlaw Corp., 164
Landrum-Griffin Act, 78, 81-82, 133,
   141, 144
Licensing, 13, 47-48, 77, 161-162

Mackay Radio (NLRB v.), 163
Manpower Development and Training
   Act (MDTA), 104
Market failure, 14, 20, 29, 35, 170
Marxian class (*See* Class)
Maximum hours, 33, 43, 45-48, 86,
   99, 157-161
McNamara v. Johnston, 81
Membership apathy, 152
*Metropolitan Life Insurance Co.
   (NLRB v.),* 80
Millwright's Local 1102, 80
Minimum wage, 13, 23-24, 33, 43-45,
   48, 77, 86-98, 104, 106, 133,
   139-140, 154, 156, 161
Mining Enforcement and Safety
   Administration, 24

Monopoly (*Also* Cartel), 7, 15-17, 21, 25-26
Moonlighting, 45, 77
Motor Coach Employees v. Lockridge, 81
Munn v. Illinois, 14

National Highway Traffic Safety Administration, 24
National Industrial Recovery Act (NIRA), 78-79
National Labor Board, 79
National Labor Relations Act (NLRA), 22, 49-74, 78, 80, 82, 86, 133, 141-154, 162, 172-173
National Labor Relations Board (NLRB), 22-24, 42, 49-74, 80, 85, 119, 137, 141-142, 165, 171
National League of Cities v. Usery, 77
National Maritime Union, 78
Nebbia v. New York, 14
Negotiating (*See* also Good faith bargaining), 59-62
Neighborhood Youth Corps, 104
New Deal, 21-22
N. Y. Times Co. (See N. Y. Typographical Union Local 6)
N. Y. Typographical Union Local 6, 80
Nuclear Regulatory Commission (NRC), 24

Occupational Safety and Health Administration (OSHA), 23-24, 28, 85, 107-109, 133, 138
O'Hara-McNamara Act, 43, 98
Organized Crime, 78, 152
Output functions, 2

Paperwork Costs, 48, 77
Phillips curve, 118
Political economy, 11, 13, 133
Political market, 42
Pollution, 15, 18, 20-21, 26-27, 31, 139
Postal Rate Commission, 24
Premium rate (*Also* Premium wage), 45, 47, 77

Price controls, 16-17
Prices (*Also* Wages), 7-8, 12, 41
Productivity, 46, 63, 79, 82, 87, 114, 133, 135, 154
Property rights, 18, 20-21
Public interest, 14, 30-31
Public review board (*See* Autoworkers Union)
Public sector unions, 137

Quit rate, 95
Quotas, 112

Railroads, 4, 49
Railway Labor Act (RLA), 49, 80, 82
Reed & Prince (NLRB v.), 60, 79
Regulation
    Costs of, 28-29
    Defined, 3, 41
    Economic justification of, 14-21
    Effectiveness of, 25-28
    Extent of, 21-25
Resignation, 72, 82
Retail Clerks v. Schermerhorn, 81
Rhodes-Holland Chevrolet Co., 79
Right-to-work, 69

Scofield v. NLRB, 80, 82
Securities and Exchange Commission (SEC), 22
Shopping Kart, 78
Signature cards (also Sign-up cards), 53-54, 78
Slavery, 7-8
Social Security, 23, 100, 127
Standardization of wages, 56, 62-63, 135-136
Steel Tripartite Committee, 12
Steele v. Louisville Railroad, 64, 80
Steelworkers Union, 4, 12, 76
Strikes, 41, 47, 72, 112-118, 142-145, 152-153
Subminimum wage, 47, 77, 96
Substantive labor regulation, 43-48
Sumner, Clyde, 81
Sweatshops, 45
Sweetheart contract, 78

Syres v. Oil Workers International, 80

Taft-Hartley Act, 50, 51, 58, 59, 78,
    79, 133-141
Taxes, 18, 20, 134, 170
Teamsters Union, 4
Teamsters v. U.S., 80
Textile Workers (See Granite State)
Treaty of Versailles, 7
Trucking, 4, 11

Unemployment, 25, 133, 139
Unemployment Insurance 13, 23-24,
    96, 100-103, 171
Unfair Labor Practice, 50, 54, 59-60,
    80, 144
United Construction Workers, 82
Union agent elections, 51-55,
    63-64, 79
Union discipline, 70, 72, 82
Union dues, 70-71, 73, 82
Union membership, 51, 64, 68-72
Union organizing, 112
Union security (*See* compulsory
    unionism)
Union shop (*See* compulsory
    unionism)
Unit determination (*Also* Appropriate
    unit), 63-64, 150, 154

Usury laws, 12

Vaca v. Sipes, 80
*Virginia Electric and Power
    (NLRB v.),* 78

Wage differential, 112-114, 135-136
Wages (*Also* prices), 112-117
Wagner Act, 5, 42, 50, 57-58, 78,
    141, 143
Wagner-Peyser Act, 104
Walsh-Healey Act, 43, 48, 86, 98
War Labor Board, 58
West Coast Hotel v. Parrish, 171
Western Cold Storage, 79
William J. Burns Agency, 164
Wirtz, Willard, 86
Work rules, 47, 48, 56, 79, 80, 82,
    154-162
Worker rights, 141, 152
World War II, 46
Woychick (Local 756, UAW v.), 82

Youth Conservation Corps, 104
Youth Employment Demonstration
    Act, 104
Youth Differential (*See* subminimum
    wage)

The following books are available from The Fisher Institute

FUNDAMENTALS OF ECONOMICS: A PROPERTY RIGHTS APPROACH by Dr. Svetozar Pejovich. The inclusion of new property rights concepts updates the field of economics in this basic textbook for beginning business/economics students and educated laymen. 258 pages, 51 charts and tables.

$11.95 (hardback)

TAX LIMITATION, INFLATION & THE ROLE OF GOVERNMENT by Milton Friedman. The Nobel Laureate has been called the most influential economist of this era. This new book will give you a broad picture of economic research and a fascinating overview of free market philosophy. It is sound public policy material. 110 pages, 15 graphs, 2 tables.

$5.95 (paperback)

LIFE IN THE SOVIET UNION: A REPORT CARD ON SOCIALISM by Dr. Svetozar Pejovich. A native of Yugoslavia, Dr. Pejovich uses new and revealing economic facts about how Soviet citizens are *really* living — a far cry from the Soviet government's propaganda. 101 pages, 11 charts and tables.

$4.95 (paperback); $9.95 (hardback)

NATIONAL HEALTH CARE IN GREAT BRITAIN: LESSONS FOR THE U.S.A. by Dr. John Goodman, professor of economics, University of Dallas. This is the first comprehensive study of the cradle-to-grave health care system in Great Britain. Its economic realities should provide lessons for U.S. proponents of similar programs. 210 pages, 15 charts and graphs.

$6.95 (paperback); $11.95 (hardback)

THOSE GASOLINE LINES AND HOW THEY GOT THERE by Dr. H. E. Merklein and William P. Murchison, Jr. A Ph.D. economist/petroleum engineer and a talented journalist combine to indict the massive government bureaucracy for America's current energy shortage. Some hard facts and incisive writing make this a book all American consumers can read and understand. 130 pages, 36 charts and graphs.

$5.95 (paperback); $10.95 (hardback)

AMERICA'S CHOICE: TWILIGHT'S LAST GLEAMING OR DAWN'S EARLY LIGHT? by James R. Evans. Foreword by John Chamberlain. An expose of government's performance as it oversees citizen affairs, exposing the fact that abandoning "value structures" for political profit does have consequences.

$11.95 (hardback)

DEREGULATING LABOR RELATIONS by Drs. Dan C. Heldman, James T. Bennett and Manuel H. Johnson. The authors conclude that: "We have conservatively estimated the social costs of labor sector regulation to be at least $170 billion annually. That works out to about $2,000 for each civilian employee in the U.S. economy."

$12.95 (hardback)

THE PRINCIPLES OF AMERICAN PROSPERITY by Leighton A. Wilkie and Richard Stanton Rimanoczy. 1981 Revised Edition. A new, updated and condensed version of this popular economics handbook. It is the distillation of the best economic and sociological thinking and writing of the past 2000 years, presented in easily understood, "bite size" units for all ages.

$3.95 (paperback)

The Fisher Institute pays for postage on all PREPAID orders. Postage and handling charges will be added to all orders which are billed. Texas buyers please add 5% sales tax.

THE FISHER INSTITUTE
6350 LBJ Fwy., Suite 183E / Dallas, TX 75240
(214) 233-1041